GREEK MYTHOLOGY FOR TEENS

GREEK MYTHOLOGY FOR TEENS

CLASSIC MYTHS IN TODAY'S WORLD

WRITTEN AND ILLUSTRATED BY **ZACHARY HAMBY**

Prufrock Press Inc. • Waco, Texas

Library of Congress Cataloging-in-Publication Data

Hamby, Zachary, 1982-
  Greek mythology for teens : classic myths in today's world / written and illustrated by Zachary Hamby.
    p. cm.
  Includes bibliographical references and index.
  ISBN 978-1-59363-717-0 (pbk.)
  1. Mythology, Greek. I. Title.
  BL783.H36 2011
  292.1'3--dc22
                              2011016960

Cover Image: ART147619
David, Jacques Louis (1748-1825)
The Oath of the Horatii, ca. 1784. Oil on canvas, 330 x 425 cm.
Photo: Gérard Blot/ Christian Jean
Louvre, Paris, France
Requested resolution : 10,000 X 7,838 pixels
© Réunion des Musées Nationaux / Art Resource, NY

Edited by Lacy Compton

Cover and Layout Design by Raquel Trevino

ISBN-13: 978-1-59363-717-0

Printed in the United States of America.

At the time of this book's publication, all facts and figures cited are the most current available. All telephone numbers, addresses, and website URLs are accurate and active. All publications, organizations, websites, and other resources exist as described in the book, and all have been verified. The author and Prufrock Press Inc. make no warranty or guarantee concerning the information and materials given out by organizations or content found at websites, and we are not responsible for any changes that occur after this book's publication. If you find an error, please contact Prufrock Press Inc.

Prufrock Press Inc.
P.O. Box 8813
Waco, TX 76714-8813
Phone: (800) 998-2208
Fax: (800) 240-0333
http://www.prufrock.com

DEDICATION

For Rachel

"All men have need of the gods."

—Homer, the *Odyssey*, Book 3, Line 54

TABLE OF CONTENTS

PREFACE

Welcome to *Greek Mythology for Teens*, a book that uses reader's theater plays to retell ancient myths and legends. This is the second book in the *Mythology for Teens* series and also the second to deal with Greek and Roman mythology. Additional information accompanies each play, explaining the myth's relevance to the modern world, providing background information and commentary on the myth, as well as suggesting other topics of discussion or exploration. Only a handful of the Greco-Roman myths are presented here, and this book does *not* claim to be a complete collection of mythology. It is a sampling—one that hopefully will leave you hungry for more. In my opinion, the myths of the Greeks and Romans are the best that the world has to offer. I hope you enjoy reading, learning, and acting from this text, as it was designed for education, as well as entertainment. Please feel free to contact me with comments and suggestions.

—Zachary Hamby (mr.mythology@gmail.com)

TEACHER'S GUIDE

The poet Homer said, "It is tedious to tell again tales already plainly told," and I sincerely hope he's wrong. The Greek and Roman myths have been told time and time again, so what is there to make this book different? Once again, I defer to the words of another: "Teach mythology not as a study, but as a relaxation from study" (Bulfinch, 1855/1967, p. 12). This is Thomas Bulfinch of *Bulfinch's Mythology* describing an approach that I am adopting as my own. The intention of this book is to make mythology fun, and I hope it succeeds.

This book presents mythology in ancient and modern contexts. As I mentioned before, it is not intended to be a comprehensive textbook of mythology. Out of many Greco-Roman myths, only nine are present. Because this is the second book in a series, I have tried *not* to retread the same ground as before. The chapters of *Mythology for Teens* were focused on (and used a particular myth) to explore certain themes and issues. This book carries on the same tradition but chooses different themes and issues than its predecessor. You will find less information about ancient Greece than was presented in the last book and more myths. After all, the culture that produced these myths is a dark age in the history of Greece, and most of what is known about that particular time period comes from the myths themselves.

A reader's theater play makes up the main part of each chapter. When acted out, these plays run between 25–40 minutes. One myth, "Jason and the Argonauts," is broken up into two plays to accommodate its length, and there are two episodes, "In the Cave of the Cyclops" and "Searching for Odysseus," pulled from the *Odyssey*. In addition to the play(s) in each chapter, there are several other follow-up sections that add to the reader's sphere of reference. Most sections include discussion questions, asking the students to analyze what they have read, and additional activities that may ask the students to draw, research, write, act, present, read, or watch outside material. These activities, designed with the intent of stimulating creativity, help to further the students' understanding and enjoyment of the myth. Their purpose is to breathe life into the old bones of myth through interactive learning. They may be utilized before, after, or perhaps even during the reading of the plays.

Even though they can be read and enjoyed individually, the reader's theater plays should be read with a group or "full cast" to utilize their maximum potential. The variety of voice and interpretation adds new dimension to the written word and links students together in a common learning experience. Students become active participants as they read because they are also required to interpret the text. Linguistic and audio processing combine, resulting in maximum comprehension. The group-learning atmosphere also makes the reading more enjoyable.

Let me stress that these plays can never replace the original works. As hard as I try to maintain the themes and tone of the poets, I will never be as good at telling Homer's story as Homer. If your students enjoy the version read here, please encourage them to seek out the source. That being said, these plays are as faithful as they can be. As you might imagine, fitting a complex story into a 30-minute play is a challenging task. A few of the stories' peripheral details have been lost, but the core is intact. At times, I have condensed events; at others, I have combined or eliminated characters. For that I apologize to all of the dead poets and mythographers who brought us these stories. If you truly wish to have the full flavor of the original, read the original. If you wish to have the condensed, but not-skimping-on-the-feel-and-emotion-of-the-story version, you cannot do better than these plays.

Writing these plays has been a process of translation, and during this process, I am sure a little bit of my own voice has snuck in. I have tried to make the plays' dialogue as engaging as possible for modern teenage audiences, while leaving it archaic enough to still be challenging. I have tried to avoid language that is *too* modern, but also lofty language that would trip up the tongue. The process is a balancing act between challenging the students' intellect without insulting it.

As for the actual reading of the play, you, the teacher, should act as the casting director. I strongly encourage you to participate in the play as well. This is helpful in breaking down a learning barrier. Instead of leaving students to learn on their own, you are becoming a participant and experiencing with them. In my own classroom, I commonly choose to be the narrator. Emotion cues in parentheses such as *(frightened)* or *(angrily)* come at the beginning of important lines. Even those students who are not strong readers can still participate (and should be encouraged to do so) by contributing through sound effects and crowd reactions. These are indicated in the script, such as *(booming thunder)*, and many can be performed by the whole class, such as *(applause from everyone)*.

Reader's theater has experienced plenty of success in lower grades, but its usefulness in middle or high school is relatively unexplored. A common rationale is this: Older students will not like activities geared toward younger students. I am here to tell you that this is not the case. Teenagers enjoy acting, playing, and creating just as much as elementary students. Even though they would hate to admit it, they are still young at heart. One draw to reader's theater for teens is that it appears "easy." Reading aloud seems like an "easy assignment." But, in actuality, when students are handed parts in a play, they are presented with a complex task: Read the written word, interpret it, and present it for others to hear—all in a matter of seconds. This process looks less like an easy assignment and more like active learning.

Reader's theater is not the only way to experience literature, but it is a great way to create a classroom learning experience where everyone laughs and learns together. As you implement this book into your own classroom, please keep these things in mind. Students will value knowledge when you make it applicable to them. I haven't yet encountered a class that didn't enjoy participating, experiencing, and learning from these stories as they are presented here.

Note on Supplemental Materials

For the films recommended to accompany certain sections, all are rated either G, PG, or PG-13. Even though your students may fall into these age ranges, please preview each film to determine if its contents are appropriate for *your* classroom.

INTRODUCTION
Wrapping Truths in Myths

British composer George Lloyd (1919–1988), who, like many composers before him, used Greek mythology as inspiration for his symphonies, made an important observation: "The ancient Greeks have a knack of wrapping truths in myths" (The George Lloyd Society, n.d., para. 7). He is playing off words that now mean the opposite of one another, *truth* and *myth*. To say something is a *myth* is to say that it is *false, untrue*, or at its very best, *a fanciful lie*. But you're here to study *myth*-ology, and mythology is not the study of *lies*. Instead it is the study of *truth (told in an interesting way)*. A truth is usually pretty straightforward—for example, "Money will not solve all your problems." It is simple. It is cut and dried. It is the truth. But it is also boring. What if, instead of simply *telling* you the truth, it was illustrated through an entertaining story? What about a story that tells of a king who desired nothing more than money and used his one and only magical wish to gain the Golden Touch? The story itself is complete hogwash. A person cannot turn something into gold just by touching it. Gods do not just go around and grant random mortals' wishes. Yet the truth is illustrated there in the story—wrapped up in layers of myth— waiting for the listeners to discover it, experience it, absorb it, and make it a part of their philosophy.

Until scientists discover that the sky does, in fact, rest on the shoulders of Atlas or that there are creatures who are half-man, half-something-else, we still classify the Greek myths as fiction. Yet you should always remember that myths were originally a way of examining humanity, and the truth of humanity is in them:

human emotion, weakness, courage, and love. And these truths will never change.

Why Classical Mythology Matters

With all of the types of mythology out there—everything from Native American to Japanese—it is important to mention why classical mythology occupies its seat as the most revered. (Classical mythology encompasses the mythology of Greece and Rome, which were basically one, but we will get to that later.) The Greeks laid the groundwork for Western civilization. Their contributions in the areas of science, literature, mathematics, art, philosophy, politics, and warfare paved the way for many successive civilizations. The Greeks invented important things like democracy, history, modern medicine, drama—things you have probably heard of. Along with all of these contributions came a complex mythology, which is at times both savage and poetic. And as Western civilization progressed, the mythology of the Greeks was passed along.

Greek culture gained significant ground when Alexander the Great, a Macedonian Greek, conquered the known world and made his own culture the "in" thing. After his empire dissolved, the Romans—Greece's neighbors to the west—picked up the slack and, adopting Greek culture as their own, continued to spread it even further. The Roman Empire ventured even further north into Europe to then-remote places like France and England. Several centuries later, when this empire had declined and ultimately fallen, the European nations—which had once been complete barbarians but were now completely "enlightened" like the Romans and Greeks before them—carried on the torch of Western civilization. (Notice how things are basically heading west, hence "Western" civilization.) The tradition went *extremely* west when the European nations began to cross the Atlantic and found colonies in the New World. Now the United States of America (about as far west as you can go without going back east again) is the heir to the Greek tradition.

At each stage of Western civilization's progression, the Greek myths found a new audience and a new fanbase. The Romans were so enamored with Greek mythology that they basically absorbed it. They kept the names of their own deities (e.g., Jupiter, Juno, Mercury, Venus) but tacked them onto the Greek gods. After a series of name changes, *Greek* mythology became *Roman* mythology. When the Europeans discovered the same mythology, they did not make it the subject of their worship, but the subject of their art. Literature, music, and art contain innumerable references to classical mythology. Only the Bible is alluded to more often.

You may not spend your spare time looking at paintings or listening to classical music, so how has classical mythology technically impacted your world? Phrases like "Achilles heel," "Oedipus complex," and "Between Scylla and Charybdis" proliferate the English language. The planets in our solar system bear the Latinized (Roman) names of the gods, and the months of the year contain references to them as well (e.g., January, March, April, May, June). Everything from young adult novels (the *Percy Jackson* series), to tennis shoes (Nike), to video games (*God of War*), to the modern Olympics uses classical mythology as a reference point. So maybe it is time you started paying attention. No other set of myths has ever—or will ever again—impact your culture so greatly.

The Many Meanings of Myths

For the original myth-makers, myths served a variety of purposes. For starters, myths helped ancient people answer their questions about the complex world around them: Why does the sun travel the same course over the sky day after day? Why do the seasons change? For this reason, myths were a primitive stab at science. In addition to Mother Nature, myths also helped explain human nature—why do humans act the way they do?—and the mystery of human existence or why men exist in the first place. Myths also served as warnings and determined the boundaries of society by illustrating which behaviors were unacceptable and resulted in punishment from the gods. Many fantastic things happen in myths—men fly, statues come to life, and men achieve the power to live forever. All of these reflect the conscious (or unconscious) desires of the myth-makers. Lastly (an often overlooked function of myth in all of the hubbub of hidden meaning), myths were made to entertain, and to this end they still succeed.

Mythologist is a term for someone who studies mythology, and this will be your title as you read the myths presented in this book. As you read, look for the various functions of mythology. Be prepared to discuss and analyze these at different intervals. These myths have been interpreted anew by each successive generation. Your interpretation will be no less valuable.

DISCUSS
- Can you think of any other references to classical mythology in the modern world?

RESEARCH
Locate a product that uses a reference to classical mythology in either its name or its advertising. Discuss how the reference helps sell the product.

The Gallery of the Gods

Zeus (Roman Names: Jupiter, Jove)

Lord of the Sky, Rain-Bringer, Cloud-Gatherer

After leading his brother and sister gods in a revolt against their forefathers, the Titans, Zeus became the unquestioned ruler of the heavens. His feared weapon is the thunderbolt, and his palace on Mt. Olympus is a place of peace, where all gods are welcome. Zeus is the husband of the goddess Hera, but it's not in his nature to be faithful. Time and time again, he enters into disastrous affairs with other goddesses, nymphs, and mortal women. Zeus is the all-father. Almost all of the second generation of gods claim Zeus as their father. Many of the mortal heroes are children of the god as well. Zeus' bird is the eagle.

Apollo (Roman Name: Phoebus Apollo)

God of Light, Truth, Poetry, Health, Prophecy, and Music

From all of the important titles laid at Apollo's feet, you can see the Greeks thought very highly of him. He is called the "most Greek" of all of the gods. He, above all others, represented the ideal man—handsome, athletic, intelligent, talented, and good. His twin sister is Artemis, Goddess of the Moon. Over time, Apollo came to replace the Greek god Helios as God of the Sun as well. The lyre is Apollo's instrument, as he is the master musician. Apollo's tree is the laurel. A wreath of laurels was awarded in Greece to those who won a contest of poetry. Apollo's oracle in Delphi was the most reliable and the most popular.

Aphrodite (Roman Name: Venus)

Goddess of Love and Beauty

Aphrodite was so lovely that the Greeks couldn't imagine her being born in the usual way. Instead she sprang from the white beauty of the sea foam. In an odd arrangement, this most beautiful goddess was married to the only ugly Olympian, Hephaestus, the deformed forge god. Some said that Zeus forced her into the marriage; others, that she chose him herself. Either way, her vows did not stop her from having many affairs. Gods and mortal men found her charms simply irresistible. Whenever on business abroad, Aphrodite is pulled through the sky by a swan-drawn cart. The swan and the dove are both symbols of her grace. In Greece her worship was popular, although the temple priestesses were rumored to be prostitutes. Our word aphrodisiac, a passion-inducing substance, is derived from her name.

Ares (Roman Name: Mars)

God of War

Ares is the cruelest member of the Olympians, hated by all. This god is known for his ruthlessness when he has the upper hand and his cowardice when the tides turn against him. Even the Greeks disliked this terrible god. There were no temples to Ares in ancient Greece. Aphrodite, in one of her many infidelities, started an affair with Ares, which was his motivation to fight for the Trojans in the war. Martial (having to do with war) and March are coined from his Latin name.

Artemis (Roman Name: Diana)

Virgin Goddess of the Hunt, Protector of Maidens and Wild Creatures
Artemis is often called upon by maidens who want nothing to do with men. Her silver arrows have slain many overzealous suitors. Artemis is also the twin sister of Apollo and revered as the Goddess of the Moon. At times her different duties contradict one other. Even though she is a hunter of animals herself, she often demands that mortals pay for killing defenseless beasts. In the most famous case, she demands that a Greek army offer her a human sacrifice in apology for trampling a family of rabbits. She asks for the life of the general's young daughter, a maiden. This is strange behavior for the protector of maidens.

Athena (Roman Names: Minerva, Pallas Athena)

Goddess of Wisdom and Battle
According to one tale, Athena was not actually born, but sprang fully grown from Zeus' head. This is symbolic of her distinction as Goddess of Wisdom. Athena's animal is the wisest of birds, the owl. As the leader of the Virgin Goddesses, those who will never marry, Athena refuses to let any man be her master. When a new city-state was founded, there was a contest between Athena and her uncle Poseidon over who should be its patron god. The competition was fierce. To win the people over to his side, Poseidon formed the first horse from the crest of a wave. In order to one-up his gift, Athena created the bridle, a tool man could use to subdue Poseidon's creation. Because her gift was the wiser, the city chose Athena as their patron goddess. From this point on the city-state was called Athens.

Demeter (Roman Name: Ceres)

Goddess of Agriculture

The Greeks and Romans felt an extremely strong connection with Demeter. The goddess was responsible for providing them with their sustenance and livelihood. In addition to this, Demeter was one of the few gods who did not reside on Olympus. She lived on Earth, where she could be close to those who needed her most. Also unlike the other gods, Demeter's existence was bittersweet. In the fall and winter, she mourned her daughter, Persephone (Proserpine), who was taken into the Underworld to be the wife of Hades. Only during the spring and summer, when her daughter returned to visit, was Demeter truly happy. All of these qualities endeared her to her worshippers. Her sacred cult at Eleusis was one of the most popular, and the secrets were kept so well that to this day researchers have no clue what their rites consisted of. From Ceres comes our word for grain-based food, cereal.

Dionysus (Roman Name: Bacchus)

God of the Vine and Wine, Patron God of the Theatre

Dionysus was a latecomer to Mt. Olympus. He is the only god to have a mortal parent. Dionysus is a two-sided god. On one side, he is the gentle planter of the vine. On the other, he is a wild drinker, inspiring his followers to commit terrible acts through their intoxication. Satyrs—half-men, half-goat creatures—were said to be the companions of Dionysus, along with his fanatical female followers (the maenads). Followers of Dionysus gathered in the wilderness and drank themselves into a wild frenzy. More often than not their gatherings ended with violence. In many stories, kings, who do not approve of the new god or the behavior he promotes, forbid his worship. This probably reflects Greek society's displeasure with the worshippers of Dionysus, whom many viewed as hedonistic drunks. Despite his late addition to the gods and his initial opposition from men, Dionysus became one of the most popular additions to the Greek pantheon. Athens dedicated its springtime drama festival to the god, solidifying his place as patron god of the theatre.

Hades (Roman Names: Pluto, Dis)

Ruler of the Dead, Lord of the Underworld

Although he has been presented as one before, Hades is no villain. He is cold and calculating. He keeps to himself, only showing up in myth when he is sought out. Hades is more a recluse than anything else. He has little to do with mortals' lives. Their deaths are a different story. Hades is not Death himself; in other words, he is not responsible for deciding when mortals die. A mortal's death is an assembly line: The Fates snip the threads of life, Thanatos (or death) causes the mortal to die, and Hermes leads the soul to the banks of the Styx. After the gods defeated their forbearers, the Titans, Hades was presented with a helmet of invisibility and given the Underworld to rule. Hades' Roman name, Pluto, came from the Greek word for wealth. The god was considered rich because of all of the precious metals that are found beneath the Earth.

Hebe

Goddess of Youth

Hebe is the most easily overlooked Greek goddess. Her only job on Olympus is to hold the holy cup from which the gods drink. Nectar, the magical liquid found within the cup, confers immortality on those mortals who drink it. Ambrosia, a food fine enough for divine lips, also is eaten on Olympus. Hebe is the daughter of Zeus and Hera. When Heracles (Hercules) completed his life of heroic deeds, he ascended to Olympus, where Zeus allowed him to drink from the holy cup. The hero then became a god, and Zeus presented him with a new wife, Hebe.

Hephaestus (Roman Name: Vulcan)

Smith-God of the Forge, God of Fire

Hephaestus, a peace-loving god, is the patron of practical arts. He is renowned for his metalworking abilities. The unparalleled armor of the gods and heroes come from his forge. His lame leg and grizzled appearance earn him the distinction of being the only ugly god. In fact, when Hera gave birth to such an unattractive son, she hurled him out of heaven, laming his leg. Ironically, Aphrodite, goddess of beauty, is his wife. The Romans pictured the fiery god Vulcan working his forge beneath the mountains, and when they saw a hilltop erupt with flame, they labeled it a volcano.

Hera (Roman Name: Juno)

Goddess of Marriage, Queen of Olympus

Hera usually is shown as a crafty schemer and jealous wife. She is the mother of a few of the second-generation gods: Ares, Hephaestus, and Hebe. Zeus and his frequent affairs are enough to keep her busy punishing his many lovers and cursing his illegitimate children. Hera is labeled as the protector of marriage, even though she cannot protect her own. Wives with unfaithful husbands could definitely sympathize with her. Hera has a fiery temper and enough venomous anger to last centuries. Her beast is the cow, and her bird is the peacock. The Romans named June, the season for marriage, after Juno.

Hermes (Roman Name: Mercury)

Messenger of the Gods

Hermes, the most mischievous and clever of the gods, also serves as a psychopomp (a guide of dead souls to the Underworld). One of the youngest gods, Hermes showed his ability to cause both trouble and delight at an early age. On the day of his birth, Hermes snuck out from his cradle and whisked away the cattle of his elder brother Apollo. Hermes was quickly found out and forced to return the cattle. But, in reparation for his actions against Apollo, the newborn god created a lyre from the shell of a turtle. He presented the stringed instrument to his older brother. Apollo's anger melted away, and he gifted Hermes with a magical sleep-inducing staff called the caduceus. Once Zeus realized his young son would cause nothing but trouble if he weren't constantly occupied, Hermes was given the job of Olympian Messenger. A winged cap and sandals were presented to him to assist him in his duties. Due to the nature of his job, Hermes appears most often of all of the gods.

Hestia (Roman Name: Vesta)

Goddess of the Hearth and the Home

Hestia never plays a part in any Greek myth. Even though she wasn't exciting enough to make it into their stories, the Greeks honored Hestia with their dinnertime prayers, asking her to bless their food and protect their homes. City-states had a central hearth dedicated to the goddess, where a holy fire forever burned. She is the third of the three virgin goddesses. In Rome she was the patron goddess of the Vestal Virgins, who kept the hearth fire of Rome forever burning.

Iris

Goddess of the Rainbow, Messenger of the Gods

Second only to the godly messenger Hermes, Iris delivers the divine decrees of Olympus. The Greeks saw the rainbow beginning at a distant point and touching down at the opposite end of the horizon. To their ancient minds, this multicolored trail could only be one thing: The path left by a goddess as she made her way through the heavens. In the modern world, the colorful part of the eye is named for this goddess. The plant iris also is named after her for its variety of colorful flowers.

Poseidon (Roman Name: Neptune)

The Blue-Haired God of the Sea

Next to Zeus, Poseidon is the god the Greeks most feared. As a sea-faring people, they knew the hazards of a stormy sea. The god was known for his mood swings—violent rage one minute, calm the next—just like the waters he controlled. In the Trojan War he favored the Greeks because of their love of shipbuilding, yet legend had it that generations before, he and Apollo had helped build the walls of Ilium.

Mt. Olympus

The Heavenly Mountain of the Gods

The palace of Zeus on Mt. Olympus is the home of the 12 Olympian gods and goddesses. When the heavens and Earth were divided between his two brothers, Poseidon and Hades, Zeus declared that Mt. Olympus would be common to all. Here is where the gods have their great debates, sipping nectar and eating ambrosia. In the earliest myths, Mt. Olympus is still associated with the mountain in Greece that bears the same name. But, by later times, it was imagined to be a mystical place, floating high in the heavens.

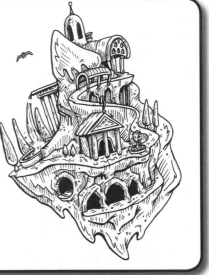

CHAPTER 1

The Nature of the Gods

THE LOVES OF THE GODS

Cast

Prometheus *Chained Titan*

Zeus *Lord of the gods*

Hera *Queen of Heaven*

Io *Mortal princess*

Hermes *Messenger of the gods*

Argus *One-hundred-eyed henchman*

Helios *God of the sun*

Hades *Lord of the Underworld*

Demeter *Goddess of the harvest, mother of Persephone*

Persephone *Goddess of spring*

NARRATOR: It was a typical day for Prometheus the Titan. The eagle that came every morning to rip out his immortal liver had not yet arrived. Over time, he had grown somewhat numb to the pain. The steel fetters that held him fast to the rock prevented any resistance, and after the daily grisly deed was done, he would writhe in constant agony until the orange of the sun touched the line of the sea. Then, by some otherworldly force, the hurting would stop, and he would feel the organ begin to form again within him.

This was his life—waiting and watching the landscape below him—but today something was different. A white speck was making its way down the coastline path that wound past his rocky perch. As it drew closer, he saw that it was a white heifer—perfectly formed.

PROMETHEUS: Hello, my animal sister.

IO: Hello.

NARRATOR: He was rather surprised that it responded. Of course, being a Titan, he could communicate with any beast, but this one had answered with the voice of a human.

PROMETHEUS: *(thoughtfully)* You are no beast. Are you under some hex from the gods?

IO: I am. How did you know?

PROMETHEUS: Zeus gives blessings grudgingly and curses easily. I myself am under one of these.

IO: I see that. You seem so kind. What did you do to deserve such a punishment?

PROMETHEUS: Ah, I offended Zeus by giving men his immortal fire. I have been trapped here ever since.

IO: That doesn't seem fair.

PROMETHEUS: Eh, I have gotten used to it. Besides, I always know that my crime was worth its penalty. Tell me, what has happened to you?

IO: I wasn't always like this. I used to be a princess—in Thebes.

PROMETHEUS: Well, the day is hot, and you could surely use a rest. I am interested to hear how a maiden came to be transformed as you have been.

IO: (sadly) It's a sad story. I have never told it to anyone. You are the first person who has cared enough to listen. I doubt I can get through it without tears.

PROMETHEUS: Speak. I will share your tears. I have much to weep over myself.

IO: It all started with Zeus. I was a naïve girl—easily infatuated with the thought of a handsome god loving *me*. I was sucked in by the excitement of it all, I guess.

NARRATOR: And so Io began her tale, and the imprisoned Titan listened intently as she recounted it. It had begun many years before, when Zeus had appeared to her in a restless dream and requested to be her lover.

ZEUS: Fair princess, I am Zeus, Lord of the Gods. I have seen your *charms* from above. The arrows of desire have pierced me. Will you consent to be mine? I will make you happier than any woman upon the Earth.

NARRATOR: Io found this quite shocking, and within her breast her heart beat desirously. To be the lover of a god—what prestige. She had no idea what gifts the immortals bestowed upon those they loved, but she was sure it was something undreamt of.

IO: I agree, my lord. Tee hee. (giggling)

NARRATOR: And so the affair was begun. As the sun rose, Zeus spirited her away to a faraway meadow and appeared to her in all his glory.

ZEUS: Long have I waited for this, my sweet. But first, let me overcast the sky so that my wife's spying eye cannot see us.

IO: (nervously) Your wife?

ZEUS: (confidently) Don't worry about her. She's a hideous old thing. I'm only concerned with *you* right now.

NARRATOR: With a wave of his mighty hand, mist filled the meadow—until the sun was all but obscured. He smiled upon this with satisfaction and swept the maiden quickly into his arms.

Within the hanging gardens of Olympus, Hera strolled casually. Her husband had left the palace early that day. "Business among the mortals," he had said. But she had her suspicions.

HERA: (to herself) I must have Iris follow him. That fool thinks he's pulled the wool over my eyes. If only I were a bit more mighty, I would punish him *permanently* for his unfaithfulness.

NARRATOR: As she said these words, her gaze happened to stray over the balcony to the world below.

HERA: What the . . .

NARRATOR: A haze lay over one portion of the countryside. Nothing could be seen beneath it.

HERA: Ha! I knew it! You arrogant fool!

NARRATOR: Swift as an arrow, Hera vaulted over the railing of the balcony and shot down through the atmosphere toward the hideaway of her amorous husband. The fog beat at her vision, and she slammed to the ground with an Earth-shaking jolt.

ZEUS: Gaea save us all! It's my wife!

IO: (frightened) Oh gods.

HERA: (screaming) Where are you, you dolt? I know you're around here somewhere—hiding in the smoke with your mortal concubine!

IO: What will she do to me?

ZEUS: Shhhh. Lie still. I will transform you until she has left.

IO: But . . .

ZEUS: Trust me.

NARRATOR: The Queen of Heaven began swiping at the clouds around her—growing angrier by the second.

HERA: (raging) I know you're here! Show yourself! Be a man!

NARRATOR: The haze was at once whisked away, revealing Zeus standing beside a pristinely white, though somewhat scared, heifer.

ZEUS: (acting surprised) Hera? What a surprise!

HERA: (calmly) Zeus, what are you doing?

ZEUS: Me? Oh, nothing. I was just admiring this gorgeous cow here.

HERA: Oh, really? And what about this atmospheric disturbance? Clouds aren't commonly found on the ground!

You weren't trying to obstruct someone's view, were you?

ZEUS: Atmospheric disturbance? Oh, you mean the fog. That must be my fault. I've had a headache today. Whenever I have one of those, for some reason, the weather seems to change. *(nervous laugh)* Ahem. Yes. That's it.

NARRATOR: Hera eyed her husband suspiciously.

HERA: Uh-huh. And why exactly were you so interested in this cow, did you say?

NARRATOR: Zeus looked nervously to his transformed lover and began to stammer.

ZEUS: Well, you know, it's a beautiful specimen . . . and, uh . . .

HERA: Fine eyes? Large udders?

ZEUS: No, no, you see, I was looking at it because, because . . . *(sudden idea)* it's a present!

HERA: For whom?

ZEUS: For you, of course!

IO: Moo?

ZEUS: I know how you . . . love . . . cows . . .

NARRATOR: His wife's frown quickly transformed into a smile.

HERA: *(fake happiness)* Well, why didn't you say so, husband? And here I was thinking that it was one of your little hussies—transformed. Whew! What a relief.

ZEUS: Nope. None of that here.

NARRATOR: Hera stepped forward and began to stroke the shaking haunches of the princess.

HERA: Thank you so much. I know exactly what I will do with it, too.

ZEUS: And what's that, my dear?

HERA: *(slyly)* I will butcher it at once, of course.

ZEUS: *(shocked)* What? Butcher it?

IO: *(shocked)* Moo?

HERA: Of course, dear. What else would I do with this? I can't have a smelly old cow stinking up my chambers, can I?

ZEUS: I meant for you to keep it—as a pet, you know. But I'll need to take it and have it groomed first, of course.

NARRATOR: The goddess stepped between Zeus and his lover.

HERA: I think it's been *groomed* enough. Very well. I will not butcher it *yet*. I'll keep it, but it's such a fine cow. I'm afraid someone will steal it. Aphrodite might want a cow of her own and try to steal mine! I'll have to put a guard on it.

ZEUS: A guard? No, no, dear. No one would try to steal this beast away. Even if they did, I would replace it immediately—with an even finer one.

HERA: I could not bear it, Zeus. I love *this* cow. In fact, I think I will name her. I'll name her Whitey. Do you like that name, Whitey?

IO: *(negative)* Moo.

HERA: See? We're inseparable. Thank you so much, my husband. This is the best gift a wife can ask for.

NARRATOR: She smiled good-naturedly at Zeus, who began to say something but stopped.

ZEUS: Well . . . I guess I'll be going . . . now that you have your . . . your . . .

NARRATOR: He waved a hand at Io, who looked back at him helplessly.

HERA: *(cheerfully)* Goodbye!

ZEUS: Hmmmm.

NARRATOR: The Lord of Olympus turned—his shoulders slumped in regret—and disappeared in a puff of smoke. Smirking to herself, Hera rounded on her animal ward.

HERA: *(gloating)* So, thought you would get away with it, didn't you? What a pathetic disguise. I mean, *really*. I'll teach you the hard way to stay away from my husband.

NARRATOR: Io cowered in fright.

HERA: I cannot undo Zeus' transformation, or I would choose a much worse form for you. What I *can* do is put a guard about you—so that no one can get near you while I think of a suitable end for a cow such as yourself.

NARRATOR: Hera cupped her celestial hands together and bellowed toward the sky.

HERA: *(yelling)* Iris! Iris! Get that good-for-nothing Argus down here at once. I need his services.

NARRATOR: The air was silent for a moment, and then a faraway sizzling sound could be heard. Spreading across the sky, a magnificent rainbow headed directly for their location. The meadow filled with color, and a towering form was shadowed within.

HERA: Argus!

NARRATOR: The shimmering light disappeared, and Argus appeared. Muscle on top of muscle padded his gargantuan body, and upon his brow were 100 eyes—all blinking and staring in different directions.

HERA: Over here! I have a job for you.

ARGUS: *(dumb voice)* Yes, my queen.

HERA: Argus, please look at me when I speaking to you.

ARGUS: *(defensively)* Argus *is* looking at his queen.

HERA: *(grumbling)* I hate that. I can never tell. *(pause)* Anyway, this heifer here is one of Zeus' hussies. Watch her. Keep her guarded until I can dream up a fitting punishment for her.

ARGUS: Duh. Yes, melady.

HERA: *(evilly)* I was thinking she'd make some nice steaks—or maybe some beef jerky.

ARGUS: *(licking lips)* Mmmm. Sounds good!

HERA: Watch her! Let no one near her! And whatever you do, don't fall asleep on the job!

ARGUS: Do not worry. Argus' eyes sleep one at a time. That way Argus is always seeing, and eyes still get rest.

HERA: *(sarcastically)* Fascinating. Apparently, being a freak of nature has its advantages. Well, I'm off. There are three other wenches I have to deal with today. My husband has been a busy man. Remember your job. If you fail me, I'll put each of those eyes out myself.

ARGUS: *(whimper)*

IO: *(whimper)*

NARRATOR: Hera raised her arms above her and with a flash of flame disappeared.

Io's monstrous guardian turned to her.

ARGUS: Moo cow, do not be afraid. Argus will not eat you. Argus is vegetarian.

IO: *(relieved)* Moooo.

NARRATOR: And so Argus of the Hundred Eyes seated himself upon the grass beside the white heifer. Io—though her mind reeled with tormenting thoughts—made the best of the situation and began to graze upon the lush turf. Every move she made, her watcher's gaze followed. So they spent the day—guard and guardian.

Up on Olympus, a frustrated Zeus had frantically called his son Hermes to him.

ZEUS: Hermes, I have a mission for you.

HERMES: In trouble with Hera again?

ZEUS: You have no idea. That woman won't give up. Of course, I can't really blame her. It is adultery. I just can't help myself, y'know? I have *needs*.

HERMES: You don't have to explain yourself to me, Father. I'm thankful for your adultery. Otherwise, I wouldn't be here—or Apollo for that matter, or Artemis, or Dionysus, or about half of the mortal world—

ZEUS: *(irritated)* I get the point. Anyway, Hera has taken captive one of my lovers, a white heifer.

HERMES: *(nudgingly)* A cow? Why, you old bull-god, you . . .

ZEUS: *(angrily)* She wasn't a cow to begin with! She was a gorgeous princess!

HERMES: Hey, I'm not judgin' you.

ZEUS: *As I was saying,* the Argus is watching her—and that's a problem. You must trick him and steal Princess Io back for me.

HERMES: Argus is the guy with the excellent vision, right?

ZEUS: Yes, I'm afraid so.

HERMES: So . . . let me get this straight. You want me to sneak up on a creature that can see in every direction and steal one of your mortal merry-makers out from under his very nose?

ZEUS: You got it.

HERMES: *(sigh)* Being the cleverest really is a curse, isn't it?

NARRATOR: Hermes flew from the mountain—wracking his brain frantically, trying to come up with a scheme and achieve the impossible.

HERMES: He can't keep all those eyes open all the time. There's got to be some way to lull him to sleep.

NARRATOR: He dug in the satchel slung at his side and produced a set of reed pipes.

HERMES: These should do nicely. I haven't found a being yet who doesn't think pipe playing is the most boring thing on Earth.

NARRATOR: Beating his way down through banks of clouds, the golden form of Hermes started to change—becoming common, coarse, and badly dressed. A ragged tunic and a large floppy hat replaced his Olympian garb. He touched down not far away from the Argus and his bovine captive.

(pipe music)

ARGUS: *(speaking to Io)* And then, moo cow, that is when mighty queen take Argus in and give Argus job. *(pause)* Argus hears music.

IO: *(surprised)* Moo?

NARRATOR: The eyes of the monster tracked to the path where a scraggly-looking man was frolicking forth—playing jubilantly upon his instrument.

ARGUS: Stop! Who are you, pipeman?

NARRATOR: Hermes stopped in his tracks and addressed 100 inquisitive glances.

HERMES: *(happily)* I am a shepherd, of course. See my ridiculous clothes and my dirty hands? I will admit at the moment I am rather sheep-less, but today is my day for pipe playing instead. Mondays, sheep watching. Tuesdays, pipe playing.

ARGUS: *(happily)* Music is very pretty. Can pipeman play more?

HERMES: Certainly, my good monstrosity. Care if I pull up a rock?

NARRATOR: The shepherd god jauntily perched himself upon a nearby boulder.

HERMES: My, my. What a wonderful heifer! Say—I'm not interrupting anything, am I?

ARGUS: *(excitedly)* Play! Play for Argus! But no funny business. Argus sees everything.

HERMES: Obviously. That's a face only a mother could love—maybe not even her.

NARRATOR: Hermes winked at the confused cow and began to produce a trilling melody from his pipes, one that recalled a brook babbling far away. The soothing sound filled the air, and after several minutes, many of Argus' lids began to droop. Almost all closed in slumber, but one—one in front—refused to sleep. Hermes played on. *(pipe music)*

An hour later, his fingers cramping from their activity, the god realized it was no use. The final eye refused to close—even while all the others slept peacefully. He stopped.

Every eye of Argus flicked open.

ARGUS: Why the pipeman stop playing?

HERMES: My fingers are killing me. I need to give them a break. Are you sure you don't want to lie down . . . take a nap? Maybe have some warm milk? I can ask the cow if—

ARGUS: Argus will *not* go to sleep! Argus said he would guard moo cow, and he will.

HERMES: Very well. How about a story? Would you like to hear a story?

ARGUS: Hmmmm. What is story about?

NARRATOR: Thinking, the god glanced at the sunlit meadow about him for inspiration. The flowers around were in full bloom.

HERMES: Spring. That's what it's about! Spring! *(speaking very slowly in a soothing voice)* It happened a very, very, very, very long time ago . . . in a place far, far, far away.

NARRATOR: The god lapsed into his tale as the Argus listened intently.

HERMES: Many years ago the seasons were not as they are today. It was always spring. The sun shone, and the ground yielded. Demeter, the Goddess of the Harvest, was eternally happy—teaching mortal man to farm and to grow. She bore her brother Zeus a beautiful daughter, Persephone, the Goddess of Spring.

DEMETER: Wouldn't you say my daughter is the most gorgeous sight you have ever seen?

HERMES: Demeter was a very proud mother and thought that nothing could ruin her happiness. But she had not counted on the eye of Hades—the Lord of the Underworld—lighting upon Persephone as she picked flowers one day.

Hades was a god of few words. Living below with the dead had made him morose and withdrawn. His skin was sickly pale, and his fingernails were in bad need of cutting.

HADES: *(mumbling, nearly incoherent)* What a beautiful maiden. I must have her as my own.

HERMES: Roaring up from a crack in the ground, his black chariot—pulled by skeletal horses—thundered into the meadow where the young Goddess of Spring was frolicking.

PERSEPHONE: *(innocently)* Who are you?

HADES: *(muttering)* I—I—am—Hades—would—you—hmmmm . . .

PERSEPHONE: I'm sorry, but I'm not supposed to talk to strangers.

HADES: But—I—

HERMES: Definitely lacking in social skills, Hades began to sweat. Most of the people he dealt with on a daily basis were *dead*. He desperately wanted to tell this stunning goddess just how stunning she actually was, but all he could do was grunt inarticulately.

HADES: Um—would—you—mind—*(cough)*—errrr . . .

PERSEPHONE: I'm afraid I don't understand.

HADES: *(angrily)* Oh, never mind!

HERMES: Spurring his steeds forward, Hades swept the terrified goddess into his chariot.

PERSEPHONE: *(screaming)* Help! Mother! Mother! Heeeeeeeeeeelp!

HERMES: The ground once again opened, swallowing its deathless master, and the cries of Persephone were sealed up within the Earth.

PERSEPHONE: Let . . . go! Let go of me, you brute! What kind of freak kidnaps a defenseless girl?

HADES: I only—want—you—to—*(cough)*—love me.

PERSEPHONE: Are you insane? You just grabbed me!

HADES: Sorry, I panicked. I just get so nervous around girls.

PERSEPHONE: So you abduct them instead?

HADES: No, I mean, yes. This whole dating thing is so hard to figure out.

PERSEPHONE: Let me give you a little hint! This is NOT the way to do it! Heeeeeelp!

HERMES: Back above the Earth, the Goddess of the Harvest was discovering that her daughter had vanished.

DEMETER: *(calling out)* Persephone! Where are you? Oh, I told you not to wander away!

HERMES: Demeter soon realized that she had, in fact, disappeared without a trace. The goddess began to wail.

DEMETER: *(in anguish)* My daughter! My daughter! Woe! *(pause)* I will search until I learn what has befallen her.

HERMES: But then a sudden thought came to her: What would happen to the Earth with no one to tend it? It would wither without the powers of Demeter to make its fields prosper.

DEMETER: Let it die. What has it done for me? It has taken my only love and hidden her from me.

HERMES: So the world wilted. Crops failed. The sky produced no rain. The sun scorched the land barren. And Demeter wandered, in the guise of a simple maid, searching for her beloved daughter.

At last, Helios, the sun himself, saw that creation would soon die if someone did not intervene. He called down from his fiery chariot to Demeter below.

HELIOS: Demeter! You must cease your wandering! Tend to the Earth, or it will die—along with all that live upon it!

DEMETER: I will not allow a plant to grow or a flower to bud until I have my daughter again.

HELIOS: Persephone? Do you not know? Hades has taken her into the Underworld. He has made her his queen there.

DEMETER: (gasping) My baby? Abducted?

HELIOS: I saw it with my very eyes. Go to Father Zeus, and tell him your complaint. He is the only one strong enough to force Hades into giving her back.

DEMETER: (gratefully) Thank you, Helios. I will.

HERMES: Demeter cried out immediately to immortal Zeus, begging him to remember his sister and the daughter whom he had fathered by her. Zeus heard her cry, and immediately dispatched the devilishly handsome and infinitely intelligent god Hermes to fetch the Goddess of Spring back from the Underworld. As the gorgeous god flew into the bowels of the Earth, he began to notice why they called them "the bowels" of the Earth. Ranks of decaying bodies waited in endless lines, foul rivers crisscrossed stinking plains, and the air smelled of rotting flesh. No wonder Hades had to abduct his dates.

Soon Hermes came to the palace of Hades and came before the grim god sitting on his throne of death. Beside him sat the emotionless Persephone—her youthful colors muted with a veil of black.

HADES: (mumbling) What are you doing here, Hermes?

HERMES: Hello, uncle. I bring orders from Dad.

HADES: Orders? What do you mean *orders?* He rules above the Earth. I rule below it.

HERMES: Interesting distinction, but what I've come about is definitely an above-Earth matter.

HADES: (angrily) Hmph. Well, I—

HERMES: You know, nobody's trying to point fingers here, but abducting a young goddess in broad daylight right out in the open isn't really the brightest idea.

HADES: I take what I want!

HERMES: Uh-huh. Well, you see, this lovely lady happens to be the daughter of Demeter. (sarcastically) And for some strange reason she's a bit depressed about her daughter getting sucked down into Hell.

HADES: Maybe she should watch her more closely.

HERMES: You're not listening. Long story short, she's so miserable that the Earth is dying, people are starving, yadda, yadda, yadda.

HADES: Why should I care?

HERMES: Think about it. Everybody's *dying.* This place is crowded as it is. Do you really want to be swamped with all that extra work?

HADES: (sheepishly) No, not really.

HERMES: Plus, I have this personal message from Zeus Almighty. (narrating) The dashing messenger god unrolled a parchment. (speaking) Ahem. He says— Don't make me come down there.

HADES: (angrily) Fine! You may take her back to her mother! I didn't want a queen anyway. It's not fair! (weeping)

HERMES: (consoling) Oh, calm down! There'll be more girls to abduct. There are plenty of maidens in the meadow.

PERSEPHONE: (emotionlessly) Am I free to go? Ever since I ate those pomegranate seeds yesterday, my heart has grown so cold. I think the sun will be the only thing to warm it once again.

HERMES: Uh-oh. Did you say pomegranate seeds?

PERSEPHONE: Yes. Why?

HERMES: How many?

PERSEPHONE: Four.

HERMES: Whoops. Well, I don't know if anyone told you this rule, but if you eat the food of the Underworld, you are bound to it.

HADES: *(excitedly)* Aha! I had forgotten that rule. Oh, well. Too bad. Guess you'll have to stay here and be my queen after all.

HERMES: Wait a minute. If she's only eaten some tiny seeds, then she doesn't have to stay here all of the time.

HADES: What?

HERMES: She may leave, but because she has eaten *four* seeds, she shall return here for *4* months out of the year.

HADES: No! I won't allow her to leave.

HERMES: *(cautioning)* Remember the note.

HADES: *(pouting)* Fine. Go. I'll see you in 8 months, I guess.

HERMES: *(narrating)* Persephone smiled and leaned in close to the Lord of Death.

PERSEPHONE: It's weird, but I kind of like it here. And underneath it all, you're cute—in a creepy kind of way.

HADES: *(stunned)* You really think so?

HERMES: *(narrating)* Hades leaned in for a kiss, but the Goddess of Spring took his hand.

PERSEPHONE: Let's work up to that, okay? *(pause)* I'll go visit mother, but I'll be back.

HERMES: *(speaking)* If you don't, he'll probably come and get you.

HADES: *(laugh)* True. Goodbye, my love.

PERSEPHONE: Goodbye.

HERMES: *(narrating)* And so every year Persephone returns to her mother, the Goddess of the Harvest, and there are 8 months of plenty. But when she once again goes away to be with her subterranean husband, Demeter mourns, and the Earth grows barren until her daughter's return. And that's why we must put up with fall and winter each year.

ARGUS: *(loud snoring)*

NARRATOR: Hermes stopped his story. All of Argus' eyes were closed in slumber. Violent snoring was escaping his huge nostrils.

HERMES: I knew that one would put you to sleep. And now that you are easy pickings . . .

NARRATOR: The mischievous god withdrew a shining sword from the pouch slung at his side.

HERMES: Sucker!

NARRATOR: With a quick slice he severed the monster's head from its body. *(snicker-snack)* The hundred eyes had enough time to open before they once again became dim with death. With its deformed head rolling helplessly onto the grass, the body slumped forward.

IO: *(excited)* Moo!

HERMES: You're free! Run while you still can! It won't take my stereotypically evil stepmother long to figure out what's happened.

NARRATOR: The transformed maiden looked to the messenger god questioningly. Was he not going to turn her back into her normal self?

HERMES: *(sadly)* Only Zeus can undo what he has done! Run! And when there is no harm of his wife finding him out, he will come to you and transform you once again!

NARRATOR: The animal turned and galloped away.

HERMES: *(loud yawn)* Wow. I almost put *myself* to sleep with that one.

NARRATOR: There was a blip, and Hermes dissolved.

Seconds later the fabric of the universe was again disturbed. Hera appeared.

HERA: What the—

NARRATOR: With suppressed rage, she flew to the carcass of her favorite sentry.

HERA: *(angrily)* Argus! What measly peon of Zeus has done this to you?

NARRATOR: She picked the severed head up into her arms and cradled it almost lovingly.

HERA: My faithful servant, let your hundred eyes never be forgotten. I will place them upon the feathers of my peacocks. There they will watch out over the world for eternity, and all will remember your greatness.

NARRATOR: With a sniff, she wiped the sadness from her face and dropped the head to the ground.

HERA: *(seething)* So, the harlot has found a way to escape, I see! Run, cow! Run!

NARRATOR: The Queen of Heaven snapped her fingers and a faint buzzing grew closer. A tiny gadfly landed in her palm.

HERA: Pursue her. Never give her rest. Drive her on through country after country. Make her regret her lust. Let her seek her death.

NARRATOR: The fly took to the air, and Hera, with a cruel smile of satisfaction on her lips, watched it wing itself away.

IO: And so I have wandered these many years—stung by the fly of Hera. Misery has been my life.

NARRATOR: The transformed maiden finished telling her tale to the chained Titan. There was a pause as Prometheus took it all in.

PROMETHEUS: You have been wronged most definitely. Your punishment is equal to my own. But I can tell you to take heart. As you spoke, I heard the future in your words. I have seen down the corridors of time. The day is not far off when Zeus will come to you and make you whole once again.

IO: *(excitedly)* Really? Wonderful!

PROMETHEUS: Then this curse will be lifted. From him you will bear mighty sons—sons to bring you joy in the later years of your life. You will be repaid all this misery through that happiness.

IO: This gives me hope!

PROMETHEUS: It is hope for me as well! From your line will come a mighty hero, the greatest hero, and he will be the one who will free me from my eternal punishment. Heracles, they will call him.

IO: *(relieved)* Finally! We both have been so wronged by the gods. Justice will be served at last.

PROMETHEUS: Indeed. Goodbye, Io. Journey well.

IO: Goodbye.

NARRATOR: Leaving the chained form upon the rock, the white heifer continued on her path with a newfound spring in her step. Relief was in sight. Prometheus smiled as he watched her leave. Beyond her he saw the eagle coming—coming to disembowel him once again. But the glorious day was nearing when he too would be freed from his torment and released from his immortal chains.

DISCUSS

- In this story, how are the gods shown in an unflattering light? Explain.
- Should Prometheus be released from his eternal torture? Explain.

WRITE

Write a short skit that contains a frame story (a story-within-a-story). In other words, a character in your story will tell another story.

PRESENT

Present this skit to your classmates.

Helios (Roman Name: Sol)

To the Greeks, the sun crossing the sky day after day could be explained only one way: It was actually a god who drove his blazing chariot pulled by four fiery steeds across the heavens. Helios could reportedly view all Earthly events from his high vantage point, and in one famous story, he informed Hephaestus that Aphrodite and Ares were having an affair. When Greek men swore oaths by the gods, they often chose to swear by all-seeing Helios. The god's palace was on the eastern island of Rhodes, and every evening, when he ended his journey far to the west, he and his team would float back to his home on Ocean (the river that encircled the Earth) in a golden cup. Because of his association with the Island of Rhodes, an enormous statue of him was erected there called the Colossus. It was one of the seven wonders of the ancient world until it was destroyed by an earthquake in 226 B.C. The terms *helium,* a substance once associated with the sun, and *heliotrope* (sunflower) are derived from Helios. The Roman sun-god Sol, which was identified with Helios, gives us modern words like *solar* and *solstice.*

The Nature of the Gods

Many myths explain the *why*'s of nature: why the seasons change, why the sun travels across the sky, why sounds echo, why the designs on a peacock's tail-feathers resemble eyes. Ancient people asked these questions, and because science was still in a primitive stage, they used myths to answer their queries.

Nature is unpredictable. The same natural forces that create peaceful, sunny afternoons can produce earthquakes, hurricanes, tornadoes, and floods just as easily. The Greeks equated nature with the gods, and, therefore, the gods must be just as unpredictable as nature. They believed that the gods must have moods like humans—otherwise, what would explain the inconsistent nature of the world?

The Greek gods were capricious—they acted on whims. Greek sailors wondered why the same sea that gave them safe travel suddenly turned violent. The answer: Somehow they had offended Poseidon, the god of the sea. Emotions are not a bad thing among mortals, but the mood swings of the gods have the ability to ruin lives and destroy civilizations. For example, Troy *used* to be a thriving city—that is, until the gods started bickering over it. Now it is a heap of rubble.

In the myths, the Greek gods are rarely, if ever, worthy of worship. Their antics seem more like the actions of spoiled children than all-powerful deities. This is partially the reason for—or maybe a reflection of—the Greeks' style of worship. The Greek gods did not love humanity. In fact, the creation of the human race was often attributed to a Titan, not a god. (More on that later.) Most Greeks worshipped a particular deity, not out of love or religious devotion, but to get something in return. Because the gods were fickle, it was important to stay on their good side. With numerous gods, it was hard to worship all of them, so the Greeks stuck to the ones who affected them the most. Sailors would not want to offend Poseidon, but if they were remiss in their sacrifices to Hera, protector of marriage, it was not a big deal. It was a buffet-style of worship, a pick-and-choose type of spirituality with heavy doses of "You scratch my back, and I'll scratch yours."

The gods were also the personifications of ideas and activities. Each god and goddess had his or her own niche, and the niches of some were quite specific: Hephaestus was the patron of blacksmiths and craftsmen, Artemis was the patron of hunters and unmarried women, Hermes was the patron of shepherds and travelers, and so on. Others embodied larger ideas, like Aphrodite (Love), Ares (War), and Hades (Death). Through these associations, the gods were equated with the forces of nature and the facets of everyday life.

Because of their irrational nature, some Greeks refused to believe the myths. Xenophanes, a student of Socrates, held that "[the poets] ascribed to the gods all things that evoke reproach and blame among human beings, theft, adultery, and mutual deception" (Brunet, Smith, & Trzaskoma, 2004, p. 433). He also accused the myth-makers of creating gods in their own human image, which he considered to be a ridiculous idea, an animal-like mentality, because if horses could create their own gods, "horses would draw pictures of gods like horses" (Brunet, Smith, & Trzaskoma, 2004, p. 433). Xenophanes had his own ideas concerning the gods (or *god*, since he was part of a monotheistic religion): "There is only one god . . . not at all like mortals in form nor yet in mind" (Brunet, Smith, & Trzaskoma, 2004, p. 433).

Whatever the myth-makers' motives, gods with human shortcomings helped explain a world filled with its own contradictions.

DISCUSS

- What events in the previous myth explain something about nature?

ANALYZE

The Greeks enjoyed hearing about the many affairs and scandals of the gods. In many ways, this parallels the modern-day obsession with celebrities. Instead of ascending Olympus, men and women flock to Hollywood to achieve "immortality" and become the latest subject of celebrity gossip. What do you think of this comparison?

Zeus' Cheatin' Heart

It is amazing how much mythological strife and anguish could have been avoided if Zeus would have simply remained faithful to his wife! In story after story, we find Zeus paying conjugal visits to Titanesses and goddesses—*not* excluding his sisters and cousins—as well as to plenty of nymphs and mortal maidens. His infidelity makes for even more conflict within his already unstable family and turns his wife Hera into a vindictive beast-on-wheels.

As the head god, it is Zeus' job to be the all-father. Excluding his brothers and sisters, almost all of the gods descend from Zeus. Likewise, many of mythology's heroes are sons of Zeus. Powerful real-life kings in the later ages would even trace their lineage back to the Almighty Thunderer.

In order to conceive this multitude of illegitimate offspring, Zeus often adopts bizarre disguises. In various myths he appears as a bull, an eagle, a satyr (goat-man), a shower of gold, and—his most bizarre choice—a swan. In order to get to the mother of Heracles, Zeus simply appears as her husband. Unfortunately, a large number of his trysts are not consensual.

Some experts believe that Zeus' various animal forms were actually smaller religions that were replaced by the worship of the Greek gods. For example, the people of Crete worshipped a bull-god. The Greeks explained this by saying that Zeus—on one of his many escapades—once visited their island in the form of a bull, and this is where the Cretan religion originated.

ANALYZE

Rather than condemning his unfaithful behavior, most Greeks considered Zeus' extramarital escapades to be humorous. The idea of Hera angrily chasing him around, trying to catch him in "the act" was comical to them. Some even called Hera a stereotypical overbearing wife. What do you think of these characterizations? Does Hera have a right to be overbearing? Explain.

In the Beginning . . . It Was Chaos!

The Greeks used their myths to answer the big questions of life, and two of the biggest are "Why are we here?" and "Where did we come from?" According to them, the universe (or *cosmos*, a word which means "in good order") was created from *chaos. Chaos* is a confusing term because it has progressed through several different meanings. *Chaos* can mean "complete disorganization" or its ancient definition: "yawning gap" (*yawning* meaning "wide," not "tired.") So was the universe formed from *nothing* (a yawning gap) or from a swirling, jumbled mass of *disorganized something*? The Roman poet Ovid retells the creation story most poetically. To his mind chaos meant "disorganized." Chaos was a primordial substance, a haphazard mess of elements—water, fire, earth, and air—all competing against one another until an unnamed creator came along, tamed them, smoothed them into their appropriate places, and formed the *cosmos*. Listen as Ovid tells the story:

> Before land was and sea—before air and sky
> Arched over all, all Nature was all Chaos,
> The rounded body of all things in one,
> The living elements at war with lifelessness;
> No God, no Titan shone from sky or sea,
> No Moon . . . walked the night, nor was Earth poised in air . . .
> Earth, Air, Water heaved and turned in darkness . . .
> Where heat fell against cold, cold against heat—
> Roughness at war with smooth and wet with drought . . .
> Heaviness fell into things that had no weight.
> Then God or Nature calmed the elements:
> Land fell away from sky and sea from land,
> And aether drew away from cloud and rain . . .
> When God, whichever God he was, created
> The universe we know, he made of earth
> A turning sphere so delicately poised
> That water flowed in waves beneath the wind
> And Ocean's arms encircled the rough globe:
> At God's touch, lakes, springs, dancing waterfalls
> Streamed downhill into valleys, waters glancing
> Through rocks, grass and wild-flowered meadows . . .
> Then God willed plain, plateau, and fallen sides
> Of hills in deep-leaved forests: over them
> He willed rock-bodied mountains against sky . . .
> As God divided regions of this world
> Into their separate parts, then all the stars
> Long lost in ancient dark began to light
> Pale fires throughout the sky . . .
> (Ovid, 8/1958, pp. 3–4)

Remembering the Titans

According to mythology, the gods were not the first group of immortal beings to inhabit the heavens. In fact, they were not even the second. After the creation of the universe, two elements appeared, Gaea (Mother

DISCUSS
- Do you like Ovid's description of *chaos* and *cosmos*? Explain. What details does he use that are particularly vivid?

MYTH-WORD
The Greek word for the created universe, *cosmos*, which means "in good order," is the root for something that puts a face in good order: *cosmetics*.

COMPARE/CONTRAST
Read the creation account from the Old Testament (Genesis 1:1–1:31). How does it compare and contrast to Ovid's account?

Earth) and Uranus (Father Heaven). Coming together, these two forces produced a first batch of children who were hideously deformed: Some were Cyclopes (one-eyed giants), and the others had 100 gangly arms and 50 heads. Disgusted by their deformities, Uranus banished them to the deepest and darkest part of the Underworld, Tartarus. Gaea grieved for her first children, yet was compelled by Uranus to produce a second batch of offspring. These beings were the Titans, elemental giants who possessed mighty powers. As they were perfectly formed, Uranus allowed them to roam the Earth freely, and there was peace for a time.

The craftiest of the Titans, Cronus (called Saturn by the Romans), heard the weeping of his mother Gaea. He saw that she mourned for her deformed first-offspring, now locked beneath the Earth. Using this to his advantage, Cronus convinced his mother that the only way to free her long-lost children was to murder Uranus. The grief-stricken Gaea agreed to Cronus' plan and gave him a scythe (or in some versions, a sickle) to help him accomplish his dirty deed. That night when Uranus materialized from the heavens to meet with his wife, Cronus leaped forward from his hiding place and, swinging his weapon, castrated his father.

Deeply wounded, his power gone, Uranus dissipated back into the sky, and there he lost substance. The blood of immortal beings had magical properties, and as the drops of Uranus' blood rained from the heavens it gave birth to new creatures as it mingled with the dust. The three Furies, demonic spirits that torture criminals, arose with their eyes dripping blood. Also, a single drop of the magical blood landed on an ocean wave as it crested. Combining with the splendor of the sea foam, the blood produced Aphrodite, the goddess of love and beauty.

With his father displaced, Cronus set himself up as the new master of the universe, and ignoring his promise to his mother, left his deformed brothers chained beneath the Earth. As his new rule began, Cronus decided to make sure his reign would last forever.

Birth of the Gods

Every king must have a consort, so the Titan Cronus took his sister Rhea to be his queen. When the union produced its first child, Cronus knew there was a chance this child might try to overthrow him just as he had done to his father. It was not a risk he was willing to take. When the baby—the first of the gods—was at last delivered, Cronus swallowed it whole. Rhea was horrified, but it did not end there: A grisly cycle of birthing and eating had begun. Time and time again, Rhea delivered yet another perfectly formed infant god only to have it gobbled up by Cronus. The newborns Poseidon, Hera, Hades, Demeter, and Hestia were all devoured in this way. As his stomach continued to swell with the bodies of his own children, it seemed Cronus' appetite for power would never be satisfied. At last Rhea had had enough.

In secret Rhea delivered her next child, a sturdy baby boy, and sent him to be raised by the nymphs of Mount Ida on Crete. When Cronus demanded to see the newborn, crafty Rhea wrapped a stone in blankets and presented it to her husband. He greedily gorged the decoy without a second thought, and Rhea smiled to herself. She knew her youngest son, Zeus, would grow to adulthood in exile and return to avenge his brothers and sisters.

Many years passed, and Zeus did return, grown handsome and strong. In secret he reunited with his mother and together they formulated a plan. Posing as Cronus' cupbearer, Zeus poisoned his father's drink. Poison could not kill an immortal, yet it would weaken Cronus long enough for Zeus to attack.

The plan worked perfectly. Cronus unknowingly drank the poisoned draught and, feeling the liquid burning, clasped his throat to halt its progress, but it was too late. As the Titan's stomach began to churn and bubble, Zeus threw off his disguise. Cronus realized his worst fears had been confirmed: Somehow one of his children had survived. At that moment the Titan's stomach convulsed, throwing him to the floor where he retched and heaved. One by one Cronus vomited up his devoured children—and last of all, a cloth-swaddled rock. Hades, Poseidon, Hera, Demeter, and Hestia stood over the prostrate form of their father—fully grown gods, seething in anger. But Cronus was not defeated yet; he called out hoarsely for his brothers and sisters to come to his aid. The palace began to shake as the great Titans drew near.

DISCUSS

- There are many folktale elements in this part of the story.
  ◊ a crafty character saves another character through an implausible trick;
  ◊ a murderous parent;
  ◊ characters are eaten, but not digested;
  ◊ a character uses a disguise to trick another character; and
  ◊ the youngest child is the most resourceful.

Identify these elements in the story, and then think of other folktales or fairy tales that use these elements in their own story.

FUN FACT

A shrine in Delphi boasted that it had found the stone that was substituted for Zeus and vomited up by Cronus. It became an ancient Greece tourist trap. Priests oiled the rock daily and on holidays decorated it.

Continued on page 30

Continued from page 29

ANALYZE

The Titans were probably deities worshiped before the gods arrived on the scene. As one religion replaced another, myths were created to explain why this occurred. This story was created during the time of the god-worship because it shows Cronus to be a monstrously cruel tyrant, begging to be overthrown. Some have even theorized that Cronus eating his children reflects a tradition of child-sacrifice that perhaps accompanied the older religion. Because such barbaric customs horrified the later Greek myth-makers, they created a story of how the "good-guy" gods overthrew the Titans.

VIEW

View the painting *Saturn* by Francisco Goya (1746–1828). (Warning: This is a disturbing painting that depicts Cronus devouring one of his children.) What details do you notice about the painting? Does it accurately capture the myth? Explain.

Clash of the Titans

What happened next was an all-out war, one that shook the heavens and the Earth—Zeus and the gods against Cronus and the Titans. The raging of the two immortal armies leveled plains and pushed up mountains. The war lasted for 10 years, and gradually the Titans—being an older and stronger race—pressed an advantage. It became clear that the gods would lose if someone did not intervene. It was then that Gaea called out to her godly grandchildren, reminding them of the malformed monsters whom Uranus had locked beneath the Earth long ago and Cronus had failed to free. Seizing upon this opportunity for aid, Zeus descended to the Underworld to free the chained creatures, the Cyclopes and the 100-handed monsters. Had they forgotten how the Titans had abandoned them to prison for so many years? Now was their chance for revenge! Roaring in freedom, the 100-handed monsters burrowed up through the Earth to face their Titan brothers and sisters. The Cyclopes paused only long enough to bestow a new weapon on Zeus—his all powerful thunderbolt—before they flew into the battle as well. Listen as the poet Hesiod describes the war as it reaches its climax:

A hundred hands stuck out of their shoulders, grotesque, and fifty heads grew on each stumpy neck. They stood against the Titans on the line of battle holding chunks of cliff in their rugged hands. Opposite them, the Titans tightened their ranks, expectantly. Then both sides' hands flashed with power, and the unfathomable sea shrieked eerily, the earth crashed and rumbled, the vast sky groaned and quavered, and massive Olympos shook from its roots under the Immortal's onslaught . . . And now Zeus no longer held back his strength. His lungs seethed with anger and he revealed all his power. He charged from the sky, hurtling down from Olympos in a flurry of lightning, hurling thunderbolts one after another, right on target, from his massive hand, a whirlwind of holy flame. And the earth that bears life roared as it burned, and the endless forests crackled in fire, the continents melted and the Ocean streams boiled. . . . The blast of heat enveloped the chthonian Titans. . . . and the incandescent rays of the thunderbolts and lightning flashes blinded their eyes, mighty as they were, heat so terrible it engulfed deep Chaos. The sight of it all . . . was just as if broad Heaven had fallen on Earth: the noise of its crashing and of Earth being crushed would be like the noise that arose from the strife of the clashing gods . . . And the battle turned. (Brunet et al., 2004, p. 150–151)

Olympian Victory

When the dust of battle cleared, the gods were victorious. Terrified and defeated, Cronus fled to the far regions of the Earth. The remaining Titans were seized by many strong arms. For their crimes against the gods, they would be eternally punished—some chained in Tartarus (as their deformed brothers had been), while others would suffer Earthly punishments similar to that of Atlas, forced to bear the awful weight of the sky on his shoulders.

Zeus now ruled on high, but he did not hoard power as his father had done. He gave his brother Poseidon dominion over the seas and his brother Hades dominion over the dead beneath the Earth. Zeus declared his palace on Mt. Olympus to be home to any god who desired peace. The Cyclopes, in thanks for their rescue, made mighty gifts for the gods. To Zeus they had already given the thunderbolt, but to Poseidon they gave a trident, and to Hades, a helmet of invisibility.

Among the Titans were some whom Zeus spared from punishment. Prometheus and Epimetheus, a pair of Titan brothers, had refused to fight the gods, and for this they were allowed to roam the Earth freely. Yet as Zeus established himself as the new ruler of the heavens, he kept a suspicious eye on the two brothers. He had learned the hard way to never trust a Titan.

DISCUSS
- Hesiod imaginatively envisions this cosmic battle and uses descriptive language to emphasize its magnitude. What are some of the best details he uses? Explain.
- The appearance of the Titans is never clearly described, even though they sound like giants. How do you picture them?

MYTH-WORD
The element Titanium, the adjective *titanic* meaning "enormous," Titan the largest moon of the planet Saturn, and a professional football team (the Tennessee Titans) are all named for the Titans of mythology.

Prometheus the Firebringer

Although they were brothers, the two Titans Prometheus and Epimetheus were very different in nature. Prometheus, whose name means "forethought," was very cunning and sympathetic toward the lower creatures of the Earth. Epimetheus, whose name means "afterthought," was basically a kind-hearted fool. It was Prometheus, according to some sources, who saw that creation was not yet complete. There was one thing left to create.

Yet [the] world was not complete:
It lacked a creature that had hints of heaven

And hopes to rule the earth. So man was made . . .
It had a godlike figure and was man.
While other beasts, heads bent, stared at wild earth,
The new creation gazed into blue sky.
(Ovid, 8/1958, p. 5)

The poet Ovid's account of creation ends with the formation of man—the one thing that creation lacks. He uses an interesting phrase to describe man: "a creature who had hints of heaven/And hopes to rule the earth." Just as he did not specify which god was responsible for making *cosmos* from *chaos,* Ovid offers two different versions of how man was created: Either the original creator God made man along with all of his other works, or Prometheus the Titan, mixing in a bit of celestial elements, sculpted man as gods made of clay. It was Prometheus as the creator of man who intrigued the Greeks the most.

The Titan had created man to be higher than the animals, to face the heavens, and to make the Earth plentiful. Yet he soon discovered that his creation was weak. Man had no way to stay warm in the winter, no way to cook his meat, and no way to keep wild predators at bay. Man needed fire. Only the gods possessed fire. It glowed in Hephaestus' forge and in the halls of Olympus, but nowhere else.

Zeus was already suspicious of Prometheus' creation. The audacity of the action, creating something new from the dust of the Earth, both frightened and angered the god. When Prometheus approached the throne of Zeus, begging him to give some of his divine fire to man, Zeus flatly refused. If man was not strong enough to live on his own, he should not live at all.

Prometheus could not and would not allow his creations to die out. Plucking a reed from a riverbed, the Titan snuck up to Mount Olympus. He crept into Hephaestus' forge and, using his reed, took some of the gods' eternal fire for himself, smuggling his prize back to Earth. It did not take long for the gods to discover what had happened. Orange fires dotted the landscape. Zeus seethed as he called Prometheus before him. Where did these miserable humans get the fire of the gods? Prometheus told the truth. He had stolen the gods' fire and given it to man.

No punishment could be painful enough for such an offense, yet Zeus managed to devise an eternal torture that pleased him. Prometheus was chained to a jutting rock at the end of the Earth. Every dawn, an eagle—the bird of Zeus—came and tore out the Titan's liver with its razor-sharp beak. Prometheus spent the course of each day writhing in agony, his stomach torn open. Throughout the night, the organ painfully grew back in order to continue the grisly cycle day after day. Prometheus took his punishment nobly and only lamented the tyranny of Zeus. To him, his torture was a small price to pay for giving his beloved children the fire of life.

Pandora, the First Woman

Because man had already learned the secret of fire, Zeus could not take it back, so he plotted another way to punish mortal men. The Almighty Thunderer remembered Epimetheus, the dimwitted brother of Prometheus, and devised a way to ruin mankind through the chained Titan's own family. His plan would require a new creation, and he went to Hephaestus with instructions at once. In the fires of his smithy, Hephaestus forged a new creation—one much like those that Prometheus had formed from mud. Only this one was different; it had grace and charm and a hidden purpose. This creation was a *she*, Pandora. Her name, "many gifts," told how the gods and goddesses heaped blessings upon her. Athena taught her how to weave and dressed her splendidly, Aphrodite sprinkled her with desire and heartbreak, and Hermes filled her to the brim with thieving morals, lies, and swindles. Zeus sent Hermes to deliver this new creation to Epimetheus to be his bride. As a part of Pandora's trappings, the god included a jar, which he told Epimetheus and Pandora never to open.

Epimetheus did not expect a trick nor have the wit to watch his wife closely. Because Hephaestus had fashioned Pandora with enormous amounts of curiosity, it did not take the girl long to give in to her desire to know, sneak into the storehouse, and pull the lid from the jar. Shrieking as they came, every evil imaginable escaped into the world—sickness, decay, death, hardships of every kind. Even the foolish Epimetheus, when he came running, realized that Pandora had cursed all mortals with

DISCUSS
- What is heroic and noble about Prometheus?
- Why is Zeus so hard on Prometheus?
- Do you find it odd that the gods are so opposed to man having the gift of fire?
- Why do they want it only for themselves? Explain.

FUN FACT
The full title of Mary Shelley's famous novel is *Frankenstein or The Modern Prometheus*. Dr. Frankenstein, who gives life to the dead, is similar to Prometheus because he is taking a divine power into his own hands. Just like Prometheus, Dr. Frankenstein is punished severely for his actions.

DISCUSS
- This male-authored myth portrays women as beautiful, thieving liars who cause nothing but suffering. Is this a fair portrayal?
- Are women more curious than men? Explain.

COMPARE/CONTRAST
The Pandora myth explains how evil came into the world. Compare this story with the Biblical story of Adam and Eve found in Genesis, Chapter 3.

FUN FACT
In the Middle Ages, *Pandora's jar* was incorrectly translated as *Pandora's box*. This is still the name by which it is most commonly known.

ANALYZE
Some cynical readers interpret the inclusion of hope within Pandora's jar as another cruel joke on Zeus' part. According to them, *hope* is actually the cruelest evil of all because it gives you false optimism. Do you agree with this interpretation? Explain.

COMPARE/CONTRAST
Almost every culture has an ancient story that involves the flooding of the world. Read the Biblical story of Noah found in Genesis 6:5–8:22.

this action. A tiny rattling from within the jar stirred their attention; one final puff floated loose into the air—a wisp of hope. Zeus, not completely heartless, had sealed it in there as well to make the troubles of the world bearable for men and women alike.

The Great Flood

When Zeus heard rumors that humans had become wicked and corrupt, he went among the mortals wrapped in a human disguise to determine their character for himself. He visited the hall of a wicked king, who offered him a dish prepared from human flesh. Appalled by this sacrilege, Zeus zapped the king's attendants with a thunderbolt and transformed the king himself into a ravenous wolf. Returning hastily to Olympus, Zeus was convinced that mankind must be destroyed. The other gods were perturbed by this announcement. Who would honor the gods if the humans were destroyed? But Zeus did not care and began to summon enough dark clouds to cover the sky. Fearing that the fire from his thunderbolts will destroy the world, he planned instead to drown the world in a divine deluge.

From where he was imprisoned, the Titan Prometheus saw the clouds gathering and sent word to his son Deucalion to build a boat. The good man heeded his father's warning, and when Zeus opened the floodgates of heaven, Deucalion and his wife Pyrrha rode the waves for 9 days before finally beaching upon the height of Mount Parnassus. Seeing that the mortals had been completely wiped out except for the kindly Deucalion and his wife, Zeus allowed the waters to subside.

Lamenting the loss of their race, Deucalion and Pyrrha called on the Titaness Themis, known for her prophetic gifts, asking her how they might repopulate the Earth. She answered with a riddle: "Throw the bones of your mighty mother over your shoulder." Pyrrha believed that the Titaness was speaking literally, but Deucalion saw the hidden meaning of the riddle. Their "mighty mother" did not refer to their earthly mothers, but Mother Earth, meaning the "bones" of the Earth or rock. Each taking stones and tossing them over their shoulders, the couple walked down from the mountaintop. Where the rocks thrown by Deucalion landed, there sprang up men, and from those thrown by Pyrrha came women. So man was awarded a new generation better than the one that came before.

CHAPTER 2

The Power of Music

ORPHEUS & EURYDICE

Cast

Apollo *God of light and music*

Orpheus *Talented musician*

Calliope *Orpheus' muse mother*

Melpomene *Muse of tragedy*

Clio *Muse of history*

Urania *Muse of astronomy*

Thalia *Muse of comedy*

Erato *Muse of love poetry*

Rock *A rock*

River *A river*

Tree *A tree*

Eurydice *Beautiful maiden*

Hermes *Messenger god*

Hades *Lord of the Underworld*

Satyr *Half-man, half-goat*

NARRATOR: It was no wonder that Orpheus could sing as well as he could. After all, his father was Apollo, the god of poetry and music, and his mother was one of the nine eternal muses. With genes like that, Orpheus was destined for greatness. His mother and her sister-muses raised him on the heights of Mt. Parnassus, which wasn't quite as ritzy as Mt. Olympus, but it worked well enough for a group of unmarried free-spirits on a budget. Every day the Muses danced and danced and danced—that's how they inspired mortal art, by dancing—until Helios' last rays passed from the sky. Some might (and did) call this lifestyle boring, but it was what amused the muses.

When Orpheus was nearly 3 years old, the god Apollo appeared on Mt. Parnassus, and after winking at a few of the dancing muses, presented his young son with a shining lyre.

APOLLO: Son.

ORPHEUS: Yes, father.

NARRATOR: Orpheus, even though only 2, was a well-spoken child.

APOLLO: This is the lyre. It holds more power than any shield or sword—and can pierce man's heart just as deeply. Use it well.

NARRATOR: The tiny boy took the lyre and plucked its six strings with his chubby fingers. New music—notes never heard before on Earth—sprang forth.

APOLLO: That's my boy! He's a musical genius already.

CALLIOPE: Sisters, our dancing is paying off! My son will be the greatest musician who ever lived! *(murmuring of the muses)*

NARRATOR: Orpheus took to the lyre like other boys took to running or wrestling. His songs were the most beautiful ever heard, and as the muses danced and danced, he played and played—his notes keeping the exuberant beat. Fifteen years passed in this manner. It was then that his aunt Melpomene, the muse of Tragedy, who had become somewhat tired of always jigging and frolicking, piped up.

MELPOMENE: *(annoyed)* Calliope, dear, would it be possible to get *your son* to slow his tempo? My feet have been numb for the last 6 months. I don't want to wear them out. We *are* dancing for eternity here.

CALLIOPE: Orpheus, dear, you know we never tire of your wonderful music, but why don't you play something slower? Something somber? All of your songs happily bounce and leap, but your tempo is exhausting.

ORPHEUS: But mother, I have never felt sadness. How can I play an emotion I've never felt? I've lived here with you and my eight dancing aunts my whole life. What do I have to be sad about?

MELPOMENE: *(shocked)* What? There's plenty of tragedy around! War, famine, death! Suicide, fratricide, matricide, insecticide! Haven't you heard? The world is full of misery!

CALLIOPE: *(shocked)* Melpomene! Please!

ORPHEUS: What are these things? I've never heard of them.

MELPOMENE: Oh, brother. That's it. Enough is enough. Calliope, it's about time you sent that boy down into the world—the real world. He's not a god! He's a mortal!

CALLIOPE: Melpomene!

MELPOMENE: Well, he should know. The boy's nearly 18 years old. You can't keep him up here in la-la land forever—fattening him up on nectar and ambrosia! He needs to go down and see what the real world's like.

ORPHEUS: What could there possibly be down there that I'm missing out on?

NARRATOR: The other muses, whose feet had also blistered because of Orpheus' happy harping, chimed in.

CLIO: History, my boy! On Earth you could study the great deeds of men!

URANIA: Astronomy! On Earth you can look up to the night sky and study the stars!

THALIA: *(laughing)* Comedy! In Athens they make the funniest plays!

ERATO: Love!

ORPHEUS: But I have love here. I have the love of my mother.

MELPOMENE: May the Fates save the boy! We're talking about *romantic* love. That's more than love for your mother.

CLIO: Unless your name's Oedipus.

(all of the muses laugh)

MELPOMENE: Go to Earth and find a girl. Maybe she'll break your heart, and then your music will know true depth.

NARRATOR: Calliope was furious at her sister for giving such advice, but the mention of love had stirred Orpheus' heart. If he were truly a mortal, his place was on the Earth. And, besides, this eternal dancing did tend to get a bit old.

ORPHEUS: I will go!

CLIO: Bravo! Now we will have a nephew who will make history!

URANIA: A nephew whose image can hang in the stars!

THALIA: A nephew to laugh at!

ALL: Thalia!

MELPOMENE: *(to herself)* Or maybe a nephew worthy of tragedy.

NARRATOR: And so Orpheus left the mountain top. The muses each unclasped one hand to wave goodbye but continued their considerably slower dancing. As he lost sight of them, Orpheus noticed tears on his mother's cheeks.

While the boy made his way down the mountainside, he sang an I-don't-know-where-I'm-going-but-I-can't-wait-to-get-there ditty. It was an upbeat song, of course, about his quest for love. There was no path to speak of on the slopes of Mt. Parnassus, but as Orpheus sang and walked in step, the rocks politely rolled to the side and made way before him.

ROCK: Best of luck to you, Mr. Orpheus. When you find love, don't take it for *granite*.

NARRATOR: Soon Orpheus saw a turgid mountain stream gushing down the slopes, blocking his way. He continued to sing, and it was no surprise to him that the stream stopped flowing for him, and he walked across its dry bed.

RIVER: Best of luck to you, Mr. Orpheus. Don't let the world *drown* your enthusiasm.

NARRATOR: And further down, where the forest began, tangled trees had grown up through the rock, making it impossible to pass. Orpheus kept walking and kept singing. The trees heard his song, unwrapped themselves from one another, untangled their thickets, and let the boy pass.

TREE: Bravo, Mr. Orpheus! If anyone or anything gets in your way, we'll tear them *limb* from *limb*!

NARRATOR: By the time he reached the bottom of the mountain, Orpheus had already learned a valuable lesson about the world: Rocks, streams, and trees make really bad jokes. More disturbing than the puns was the fact that he had no idea where to go next. He had set out on a quest to find love, yet no one had explained to him where love lived or how love worked.

ORPHEUS: Does it just happen . . . like lightning? Or is slow and steady like the growth of a tree?

NARRATOR: Orpheus did not have to walk far until he saw someone sitting on a large rock in the midst of a field. It was a girl. She had raven-black hair pinned behind her ears and was watching a few tufts of sheep nibble on the grass.

ORPHEUS: Hello, I am Orpheus.

NARRATOR: The girl turned to him in surprise.

ORPHEUS: I've come to Earth to find love. My songs can move stone, divert streams, and bend mighty trees.

EURYDICE: Sounds dangerous.

ORPHEUS: Would you like to hear one of my songs?

EURYDICE: Sure. Why not? I've just been sitting here watching sheep all day.

NARRATOR: Orpheus began to play an I-have-found-the-love-of-my-life tune, and something inside the girl's mind shifted. Up until then she had seen only a boy—one who seemed a little off in the head. Now she was looking upon someone she loved.

EURYDICE: *(lovey-dovey)* Beautiful boy, thou hast charmed my heart!

ORPHEUS: Is that a good thing?

NARRATOR: The girl jumped from the rock into the surprised arms of Orpheus and planted on his lips a first kiss of magnitude 10.

ORPHEUS: *(breathlessly)* I have found love after all!

NARRATOR: The current of their love threatened to sweep the two young people away, so marriage followed quickly. Eurydice—that was the girl's name—made all of the arrangements, and Orpheus sang a I'm-getting-married-and-I'm-happy-about-it melody. During the marriage ceremony, the god Hymen appeared among the shadows, holding aloft a burning torch.

EURYDICE: Orpheus, look. This is a good sign. There is the god Hymen, come to bless our marriage. My sister will be so jealous. He never showed up at her wedding, and, as it turns out, her husband already had a wife in another village.

NARRATOR: But instead of burning cleanly, the god's torch started to smoke. It smoked so much that it stung the eyes of the guests and caused the bride to cough.

EURYDICE: *(coughing)* Maybe I spoke too soon.

NARRATOR: Yet after the god had disappeared and Orpheus had struck up his lyre with a never-mind-bad-omens song of celebration, the lighthearted spirit of the wedding returned.

Each day of their married life, Eurydice went to the meadow where they had first met to watch her sheep. Orpheus went with her and sang a sheep-watching song. At the sound of his lyre, the sheep would clump up or scatter just as he desired.

In the fall, a nearby village requested that Orpheus come and sing for them. They'd been hit by a plague, and their hearts needed revival. Orpheus agreed to go and sing them a cheer-up-and-heal-up tune, so Eurydice went to the meadow alone during his absence.

EURYDICE: Watching these sheep is so much harder without my wonderful husband. Thanks to his lyre music all I had to do was leave them alone, and they came home, wagging their tails behind them.

NARRATOR: Eurydice realized that she was talking to herself and dissolved into a reverie, which further dissolved into a noonday nap. This is why she did not notice the mischievous goat-man who tender-hoofed his way up to her rock.

SATYR: A beautiful nymph—asleep on a rock! Easy pickings!

NARRATOR: It should be a testament to Eurydice's beauty that the goat-man mistook her for a nymph, because it is the sole job of goat-men to pursue nymphs day and night. This is one reason why they're frowned upon in polite society. (The other is that they don't wear pants.)

When Eurydice awoke with the shadow of a wormy goat-man hovering over her, she let out a shriek.

EURYDICE: (scream) Get away from me, you horrible goat-man!

SATYR: Actually we prefer the term *satyr*.

NARRATOR: Not in the mood to debate terminology, the maiden jumped from the rock and tore through the tall meadow grass.

EURYDICE: Help! Help!

NARRATOR: This is exactly what the goat-man had hoped she would do. Goat-men love a chase. Although the girl ran with all her speed, he clipped and clopped along at her heels.

SATYR: (amorously) My sweet, my sweet! Let us end this ridiculous charade! You know you want the goat-man.

EURYDICE: Dream on, weirdo!

NARRATOR: Unfortunately, in their chase, the maiden stepped upon a very poisonous snake slinking in the proverbial grass. (Everyone has been told that snakes are more afraid of you than you are of them, and this is supposed to be comforting. Yet, in most cases, humans

don't have fangs and bite when frightened—while snakes do.) This snake sunk its fangs into Eurydice's tender ankle.

EURYDICE: (cry of pain)

NARRATOR: The snake, which was about to have cardiac arrest over its terror of humans, slithered away, and Eurydice fell into the grass. The poison worked quickly.

SATYR: Whoa! I've never seen an ankle swell up that quickly! Is that oozing pus? (nervously) Uh . . . well . . . I'd better be going now.

EURYDICE: Get back and help me! This is all your fault, you stupid goat-man!

SATYR: (distantly) Satyr. Goodbye.

NARRATOR: When Orpheus returned to the meadow from his journey, he did not see Eurydice where she normally perched on her rock. He searched the meadow until he saw the sheep gathered in a clump around her fallen body. The girl's lips were blue, and her ankle was grossly swollen. He held her tenderly in his arms.

ORPHEUS: What has happened?

EURYDICE: (weakly) Goat-man!

ORPHEUS: What?

EURYDICE: (weakly) Snake in the grass!

ORPHEUS: (between tears) Please! Don't call me names, my love, or I will die!

EURYDICE: Oh, never mind.

NARRATOR: With that Eurydice's irritated soul sank down into the Underworld.

It is said that Orpheus cried enough tears to make their own salty river. He had found love only to lose it. His songs, which had up till then brought mirth, were now haunting dirges for Eurydice. He wandered the countryside—his body thin and his eyes sunken from fasting—playing his languid laments. Although their tone had changed, his tunes still held power. To those villages who wanted rain, his music brought drought; to those whose homes were nearly flooded by spring rains, dismal deluges accompanied his dreary notes. Each day he sang for the night to come quickly; he forbade the stars to shine and told the darkness to linger past the dawn. Those who heard him approaching—men and women who once welcomed him—closed their windows tight and snuffed their lamps, so he would pass on and take his gloom elsewhere. His lamenting at last reached the ears of Olympus and moved the hearts of the mightiest of the immortals. One night as Orpheus staggered forward mumbling and plucking with bleeding, feeble fingers, a dark form blocked his path. The bard paused in his song.

HERMES: *(booming)* Mortal Orpheus! I am come from high Olympus to tell you to stop your mourning!

ORPHEUS: *(angrily)* Why do you gods care if I mourn? You are the ones who created my suffering! I want *all* of the gods, *all* of the mortals, and even the Earth herself to suffer—*as I suffer*!

HERMES: Creepy. But, pray tell, what is the source of your suffering? Why do you sing?

ORPHEUS: For my lost love, Eurydice! Taken from me in the blossom of youth! *(begins to sing again)* Eurydice! Eurydice!

HERMES: Please! No more! Your music has had its desired effect among the immortals. It has even sobered Dionysus—and that takes some doing. So you're mourning for your love. That's tough, it really is, but there are other fish in the sea. Take my father Zeus for example. I can't tell you how many mortal women he's incinerated . . . or flattened . . . or mutilated . . . or turned into bears. But, you know, he doesn't let it get him down! He gets right back out there—and usually the same day. *(pause)* Hmmm. Okay. Maybe *he* isn't the best example.

NARRATOR: The musician's nostrils flared with anger.

ORPHEUS: I could never find another love like Eurydice! She was my sun! My goddess! My *very life*!

HERMES: Hmmm. I never thought of that. You could kill yourself—but that's too stagey. But listen, the gods have sent me with a suggestion for you.

ORPHEUS: They know of a way to get my love back?

HERMES: Of course we do. As the poets say: Death is not the end, just an intermission.

ORPHEUS: Do you mean—?

HERMES: Yes, Orpheus, the gods are telling you to go to hell. Hades! The Underworld! Take your golden lyre, go to Hades himself, and melt his heart with your music. It just might work. Your songs have all of us on Olympus absolutely depressed. I promise. Zeus hasn't had an affair in weeks, Dionysus hasn't touched a drop of wine, and Hebe can't bear to bear her cup. If we want a drink, we have to get it ourselves! It's barbaric!

ORPHEUS: But it's impossible. I'm not a hero like Heracles.

HERMES: Listen to me, my boy, *you* have the greatest weapon of all. I should know; I invented it. That lyre right there is stronger than any sword or shield. They may pierce the body, but music pierces the soul!

ORPHEUS: You're right! What do I have to lose?

HERMES: Well, your life, but—

ORPHEUS: I will do it! I will get back my love!

HERMES: That's the spirit! You'll find a foul-smelling cave to the west. Follow it down. It goes into the Underworld. Hades is filled with all types of creepies and crawlies, but your music will keep them at bay. Farewell, Orpheus!

ORPHEUS: Farewell.

NARRATOR: As the messenger god disappeared, Orpheus steadied his nerves by playing a prepare-to-do-the-impossible serenade upon his lyre and struck out toward the foul-smelling cave. Within the depths he faced many frightening specters, but his melody was stronger than them all. When the musician neared, the six eyes of Cerberus moistened with tears, his three snouts sniffed, and three necks bowed submissively as he whimpered to the side of the path. When Orpheus came to the banks of the river Styx and beheld Charon, the miserly boatman, leaning heavily upon his oar, a song of sorrow was the only toll he had to pay. As Charon poled the singing boy across the river, he shook his head. Orpheus was the only passenger he had ferried without a coin. At last Orpheus came before the grim god Hades, whose eyes—like those of an insect—held no feeling of any kind.

HADES: Since you have made it this far, you may play, mortal. But, be warned: My heart is made of stone.

NARRATOR: Yet as Orpheus played his love-is-love-even-in-Hades anthem, something hitherto unseen in the Underworld happened. A bit of sediment slowly collected in the corner of Hades' eye. It formed into a tear-shaped deposit on the god's grey cheek. Then the Earth—above and below them—shook with a deep tremor, and a crack like a pick on stone was heard. It was the sound of Hades' heart breaking.

HADES: Very well. Take your love. Her spirit will follow you out. But you cannot look on her face until you are both fully in the light of your father Apollo—the Earth-light—once again. If you do, she will return to me. Light to light; shade to shade.

NARRATOR: The god's finger flicked and crumbled the newly-formed stalactite from his eye.

As he walked back to the surface, Orpheus sang a love-is-not-swallowed-up-in-death chorus. The guardians of the Underworld—as before—did not hamper his progress, but bowed in acknowledgement of his supreme gift.

Orpheus knew he could not look behind him, but as he drew nearer and nearer to the surface, he became more and more eager to know for certain that the spirit of Eurydice followed behind. When he crossed back over the Styx in Charon's ferry, he tried to gauge whether or not the craft seemed burdened with the weight of three—or only two. When he passed before the glittering eyes of Cerberus, they tracked his progress but never even once glanced behind him to where his Eurydice supposedly followed. Doubt redoubled its gnawing at his heart.

ORPHEUS: *(to himself)* Is Hades making a fool out of me?

NARRATOR: The end of the tunnel appeared like a lamp in the darkness. He was nearly home free. The very moment his foot crossed the threshold of light, he whirled anxiously around. *She* was there, behind him in the tunnel—shimmering on the air like a mirage. There was a look of sadness on her face, a look of disappointment, as if he had forgotten her birthday.

EURYDICE: Oh, Orpheus. Too soon. Too soon.

NARRATOR: Then he saw what she saw. Although he stood in the light of the world, she still stood in the darkness of the Underworld.

EURYDICE: Farewell, my love.

NARRATOR: Orpheus lunged out toward her, but his arms embraced only air. The spirit of the girl bowed its head and, to the music of Orpheus' staccato sobs, faded out.

DISCUSS

- What is Orpheus' main flaw? Explain.
- What do you think happened to Orpheus after the events of this story?
- As this story shows, music is a powerful weapon. How is music powerful in your own life?
- What power or prestige is given to those who are musically talented in society? Why do you think this is so?

ANALYZE

Some have said that the myth of Orpheus illustrates that love is more powerful than death. But it is not necessarily Orpheus' love that earns him entrance into the Underworld, but rather his ability to express his love through music. Is the theme of the story more about the power of love or the power of music? Explain.

WRITE

If Orpheus lived in your society, how would his life have been different? Pretend that Orpheus became a famous musician in modern time. Write his story as it would happen today.

PRESENT

Bring a song that means something to you to your class. Play the song, and explain its significance.

VIEW

View the film *Black Orpheus* (1957), directed by Marcel Camus, which modernizes the myth of Orpheus and Eurydice. In this version of the myth set in Brazil, Orfeo (Orpheus) is a musically talented streetcar conductor who falls for Eurydice during Carnivale, the Brazilian equivalent of Mardi Gras. When Eurydice dies unexpectedly, Orfeo consults with a voodoo priestess to find out how to bring her back from the dead.

"Eurydice to Orpheus"

The idea of a second look, one last glance, is a powerful one. A similar story to Orpheus' exists in the Bible, when Lot's wife turns back to look at Sodom and Gomorrah as the cities are being destroyed for their sins. For her defiance of the angels' command, Lot's wife is turned into a pillar of salt (see Genesis 19:26). In addition, Robert Browning (1812–1889) wrote about the mistaken look back of Orpheus in his poem "Eurydice to Orpheus," reprinted here:

> But give them me, the mouth, the eyes, the brow!
> Let them once more absorb me! One look now
> Will lap me round for ever, not to pass
> Out of its light, though darkness lies beyond:
> Hold me but safe again within the bond
> Of one immortal look! All woe that was,
> Forgotten, and all terror that may be,
> Defied—no past is mine, no future: look at me!

DISCUSS
- Who is the speaker in this poem?
- Why is the speaker's request contradictory to the original myth?
- What is the meaning of the poem?

The Muses

The muses were nine eternal beings who inspired every form of Greek art. Artists invoked the aid of the muses before they began any artistic project. Both the *Iliad* and the *Odyssey* begin with an invocation for the muses to make the work divinely inspired. The muses made their home on Mt. Parnassus. The muses and their offices were as follows: Calliope (epic poetry), Clio (history), Erato (love poetry), Euterpe (lyric poetry), Melpomene (tragedy), Polyhymnia (songs to the gods), Terpsichore (dance), Thalia (comedy), and Urania (astronomy). Many modern words come from the muses: *amuse, music,* and *museum* are a few.

The Power of Music

The story of Orpheus can be viewed in more than one way. In one regard, it is a story about the power of love because a man loves enough to brave the terrors of death in order to recover the soul of his lost bride.

DISCUSS
- What is your favorite type of music? Explain.
- Are there any types of *noise* that you would not classify as music? Explain.
- Why does music change from generation to generation? Parents often disapprove of the music their children listen to. Why do you think this is so?
- Describe a time when a certain song moved you.

But in another regard, it is a story about the power of music. It is not Orpheus' love itself that allows him to (temporarily) regain his love; it is his ability to artistically express his love that ultimately brings success. The message of this myth is that music moves us all—even the gods.

Since music was invented, it has maintained a strange power over the human soul. Defining what is actually *music* and what is *noise* has been an ongoing debate. Surely you have heard someone comment, "That's not music!" Apparently, there is a boundary between what is and what is not music. Music *could* be defined as the combination of musical notes and lyrics. But rap music is often lyrics only, is spoken in a certain rhythm, and uses musical notes sparingly. Other types of music, such as most classical pieces, are simply instrumental and have no need for lyrics.

To make things even more complicated, there are people who listen to "music" that sounds more like the destruction of an electric guitar via sledgehammer. Not to mention the "lyrics," which are yelled so loudly that it is debatable whether or not they are actual words. Is this still music?

To fully capture the meaning of music, it must be given a broader definition: Music is something that speaks to your soul. If the hitting-a-guitar-with-a-sledgehammer-whilst-screaming-indecipherable-words type of music moves you, it *must* be accepted as music—even if it is not everyone's cup of tea. Just remember: For some people, accordion music speaks to their soul. There are many different genres of music—country, rap, reggae, soft rock, hard rock, alternative rock, techno, bluegrass, southern gospel, scream-o, and so on—because there are many different types of souls out there to speak to.

Creature Feature: Pan and the Satyrs

Pan is the patron god of shepherds and, because of this association, is often represented as half-man, half-goat. He plays upon the reed pipes or *syrinx*, named for a nymph who transformed into a reed to escape him. Pan is considered to be the source of a fear that creeps up on those who are alone in the wilderness called *panic*. Satyrs, woodland spirits who were the brothers of the nymphs, eventually became associated with Pan and took on his characteristics. Therefore, satyrs are often pictured as having the haunches and horns of a goat. They are the devout followers and constant companions of the god Dionysus and are known for their crude and unpredictable behavior. *Satyr plays* were a type of play performed in ancient Greece characterized by their low-brow antics that parodied popular myths. For these plays, the chorus, which was typically dressed as men, wore anatomically correct satyr costumes.

Greek Music

The Greeks, too, believed that music nurtured the soul and considered musical education one of the highest pursuits that young men could undergo. Even the hero Heracles, who had obviously honed his physical strength, was also expected to cultivate his character by learning to play the lyre. Heracles, the epitome of impatience, was not cut out for music, and when Lycus, his elderly music teacher, ridiculed his horrible technique, Heracles cracked the old man's skull open with his lyre. Some ancient Greeks believed in the spirituality of music so deeply that they swore that the universe moved to a certain type of music. Each layer of atmosphere created a different note when celestial bodies moved through it, and the whole world swayed to the "music of the spheres."

Music in ancient Greece was obviously much different than modern music. The lyre, a six-stringed harp, was one of very few instruments used. (Ironically, the term *lyrics,* meaning the words of a song, comes from the instrument, the lyre.) Two other common instruments were the Greek flute, which is very similar to a modern clarinet, and the shepherd's pipe, which we typically refer to as a *pan flute.* The instrumental portion of a musician's performance always took a back seat to the words. Greek music was first and foremost poetry. It is believed that even the *Iliad* and the *Odyssey* were chanted to the accompaniment of background music like some kind of ancient rap.

The development of music over the centuries has caused this Greek lyric-focused approach to flip-flop. If asked, most people would now say lyrics are secondary to the accompanying tune. Not that the words are unimportant; they are just no longer the main focus of the music. To honor the Greek ideal, the next time you listen to a song, pay special attention to the lyrics and see if there is something there that you have been missing.

Love Stinks?

Most of the love stories found in Greek mythology end tragically. This may be a reflection of the many hardships faced and customs practiced in ancient times. Disease and death were much more frequent than they are now—many people died young. Fathers arranged the marriages of their daughters, and "true love" rarely entered into their matchmaking. Maybe the Greeks as a whole enjoyed tragic love stories more than the happy endings modern audiences have come to expect because their love existed in a much more limited world.

Ultimately, Orpheus and Eurydice are denied a happy ending, but at least they are not alone. Pair after pair of lovers finds its love limited by circumstance and fate. Below are three love-myths: one happy, one tragic, and one bittersweet. Each says something different about love.

The Lamentable Tale of Pyramus and Thisbe

In Babylon, two families lived under a single roof, their two living quarters separated by a single wall. A boy of one family, Pyramus, fell desperately in love with Thisbe, a girl of the other. Apparently, being neighbors had made enemies out of their parents. When Pyramus and Thisbe announced their love, both sets of parents objected and forbade the couple from seeing one another. This only made the love of Pyramus and Thisbe grow stronger. The teenagers discovered a fault in the wall that separated the two living spaces. While their parents slept, the lovers would sneak to the wall and whisper words of passion through the crack.

After weeks of secret meetings, they decided they could stand their separation no longer and agreed to run away together. Pyramus instructed Thisbe to meet him at the Tomb of Ninus, a local landmark, after nightfall. From there they would escape into happiness. The night came, and Thisbe stole silently from her home. She arrived at the tomb. Something stirred in the darkness of the mulberry bushes, but it was not Pyramus. She saw two glowing eyes. The girl turned to flee, and as she did, a lioness (for that is what was hiding in the bushes) moved toward her. Thisbe's cloak caught upon a branch. The lioness licked its blood-stained muzzle and crept closer. Jerking violently, Thisbe tore from the branch, leaving her outer cloak behind. The girl disappeared into the night, and the lioness, who had a full belly from a recent kill, curiously examined the cloak, nuzzling it with her bloody muzzle. After the lioness lost interest, she sauntered back into the night.

Pyramus arrived soon after. He had been delayed by his parents, who questioned where he was headed at such a late hour. When he found that Thisbe was not there to meet him, he desperately searched the thicket. What he found there forced him to his knees: Thisbe's bloody cloak and the pawprints of a lion. The pieces of the puzzle formed quickly in his mind. The lion had mauled Thisbe and dragged her body away to its den. In a frenzy, Pyramus drew forth his dagger and, calling out the name of Thisbe, drove it into his breast.

You might guess what happened next. Thisbe returned to the tomb, suspecting the lioness was now gone. There she found Pyramus, dead by own hand, his blood staining the ground and bushes. As she interpreted the scene before her, she took up the dripping dagger that had pierced her lover's heart and plunged it into her own.

The blood of the two lovers had been spilt on the fruit of the nearby mulberry tree. As a testament to Pyramus and Thisbe, the gods turned the white berries of the mulberry tree eternally red.

Baucis and Philemon

Frequently, Zeus would take it upon himself to journey through the mortal world rewarding the kind and punishing the evil. On this particular trip, he took his clever son Hermes along and disguised them both as penniless travelers. The first country they journeyed through was very inhospitable. When they knocked on doors to ask for food and shelter, they were denied. Only one household showed them hospitality. Philemon, an elderly country farmer, and Baucis, his wife, let the disguised gods sit next to their warm fire while they prepared dinner. But when Baucis went to fetch the goose for dinner, she could not catch it. No matter how quickly she moved, it was always quicker. She returned inside, exhausted. Philemon asked where the goose was, but she only motioned for a drink. To his astonishment, the old man realized that the pitcher he and the strangers had drunk empty was now completely full. The elderly couple whispered to one another. There could be only one explanation for these things: Their guests must be gods. Zeus and Hermes happily admitted that this was so and thanked Baucis and Philemon for their generosity. There was a flash of light, and the couple's humble dwelling was transformed into a magnificent temple. All of the land around them, where their neighbors' houses had been, lay covered in water. Zeus asked Baucis and Philemon to serve in his temple the rest of their days. In return for this, he said, he would grant them one request, and they immediately agreed to his arrangement. As for their request, they asked to never be separated from one another—to die at exactly the same moment. Zeus consented to this noble wish. After years of happy servitude, the time came for Baucis and Philemon to die. As their souls slipped down into the Underworld, their bodies changed forms, turning into two trees that grew from a single trunk.

DISCUSS
- What does each story say about the nature of love?
- What similarities exist between the myth of Pyramus and Thisbe and Shakespeare's *Romeo and Juliet*?
- Why is it significant that Baucis and Philemon turn into two trees that share a single trunk?
- How is the sculptor Pygmalion similar to Orpheus?

LISTEN

Listen to the song "Love Hurts" performed by the band Nazareth. What does this song have to say about love?

WRITE

Write your own ode to love.

ANALYZE

As you have learned, most Greek love stories had tragic endings. Do most modern love stories tend to have happy or tragic endings? Think about Hollywood, a movie-making machine that cranks out dozens of love stories every year. Yet Hollywood caters to its audience and frequently shows us what we want to see. Think about romantic movies. Which type of ending do you think modern society prefers, and what does this tell you?

Pygmalion and Galatea

Pygmalion was the greatest sculptor on the isle of Cyprus. From his earliest days, he had no use for women, scorning them for their simple-minded ways. Because he was surrounded by *im*perfect women, he decided to use his art to create the perfect woman. His statue was a labor of love. He sculpted its delicate features with the greatest care. As he worked, the statue became more and more lifelike, and Pygmalion began to fantasize: What if she really did come to life? Oh, how he would love her! His frenzied work led to what his friends considered insanity. He would bring the statue gifts, dress it in clothes, and lay with it beside him, cradling it in his arms. When his masterpiece was complete, Pygmalion realized that he had truly made the perfect woman, but he wept for he knew she would never live. The goddess Aphrodite saw the love that the sculptor put into his creation, and in recognition of his talents, she breathed life into his stone maiden. When Pygmalion returned to his workshop one day, he noticed that the statue's skin felt warm, and its chest moved with breath. With a cry he realized that his statue had come to life. Now it would be his wife, the beautiful Galatea.

Through Hades and Back

Even though the terms *Hades* and *Hell* are used interchangeably, the two places have little in common. In the Greek Underworld, there were no consuming flames, and in fact, it was described as a cold place, rather than hot. And it wasn't just the wicked who went there—everyone did; there was no escaping it. Immortal judges saw to it that the deceased got just what they deserved. Greeks who were kind and generous might spend eternity plucking a lyre by a dark river or wandering through the Plain of Asphodel (named for asphodel, the unattractive gray weed that covered it). Definitely not an exciting fate, but better than the alternative (as you will see).

No one—not even the greatest of heroes—seemed to enjoy being dead. Achilles, who during his lifetime considered dying young an easy price to pay for long-lasting fame, regrets his foolish life when he says, "Better to be a slave and see the sun, than be the greatest king in Hades." On the other hand, those who filled their lives with wickedness had even crueler fates awaiting them—eternal punishments that were sadistic reflections of their crimes. Sisyphus, a mortal who had ratted on one of Zeus' affairs, was forced to roll a boulder up a steep hill, only to lose his grip before the summit was reached. Time and time again the boulder rolled back to the bottom of the hill, and Sisyphus would start his ascent once again. Tantalus, a man who murdered his son and served him as a dish to the gods, was forced to stand knee deep in a pool of water with a fruit-bearing branch hanging just out of his reach. No matter how thirsty or how hungry he became, he could never bend down and drink of the water or reach up and partake of the fruit. (Tantalus gives us the word *tantalize* for obvious reasons.)

In their typical way, the Greek myth-makers made the afterlife seem as real and concrete as possible by giving it location and geography just like any other spot on the map. For starters, it was called the *Under*world because it was literally *under the world.* Getting there was no big chore. The Greeks knew which caves ran deep enough to actually penetrate Hades. Getting *out* was the hard part. Yet hero after hero—Heracles, Psyche, Orpheus, Theseus, and even Odysseus—visited there for various errands and returned to tell about it.

As for the geography of the Underworld, the Greeks knew it was intersected by several rivers. As the first and most famous of the rivers, the Styx formed the boundary between the world above and the world below. It had magical powers as well. Its waters were responsible for Achilles' near-perfect coating of invincibility. When the gods wanted to swear an oath, they swore on the Styx, and then there was no going back on their word or they suffered a horrible fate. Charon, the aged boat-man of the Underworld, ferried the dead across the Styx. One could not pass without the coin or coins (placed under the tongue) that signified a proper burial. Those souls not properly buried could not pass. Some said they would be forced to wander for eternity; other said they had to wait for 100 years to cross the river. Either way, wandering or waiting, it was not a desirable end.

If a mortal, trespassing where no mortal should, was wily enough to get past the boat-man, there were plenty of other guardians to bring the trip to a quick end. Cerberus, the three-headed hell hound, attacked those who trespassed. There were also the Furies, tormenting demons of guilt whose eyes wept blood. Down in Tartarus, the deepest and darkest pit of Hades, chained Titans groaned, still suffering Zeus' wrath. In the midst of this dark land lay the hall of Hades, where the Lord of the Underworld sat on his throne, stone-faced, with his queen, Persephone, beside him. Only one thing was ever said to melt his frozen heart: the magical lyre-playing of Orpheus.

Certainly all of these elements worked together to make the Underworld an unfriendly place, one that only the noblest and most adventurous could navigate. The geography given to it by the Greeks made it easy

DISCUSS
- How is the Greeks' concept of the afterlife different than what most people believe today? Explain.

READ
Read a canto of Dante's *Inferno*. How are the punishments that Dante witnesses in Hell inspired by the Greek concept of the Underworld? Explain.

DRAW
Using the geographical details given in this section, draw a map of the Underworld as the Greeks imagined it.

for the Roman poet Virgil to lead his hero Aeneas into the depths. Virgil's poem *The Aeneid*, in turn, inspired a medieval Italian poet named Dante Alighieri to write about his own excursion into the afterlife. By Dante's time, the Underworld had gotten quite a bit hotter, undergone a name change, and was under new management. Dante made sure to take plenty of notes on the changes.

Put Your Money Where Your Mouth Is

As a part of their burial ritual, Greeks placed one or two *obols* (coins) in the mouth (or sometimes hand) of the deceased. This way when the spirit reached Charon, the aged boatman of the Underworld, he or she would have the required fee.

Talking Heads: The Fate of Orpheus

Immediately after his failure, Orpheus tried to re-enter the Underworld, but this time his songs had no effect. He had already had his one chance to save Eurydice. Miserable from the loss of his one and only love, it is said that Orpheus swore off the fair sex. If he could not have Eurydice, he would have no other woman.

It was during this time that the worship of the wine-god Dionysus was becoming widespread in Greece. *Maenads* were his female followers, infamous for performing all kinds of crazed, horrific rituals. (The word *maenad* can be translated as "raving one.") Working themselves into a "divinely inspired" frenzy (probably through the help of plenty of wine), the maenads ran as a pack through the wilderness, wearing deer pelts and bearing pinecone-tipped scepters. In some of their ceremonies, they ripped apart living animals. In one famous story, they even ripped apart Pentheus, a wicked king. Maenads were also known for their incredible lust. According to the myth-makers, encountering these frenzied women was both frightening and dangerous.

As Orpheus wandered through the forest, he stumbled upon a *maenad* ceremony. The crazed women turned from their rituals and approached him lustily, but when he rejected their advances, they began to hurl rocks and sticks at him. Orpheus struck his lyre, and their projectiles fell harmlessly to the ground. The maenads became so enraged that they rushed forward and—amid frenzied howling—tore the musician limb from limb. Wrenching his head loose, they threw it into the nearby river along with his lyre. Hearing of his death, the Muses came and buried what remained of Orpheus' body, yet they could not find his head. The head had floated downstream and, although it was no longer attached, began to prophecy. Likewise, the lyre continued to play all the way down to the sea. The people of Lesbos who later discovered Orpheus' head established it as an oracle. Any who wished to know the future could come and listen to the prophetic words of the talking head. Meanwhile, the soul of Orpheus had at last found happiness; it was reunited with Eurydice in the Underworld.

Another Great Musician: Marsyas

Not long after the goddess Athena had invented the Greek flute (which was played like a modern clarinet), the other goddesses mocked her, saying that because the instrument caused her cheeks to puff out, she looked completely ridiculous. In anger, Athena threw the instrument away. It was found by the satyr Marsyas, who immediately took to the flute and mastered it. He became quite renowned for his talent, and one day he rashly challenged Apollo, the God of Music himself, to a contest. The rules were simple: Apollo would play his lyre, and Marsyas would play his flute. The muses would act as the judges, and whoever produced the most pleasing music would be the winner. As for the fate of the loser, the winner could do with him what he willed.

The contest began, and the musical skills of the god and the satyr seemed nearly equal—that is, until Apollo played a crafty trick. In order to one-up Marsyas, the god flipped his lyre upside down and, without missing a beat, continued to play as gracefully as before. He challenged the satyr to do the same with his instrument. Obviously, Marsyas could not, and Apollo won the contest. In one of his cruelest moments, Apollo tied the satyr to a tree and flayed him for daring to challenge a god. The woodland nymphs cried many tears over the satyr's death, and these were said to have formed a river that bears the name Marsyas.

CHAPTER 3
Teamwork

THE GOLDEN FLEECE:
THE VOYAGE OF JASON AND THE ARGONAUTS, PART I

Cast

Jason *Young hero*

Pelias *His evil cousin*

Hera *Queen of Heaven*

Zeus *Lord of the gods*

Orpheus *Morbidly depressed master musician*

Heracles *Famous strongman hero*

Atalanta *Famous female hero*

Chiron *Centaur, trainer of heroes*

Iris *Rainbow messenger of the gods*

Guard *Guard to Pelias*

Man *Man from the crowd*

CHIRON: In the distant land of Colchis, on a withered tree amid a barren field, hangs a Golden Fleece. This fleece is a symbol of heroic virtues. To claim it one must be blessed, above all others, by the gods.

NARRATOR: The centaur Chiron had been lecturing on this subject for some time. He paused in his story and glanced at the young man half-asleep on a nearby rock.

CHIRON: *(sternly)* Jason—have you been listening?

JASON: *(sighing)* I'm sorry, master. I have so much on my mind.

CHIRON: So it seems—everything but your lessons.

JASON: I'm just sick of sitting! I've been sitting since I can remember.

CHIRON: Patience is a virtue many centaurs do not have. So it is with humans. But I have learned it and so shall you.

JASON: *(angrily)* Every time I think about *him* my blood boils. I can't think about anything but running a sword through his guts!

CHIRON: Think, young one. What would happen then? Many men would strike you down before you had time to savor your revenge. Your cousin is a king, after all.

JASON: On a throne that's supposed to be mine!

CHIRON: What good is a throne if you're not smart enough to use it? Instead of desiring to be powerful, perhaps you should desire to be good.

JASON: *(childlike)* Being good is boring.

CHIRON: Which brings us to mathematics. Get out your abacus.

NARRATOR: Jason, a young prince, had been raised in a mountainside dwelling by the wise centaur. His father had been king until Jason's cousin had violently seized the throne. With his father missing and presumed dead, his mother had fled, leaving the boy in the care of Chiron.

His whole life, he had been trained—trained for the day when he would go back to his father's kingdom and challenge the tyrant who now ruled it.

Chiron had taught him everything he knew: the ballads of the gods, the layout of the stars, the stories of the old heroes, learning that filled Jason's head to the point of bursting. Yet he had never taught him how to swing a sword or to shield himself from a heavy blow.

Then one morning, the centaur woke him. It was early, the stars were still in the dark sky—

CHIRON: Get up.

JASON: *(groggy)* Heh—what's going on?

CHIRON: The time has come.

JASON: To what?

CHIRON: To leave. I have taught you all that I know. Now, you must go face your cousin and claim your right.

JASON: But—but—you haven't even taught me how to use a sword!

CHIRON: There is not much to it. There is a blunt end and a sharp end. Hold it by the blunt end. Swing the sharp end toward your enemy. Stop swinging when either he or you are dead.

JASON: I mean, how to fight! How to be a great warrior!

CHIRON: Great warriors accomplish nothing. What can a sword gain you but death? What can death gain but more death? Do not desire a cycle of killing. The mind is the weapon of greatness.

JASON: Nice philosophy, but what am I going to do? I can't *think* him to death!

CHIRON: The gods willed that I be your teacher. I do not train mindless warriors. I train great men, and you, my boy, have become a great man. It is time for you to go.

JASON: *(grudgingly)* I will, but I'm sure to fail.

CHIRON: Do not defeat yourself. You are destined for great things. I will give you this before you leave.

JASON: *(excitedly)* What is it? A weapon? At last!

CHIRON: No, but rather a garment to turn away the rain as you travel.

JASON: *(not impressed)* A leopard skin?

CHIRON: Do not look down upon it. The mighty leopard gave you his skin. It is a wondrous gift. Wear it well.

JASON: *(hopefully)* And?

CHIRON: And the dawn is coming, you must be off—follow the road. You have learned the way. Claim your birthright, but along the way, do not forget wisdom, for often will it save you.

NARRATOR: And so Jason left the only home he had ever known.

The road moved quickly; he was soon out of the mountains and approaching his father's former kingdom. Deep down, he knew the centaur was right. He would be a wise king, not a tyrant. He would bring peace and thought and majesty back to the throne. The only problem was *how* to get it back. But, in spite of this, he felt his spirits rise. He was Jason, son of a king, trained by Chiron the Wise.

JASON: This may not be so hard after all!

NARRATOR: At this moment, the strap on his left sandal gave way, and in his shock, he tripped and fell face first to the ground.

JASON: *(angrily)* Great. This is just what I need. I guess I'll have to limp into the palace with one sandal. That'll strike fear into him—a limping teenager.

NARRATOR: But little did Jason know that what he wore was *exactly* the thing to strike fear into his cousin. After seizing the throne, the evil King Pelias had consulted an oracle. The oracle had told him that while his fortune was great, he should fear one who came wearing only one shoe. Bitterly, the king had harbored this news in his heart and had set the palace guards to watch for a man who wore only one shoe. If a man fit this description, they were to bring him immediately before the throne—for a speedy execution.

GUARD: Stop, boy!

JASON: Me?

GUARD: Why do you only wear one shoe?

JASON: *(jokingly)* I'm making a fashion statement.

GUARD: Come with me.

NARRATOR: The guard grabbed Jason and started to drag him toward the palace.

JASON: *(frightened)* I was only joking!

NARRATOR: Thrown roughly to the ground, Jason was shocked when he looked up to behold the king—the repugnant swine he had come to see. He was even a bit more swine-like than Jason had imagined—weight hanging from his rotund body.

PELIAS: *(booming)* Who are you? *(to guard)* Bring me a sword.

JASON: Wait—you can't do this!

PELIAS: Why not? I am a king. You will tell me your name. Then I will *kill* you.

JASON: Why? Because I'm wearing one shoe? Is there a law that no one can wear one shoe? That's the stupidest thing I've ever heard!

PELIAS: This is my kingdom. I make the laws. Everyone wears two sandals at all times. The *most* loyal wear *three*. Any who wear only one are put to death. Now, give me your name, or I will cut it out of you.

NARRATOR: The fat king advanced with his sword—his eyes glittering with hate. It was then that Jason found his courage.

JASON: *(growing angry)* You know me well, you coward. It was my father who you drove from this very throne. I am Jason.

PELIAS: *(shocked)* Jason?

JASON: You cannot kill me. I am your relative. If you murder me, the Furies will haunt you forever!

NARRATOR: He saw the king's face twist into a look of extreme anger—then melt away into a smile.

PELIAS: *(sugary tone)* Jason, my boy. Guards, put the sword away, please. There will be no need for that today. *(happy laugh)* So, tell me, my cousin, where did your father manage to hide you all these years?

JASON: I was raised in the countryside by Chiron, the centaur.

PELIAS: Ah, Chiron. He's a very wise man—or should I say horse? But royalty should not associate with such creatures. Gives the wrong impression. It is no matter though. Welcome home.

JASON: I see through your sweetness. I've come to claim a throne that is rightfully mine. One that you've been keeping warm with your enormous rear.

PELIAS: *(gritting teeth)* But, young prince, I have only been keeping it for you. I will gladly step aside and let the true heir take his place.

JASON: Thank you.

NARRATOR: Could it really be this easy? Chiron had been right. He hadn't needed weapons at all.

PELIAS: But first, let us call in all the nobles. *(to guards)* Guards, send for the nobles. They are gathered in the main hall. Tell them that my cousin has returned.

JASON: I expect you to stay true to your word.

PELIAS: Of course, of course. True as day.

(murmuring from the nobles)

PELIAS: Ah, here we are. Great men of this realm, look who has returned! The son of the former king!

(murmuring from the nobles)

JASON: *(loudly)* I have come to claim my father's throne.

PELIAS: And so he has—but, dear nobles, I must pose you a question: How do we know that this boy is who he says he is? Any shepherd or beggar may wander into a throne room and profess himself a prince—especially one dressed as this boy is. How can you prove that you are the heir to the throne?

JASON: I . . . I . . .

PELIAS: *(Snakily)* Gentlemen, I suggest a task for our young prince. We have all heard stories of the Golden Fleece, a prize fit only for a king. If eager Jason here is ready for the throne, it wouldn't be beyond his means to, say, nip out and get it for us.

(murmurs of approval, "Yes" from the nobles)

JASON: *(in shock)* What? I mean, that's on the other side of the world.

PELIAS: Oh, now, it's a very simple test, young Jason—if that is your name. Bring back the Golden Fleece and with it receive your kingdom.

NARRATOR: Jason's face stayed emotionless, but inside his stomach was churning. He had been tricked. He had no choice.

JASON: *(numbly)* I will do this thing you have asked of me.

PELIAS: Wonderful. Spoken like a true relative of mine.

JASON: *(hatefully)* Do not speak to me. I'm no relation to a reptile like you. I will bring this fleece, and with it your destruction.

PELIAS: *(laughing)* We shall see, boy. We shall see.

NARRATOR: Jason felt heat boiling behind his eyes as he left the palace. Had he spent his whole life in exile only to die on a wild goose chase? Colchis was leagues away—he had no ship, no crew, no hope. In his despair, he wandered the lonely streets of the city and came to sit at last on the sands that looked out over the ocean he had pledged to cross.

It was here—his will lost—that he caught the eye of Hera gazing down from high Olympus.

HERA: This boy, Jason. What do you know of him, husband?

ZEUS: *(distractedly)* Hmmm, nothing, dear, nothing.

HERA: *(annoyed)* No, I didn't think so. He isn't a nymph or one of your mortal hussies.

ZEUS: *(ignoring that remark)* I should say he could pass for either. A weak-looking lad.

HERA: But his heart—his heart is good. His destiny is to become a hero. He will need much help to fulfill his task.

ZEUS: Dear, we should not interfere with the destinies of mortals.

HERA: *(coyly)* Really? I believe it is *you* who have been interfering to the point of exhaustion. Why shouldn't this hero receive the help of Olympus?

ZEUS: Hera . . .

HERA: Is it because he—among all others—is not the putrid offspring of your insatiable loins?

ZEUS: *(grumbling)* You have said your piece.

HERA: Have I? I am not a thing to be ordered about. *(softly)* I will help this boy because no one else will. He is no son of Zeus, yet I will see to it that he goes on the greatest quest man has ever known—and succeeds.

NARRATOR: So Hera sent her messenger, Iris, throughout Greece, spreading the word of the great quest. Many heroes heard of this mighty undertaking and started to make their way to Pelias' kingdom. Such a magnificent voyage attracted the greatest and most powerful champions in all of ancient Greece.

Meanwhile, back in his forsaken father's kingdom, Jason wandered aimlessly—ignorant of what was happening thanks to Hera.

JASON: How am I ever going to do this?

IRIS: Sir.

NARRATOR: Jason looked up and saw a young girl with a plain face standing before him. It was odd, but for a second, he thought he saw her eyes glowing with a purple light.

IRIS: You are Jason, correct?

JASON: Yes, why? Do you have a message for me from the king?

IRIS: No, a message from Argus, the shipmaker.

JASON: Argus?

IRIS: Your ship will be seaworthy in a month. He has received your order.

JASON: My order? What do you mean?

IRIS: *(pointing)* He lives just over there.

NARRATOR: He looked where she pointed—toward a distant part of the shorefront.

IRIS: You may ask him yourself.

JASON: But I didn't order any . . .

NARRATOR: He turned back to argue, but the girl was gone. A giant rainbow had spread across the bay. Iris had done her duty. Even though he did not understand, Jason was overjoyed. He couldn't believe it. He wanted to run back to Chiron, tell him of his good fortune, but he needed to stay. There was so much he needed: weapons, supplies, maps, men—where would he get men?

Over the next week, Jason asked among the people of the kingdom: Who was brave enough to go with him? He found that working a trade and making a harvest easily outranked a dangerous mission to the far ends of the Earth.

He had hit another wall . . . until one day . . .

ATALANTA: Excuse me, man.

JASON: *(annoyed)* Look, miss, I'm really busy. I'm trying to—

ATALANTA: Get people to go on your voyage. I know.

JASON: You know?

ATALANTA: I've come to tell you that I'll come with you.

JASON: Well, that's very nice, sweetie, but we won't be needing any women on this . . .

NARRATOR: He suddenly felt his arm being painfully pinned behind him.

JASON: *(in pain)* On second thought—welcome aboard.

ATALANTA: I am Atalanta. You will find that I am as strong as any man, though somewhat smarter.

JASON: Nice. Who is that with you?

NARRATOR: He had noticed a sad-looking boy behind her—golden haired with fair skin and a lyre thrown over his shoulder. He seemed to be moaning softly to himself.

ATALANTA: This is Orpheus. We traveled the road together. He's a bit mopey, but you'll find that his music is as good a weapon as any. And that's not necessarily a compliment.

JASON: Well, I welcome you both. *(under his breath)* Great. A girl and a harp player. What a fearsome group.

NARRATOR: Suddenly, angry shouts came from across the marketplace. A crowd was gathering around some sort of scene.

MAN: *(screaming)* Put it down, you brute, put it down!

ATALANTA: What is that noise?

JASON: I don't know.

ORPHEUS: *(sadly, monotone)* Some man is holding an ox cart in the air.

JASON: What?

NARRATOR: They ran to see what all the commotion was about. A large man—like Orpheus had said—was holding an ox cart over his head. An old cart driver was screaming irately at him.

MAN: *(screaming)* My cart! My cart! Thief!

HERACLES: Quiet, puny man. Do you not know who I am? You almost ran me over with this tiny cart!

MAN: Help! Guards! Help!

HERACLES: *(annoyed)* Here, I'll put it down.

NARRATOR: The large man dropped the ox cart onto the screaming driver. They heard a groan rise up from beneath it.

HERACLES: Some people have no manners.

JASON: *(to Atalanta)* Who is that man?

ATALANTA: Isn't it obvious? It's Heracles.

JASON: What's he doing here?

ORPHEUS: *(dryly)* He's come to join you.

JASON: Me? Why me?

ORPHEUS: *(even drier)* Maybe he's like me. Nothing better to do.

ATALANTA: Heracles! Over here! HERE! *(under her breath)* Big dumb brute.

HERACLES: Hello, small people. I am Heracles. Can you tell me where to find Jason?

NARRATOR: With the giant man so close, Jason suddenly found that he had lost the ability to speak. He had heard stories about what those huge arms had done.

ATALANTA: This is he. Jason, speak up.

JASON: *(weakly)* Hello?

HERACLES: You're smaller than I thought. Such a great quest for a small man?

JASON: Errrr . . .

HERACLES: Can you not talk, little one? I have come to join you. With the mighty Heracles on your journey, you shall not fail.

ATALANTA: Riiiight . . .

ORPHEUS: *(sighing loudly)* I'm tired. *(sigh)* Life used to be so good . . .

HERACLES: What's his problem?

ATALANTA: His one true love died.

HERACLES: *(sadly)* I know how he feels.

ORPHEUS: *(somewhat hopefully)* Did you lose your love to Hades as well?

HERACLES: Err . . . sort of.

ATALANTA: Did a wild animal kill your closest friend?

HERACLES: No, I sort of murdered my wife and kids, *(quickly)* but it wasn't my fault—exactly.

ATALANTA: Well, I'll be keeping my distance now.

NARRATOR: Jason couldn't believe it. In front of him stood two of the greatest heroes Greece had ever known—and Orpheus—all of them offering to accompany him on his journey.

HERACLES: So, when do we leave, captain? We are a hearty crew, thirsting for adventures!

NARRATOR: Jason realized he was talking to him.

JASON: Tomorrow. I just received word that our ship was ready.

HERACLES: What is our ship's name?

JASON: The Argo.

ORPHEUS: *(emotionally drained)* Catchy.

NARRATOR: And so this band of heroes retired for the evening, preparing themselves for their voyage the next day. But Hera's full power hadn't yet been revealed. There were more—many other heroes—late arrivals yet to come.

That night, stranger after stranger made his way into Jason's tent, pledging loyalty to his cause, and all vowing to follow little Jason to the ends of the Earth. Hera had done well.

On the beach, his new vessel rocking silently in the bay, Jason stared up at the stars—the same stars that had seen him off only a short time ago. He felt so much older now, so much wiser.

JASON: Chiron, you were right. I only had to trust myself. There's still a long way to go, but look at all my help! Suddenly, it doesn't seem so impossible.

NARRATOR: As he spoke, several stars in the night sky started to glimmer and dance. To his astonishment, they shifted and formed a shape. In that shape, Jason saw his old teacher.

JASON: It can't be! Chiron! *(shouting)* Chiron, can you hear me?

CHIRON: Yes, little one, I can.

JASON: I don't understand. What's happened to you?

CHIRON: I knew that you would need help, so I went in search of Heracles. I ran into him at my cousin's wedding. He's a sucker for centaur weddings, apparently. Anyway, things went sour. Too much wine was drunk. Long story short: Heracles got into a big, drunken brawl, and I caught a stray arrow in the hoof.

JASON: *(sadly)* I . . . I didn't know.

CHIRON: It's not the worst way to go. The good news is that Zeus has placed me in the stars so that I might watch over you.

JASON: That's great! I think I'm going to need all the help I can get.

CHIRON: You have mighty helpers—helpers of legend. I have trained many heroes, Jason, but you, my son, will accomplish the most.

JASON: If you say so.

CHIRON: I know so. Take care. It won't be an easy journey. You will face many challenges. But you are favored by the gods—no small feat. Remember to follow my form in the stars as you sail, and it shall take you to the land you seek. Do not forget your old teacher, Jason. I hope that I have taught you well. Now is the test. Farewell.

JASON: Farewell.

NARRATOR: The stars faded from his eyes. The dawn was breaking.

DISCUSS
- Is Jason overeager to grow up? Explain.
- What is added to the story by including outside characters who already have their own legends? Explain.
- Are Hera's motives for helping Jason noble? Explain.
- Predict what will happen in the second half of this story.

THE GOLDEN FLEECE:
THE VOYAGE OF JASON AND THE ARGONAUTS, PART II

Cast

Jason *Young hero*

Pelias *His evil cousin*

Hera *Queen of Heaven*

Orpheus *Morbidly depressed master musician*

Heracles *Famous strongman hero*

Atalanta *Famous female hero*

Iris *Rainbow messenger of the gods*

Hylas *Heracles' young armor-bearer*

Phineus *Tormented prophet*

Aphrodite *Goddess of love*

Nymph One *Water spirit*

Nymph Two *Water spirit*

King Æetes *Ruler of Colchis*

Medea *Witch daughter of Æetes*

NARRATOR: In the faraway land of Colchis, the desert nation that housed the legendary Golden Fleece, the Princess Medea was awakened by a vision. She at once went to report it to her father, the king.

MEDEA: *(somberly)* Father . . .

ÆETES: *(so hoarse he can barely talk)* What is it, girl?

MEDEA: Father, I have had another vision.

ÆETES: *(suddenly interested)* Speak . . .

MEDEA: I saw the young Greek. He and his crew have set sail. They are being aided by Hera, Queen of the Gods. They come for the Fleece.

ÆETES: *(calmly)* Good, daughter, good.

MEDEA: *(angrily)* Father! We cannot let them have the Fleece. They are filth! They do not deserve to set foot in our land.

ÆETES: Patience, Medea. It is with patience that the spider, Arachne, spins her web—not haste—and so she catches her prey. We must do the same.

MEDEA: *(irritated)* Your will be done, father. Good night.

ÆETES: Good night.

NARRATOR: What the Princess of Colchis had seen in her dream was true. Jason and his Argonauts had finally embarked.

The first day of the journey had burst forth in a blaze of glory. The crew had hoisted the sail. The keel had pulled across the shoal. They had taken the first step on the greatest quest of all time.

HERACLES: A fine day for sailing, little Jason. *(claps his hand on Jason's shoulder)*

JASON: Oof! Yes, a perfect day.

ATALANTA: So, do we have any idea what stands between us and Colchis?

JASON: Open sea.

HERACLES: Monsters to be sure.

ORPHEUS: *(hopefully)* Death—I hope.

ATALANTA: It will be no easy feat. That's for sure. We'll have to stay on our guard.

NARRATOR: They sailed for many weeks. Day after day, Orpheus sang of his lost love, Eurydice, and moved even the manliest of men to tears.

After time, supplies grew low, but fear had kept them from going inland to hunt and forage on the islands they moored by. Need was growing greater with each passing day. Soon, they would have to risk a journey inland.

ORPHEUS: *(depressed)* And that is how I lost my love.

HERACLES: *(sobbing)* It's sooo sad!

ATALANTA: Oh, please. He sings that song about 10 times a day. Maybe he should row a bit, huh?

JASON: We need water and food.

ORPHEUS: There's a rather dangerous-looking bit of land to the east.

JASON: That is where we will have to go ashore. Who's coming with me?

HERACLES: Hylas, fetch my armor!

HYLAS: *(eagerly)* Yes, sir.

HERACLES: Hylas and I have been together on many voyages. He is an orphaned lad. I have taken him under my wing. I think of him as a son.

ORPHEUS: That could be dangerous.

HYLAS: Here you are.

HERACLES: Thank you, boy. I'm ready to go ashore.

NARRATOR: As they pulled in close, Jason and Heracles stepped off the boat. The forest was thick with vegetation—tangled vines and large-leaved plants prevented easy travel. But they trudged ahead and soon found the wild game they sought.

HERACLES: Now that we have our deer and piggies, Hylas, boy, go fetch us some water.

HYLAS: Yes, sir.

NARRATOR: The men began to butcher the game and offer the proper sacrifices as Hylas sped away on his errand.

HYLAS: I must hurry.

NARRATOR: Several miles away, Hylas knelt beside a clear pool and lowered his jar beneath the lip of the water.

NYMPH ONE: *(seductively)* My, my, what a handsome young man!

HYLAS: *(nervously)* Who's there?

NARRATOR: Two slinky forms rose from the depths of the pool—two young girls—perfect in every way. They were the nymphs who lived there.

NYMPH TWO: What a strong lad you seem to be.

NYMPH ONE: Perhaps you should stay here with us, pretty one.

HYLAS: N-N-No, I must be getting back to Heracles.

NYMPH TWO: We will make it worth your time. Tee hee.

HYLAS: No . . . I think . . . Let me go!

NYMPH ONE: I have his hand, sister. What a strong hand!

NYMPH TWO: Come into the pool with us, beauty.

HYLAS: I . . . no . . .

NYMPH ONE: *(angrier)* Stay with us.

NYMPH TWO: Forever.

NARRATOR: Before he could react, the two nymphs pulled the poor young boy into the pool. Below the surface, they caressed him as he struggled for breath.

Soon, amid their adoration, he stopped thrashing, and life left him. The nymphs cooed bubbles of pleasure. And there, in the bottom of their enchanted pool, they kept the body of Hylas as their eternal plaything—his beauty forever still.

HERACLES: *(shouting)* Hylas! Hylas!

NARRATOR: The Argonauts, fearing the worst, had swept the woods for a sign of the missing boy. There had been no trace of him, but Heracles refused to leave without his precious armor-bearer.

ATALANTA: Heracles! We must go! Whatever got him might come back for us!

HERACLES: *(emotionally)* I refuse!

JASON: But that means you have to stay behind!

HERACLES: So be it.

ORPHEUS: Oh well.

JASON: You've got to do what you think is best. Farewell, Heracles. Thank you for your help.

HERACLES: I am sorry that I could not have been of more help, but the lad is like my son. I must find him, no matter how long it takes. Farewell.

NARRATOR: With that, Heracles turned and started walking. His shadow was lost amongst the trees.

He would wander for many years, searching for Hylas, shouting his name at every step, scouring the Earth, but the young boy would never be found.

JASON: Well, let's go.

NARRATOR: It was with sad faces that the crew hoisted the sail and set the Argo back out to sea. They continued toward Colchis.

The next leg of the voyage proved uneventful. Atalanta kept watch on the sea for signs of danger, but no danger came. Supplies once again ran low, but the last time they had gone inland, they had lost two of their men.

JASON: We must go ashore. We will take only a few men—as many as can be spared.

ATALANTA: I'm coming, too.

JASON: Of course, I count you among the men.

ATALANTA: *(satisfied)* Good.

NARRATOR: So they went ashore on a dark island—Atalanta, Jason, and Orpheus—taking a few Argonauts along. There could be no telling what they would find and the fewer lives risked, the better.

ORPHEUS: *(matter-of-factly)* There are Harpies on this island.

ATALANTA: Sssshhh! How could you know that?

ORPHEUS: Just a sixth sense. Whenever something bad's about to happen, I always feel it.

ATALANTA: What about something good?

ORPHEUS: *(surprised)* Something good? I don't think that's ever happened.

NARRATOR: Above the trees far ahead, a plateau rose before their view. In the middle of this high spot, there was set a long table and seated at it, the figure of a one old man.

ATALANTA: A man! There! Let us ask him where to find fresh water!

NARRATOR: They climbed the steep embankment that led up to where the man sat. The table before him was covered with food—exotic dishes, suckled meats, fine pies, anything the body could wish for—yet the man sitting at it looked feeble and emaciated. When the group approached, he did not look up.

JASON: Old man, can you tell us where we might find . . . ?

NARRATOR: The old man looked up—his eyes unglazed—and he jumped.

PHINEUS: Ghosts? Or are you real?

JASON: We are real. We don't want to hurt you, we just need information.

PHINEUS: *(crazy)* Visions of the future! Spirits from the past! What is the present? Who knows, who knows?

ATALANTA: I think he has gone senile.

ORPHEUS: Lucky.

JASON: We only need to know where to find . . .

NARRATOR: But he was cut off. The old man began to scream, falling from his chair, shrieking to the skies.

(screeching of the Harpies)

PHINEUS: *(screaming)* The Hounds of Zeus!

NARRATOR: Swooping low, three winged creatures darted from the sky. Atalanta pulled Jason to the ground. The beasts shrieked as they came—Harpies, head of a woman, body of a bird. A stench came with them, a stench that made it impossible to breathe.

ATALANTA: We're trapped!

NARRATOR: But they did not move to attack the travelers or the old man. They stopped their dives and flapped their foul wings above the food on the table. As the three watched, the green of their stench caused the food to wilt—puckering with foulness. The Harpies let out laughing cries as they watched with crazed eyes.

(Harpy screech)

ORPHEUS: What are they doing to the food?

NARRATOR: The old man had crawled close to them. At this question, he flinched and looked Orpheus' way.

PHINEUS: They are my curse, my curse. I have offended Zeus with my prophecies. I am doomed to stay on this island—starving—for eternity.

JASON: *(whispering)* Why do you not eat?

PHINEUS: The Harpies, the Harpies come and ruin my food before I can even think of touching it. That is my punishment. Tomorrow, the food will be restored, and a new day of torture will begin! Food, oh precious food! *(pause)* Do you perhaps have some on you?

JASON: No, we were hoping you had some.

ATALANTA: *(angry)* Gods or no gods, no creature should suffer such a fate!

NARRATOR: Atalanta raised up, bow in her hand, and released a shaft. A nearby Harpy shrieked—an arrow in its shoulder—and turned its cruel talons toward her. Atalanta already had another arrow notched into her bow.

But the Harpies did not fly forward. They hovered in midair, perfectly still. To her surprise, Atalanta found that she was not able to move.

PHINEUS: Gods above! What's happening?

NARRATOR: The air started to flash, color coming from everywhere—blue, red, green, yellow, orange—and then there was the outline of a woman in the midst of the light, a regal woman with purple eyes.

IRIS: I am Iris, the messenger of Hera. *I* have stopped you.

ATALANTA: *(through clenched lips)* Why?

IRIS: No man or woman may kill the Harpies. They are the Hounds of Zeus.

ATALANTA: Watch me.

IRIS: You would do well to learn some respect for those above you, girl. There is no need for your theatrics. Because of your bravery, Heaven has declared Phineus' punishment ended. The Harpies will no longer plague him.

NARRATOR: Atalanta found she could move again.

PHINEUS: Thank you, oh thank you, beautiful messenger of the gods.

IRIS: I have not saved you. These Argonauts have. Give them your thanks.

PHINEUS: *(turning to Jason)* I am a great seer. Tell me where you are going! I know the way from here to any country.

JASON: We seek Colchis and the Golden Fleece.

PHINEUS: The Fleece! A mighty quest! But know this: Between this shore and that, two great rocks rise out of the ocean. A terrible danger awaits between them. They rise out of the water and smash ships to smithereens!

ATALANTA: I have heard of these rocks.

PHINEUS: If you sail between them, they shall crush your craft.

JASON: Is there a way around them?

PHINEUS: No, not to Colchis. But do this: Capture a bird on these shores. Let the bird fly between the rocks. They will crush *it*. Then, when they are lowering from their attack, quickly sail through.

JASON: Will that actually work?

ORPHEUS: Probably not.

PHINEUS: You shall reach Colchis. I have seen it. Many thanks to you, Jason, for saving me, an old man.

IRIS: The voyage must be continued. Hera has smiled upon you, but you must be quick. The Colchians already know of your coming. Sail well, young Jason.

NARRATOR: Iris raised her hand, and the world about them filled with radiant light. They blinked. They were back on their ship—supplies piled around them.

ORPHEUS: That was easy.

NARRATOR: And so they set sail once again. When they neared the two gigantic, clashing rocks that Phineus had spoken of, they released a dove. It met its death between the crags, but as the rocks lowered into the water, the Argo sailed between them.

In front of them in the distance spread out a flat, dry country: Colchis. They had made it.

MEDEA: Visitors to the throne, father—Greeks.

ÆETES: *(hoarsely, almost a whisper)* Let them in, let them in.

NARRATOR: The band of travelers now stood before the throne of the King of Colchis. King Æetes, aged beyond time, still remembered when young Phrixus had visited his realm. Times had changed. He was no longer the trusting, kind man he once was. Age had soured him.

ÆETES: You must speak for me, daughter. My voice is nearly gone.

MEDEA: *(sarcastically)* Yes, Medea the witch. Medea, the speaker for those who cannot speak.

JASON: Hail, King Æetes, ruler of Colchis and keeper of the Golden Fleece.

MEDEA: Greeks, to what do we owe this honor? His majesty is not lightly troubled. If we were not civilized people, your heads would have been cut from your necks before you reached the shore.

ATALANTA: *(under her breath)* Hardly.

JASON: We have come to claim the Golden Fleece.

MEDEA: The Fleece? *(laughs)* My father will give the Fleece to no one, especially not a filthy Greek.

JASON: We have come for the Fleece. If you won't give it to us, we will have to take it.

MEDEA: Yes, you are all quite frightening—all five of you. I see no danger of the Fleece going anywhere.

ÆETES: *(hoarsely)* Medea, Medea, tell them that we will give them the Fleece.

MEDEA: *(quietly)* What? Father, are you mad?

ÆETES: They must first complete a task for us—one that can never be completed. In this manner, we can kill these trespassers without spilling our own blood.

MEDEA: *(sarcastically)* What a wise father I have. *(loudly)* Greeks, we have decided that we shall give you the Fleece . . . if you pledge to complete a task of our choosing.

ATALANTA: It's a trap. Don't do it, Jason.

JASON: How else will we get it?

MEDEA: If you complete this task successfully, the Fleece shall be yours. If you fail, your men shall return home—empty-handed.

JASON: We will take this challenge.

MEDEA: Good. We shall meet on the plain that lies between this palace and your ship tomorrow. Bring nothing but your sword. You shall face the challenge alone, bold one. If you fail, I will dance upon your corpse.

ORPHEUS: That's a pleasant thought.

NARRATOR: And so they were dismissed. As they walked back to the ship, Atalanta stalked ahead.

ATALANTA: Stupid, stupid, stupid! They will give you an impossible task! Then where will we be?

JASON: At least only *I* will lose my life. This is *my* quest, after all.

ATALANTA: Stupid!

NARRATOR: Night fell, but Jason found he could not sleep. Tomorrow he faced his destiny, but what would the task be? How can you prepare for a trial if you do not know what it will be? His mind continued to conjure up one fearsome creature after the next. He was no Heracles.

High above, Hera was looking down upon him. She had seen him safely thus far, but success in this matter would take more power than just hers.

She walked silently through the halls of Olympus to the sitting room of her cousin and nemesis, the mighty Aphrodite.

APHRODITE: *(sweet voice)* Hera? To what do I owe this pleasure?

HERA: Oh, please. Drop the act. You hate me as much as I hate you, but I have come to strike a deal.

APHRODITE: *(sarcastically)* Getting right to the point, I see. What do you want?

HERA: I know that your cuddly little son, Eros, has a certain bow and arrows that produce love. I require his services.

APHRODITE: Ah, but these services do not come lightly. If you, Queen of Heaven, require my help, you must give me something in return …

HERA: *(coldly)* You may name your price.

APHRODITE: Gladly. My ugly husband no longer excites me. His looks leave something to be desired. I grow bored. Therefore, I have turned my attentions elsewhere.

HERA: It is not my concern that you are sleeping in someone else's bed. If it were, I would *always* be concerned.

APHRODITE: Nice, but Hephaestus grows suspicious. He suspects that I share a bed with the God of War, your mightier son.

HERA: Is there a bed you do not share?

APHRODITE: Cute. *(pause)* You are his mother. Soothe his concerns. Blind him to my actions, and I will grant you this favor.

HERA: It will be done.

APHRODITE: Now, this arrow doesn't have anything to do with the handsome Jason, does it?

NARRATOR: And so a bargain was struck. That night as Medea watched the Greek ships from afar, Eros fired one of his magical arrows into her heart.

The sorceress was overcome with instant passion for the man who had so infuriated her before. What was happening? She nearly swooned when she realized that earlier that day she had sentenced him to death.

JASON: Master, master, what do I do now?

MEDEA: Pssst.

JASON: *(startled)* Who's there?

NARRATOR: A cloaked figure approached across the sands to where the Argonauts were encamped. The hood was thrown back, revealing a face: It was the Princess Medea.

JASON: *(surprised)* You!

MEDEA: *(passionately)* Yes, me. There is little time. I have sent you to your death.

JASON: What do you mean?

MEDEA: The task you will face tomorrow is impossible. My father owns a pair of fire-breathing bulls—fearsome creatures that are untamable—but he will ask you to yoke them, drive them, and use them to plow the field.

JASON: That doesn't sound easy.

MEDEA: That's not all. He will ask you to sow the field with the teeth of a dragon. Once these teeth have been planted, they will instantly grow into an army of phantom warriors—too many to conquer. Even if you managed to harness the bulls, you could never defeat this army.

JASON: I don't understand. If I can't change anything, why are you telling me?

MEDEA: But you can. That is why I have come. I cannot bear to see you die.

JASON: *(confused)* Has something changed?

MEDEA: Everything. *(pause)* I am a sorceress. I can help you. Here, take this ointment. Cover your body with it. It will protect you from the fire of the bulls.

JASON: Great, but what about the army?

MEDEA: This.

NARRATOR: She held up a simple rock.

JASON: A rock?

MEDEA: Yes, there is a secret to defeating the men who spring from the dragon's teeth. Throw this rock into their midst, and they will turn upon one another—slaying themselves.

JASON: Fantastic.

NARRATOR: Suddenly, Jason paused. Was this another trick? Medea had seemed so cold and cruel in the throne room earlier that day.

JASON: Why are you doing this?

MEDEA: *(sadly)* Isn't it obvious? *(pause)* I do all this for you, but I ask one thing.

JASON: Name it.

MEDEA: You must take me back to Greece with you and make me your wife.

NARRATOR: Jason thought. He barely knew this girl—a girl who had recently smiled at the prospect of his death. Now, she was asking to be his bride?

He knew he had no choice. He could not do this task on his own.

JASON: I swear it.

NARRATOR: Medea smiled in spite of herself.

MEDEA: Until tomorrow then, handsome Jason. Fight well.

NARRATOR: She slipped back into the night as quickly as she had come.

Even with his victory at hand, Jason still couldn't sleep. Had he done the right thing?

The morning broke bright on the barrenness of Colchis. The King Æetes was seated, overlooking the testing field, with his nobles. Medea was at his side, hiding the emotions she felt welling up inside of her.

Jason took the field—sword and stone in hand. The Argonauts crowded eagerly around, anxiously watching their leader.

MEDEA: *(shouting)* King Æetes wishes that you die well. You have been given your task. Release the bulls.

NARRATOR: From a great iron wagon, two giant bulls charged forth—their thick hide bristling with spikes—their breath flaming out before them. Atalanta and Orpheus watched from the sidelines.

ATALANTA: Stupid!

NARRATOR: At once, the bulls consumed Jason with a fiery blast from their heaving nostrils. The crowd gasped, but when the smoke cleared, Jason was still standing.

He picked up a long chain that lay in the dirt and threw it about the two beasts' necks. They pulled away in surprise, but he had already hooked them to a large stone plow. As they pulled, the plow furrowed deep rows. Into these rows from a sack at his side, Jason dropped the dragon's teeth he had been given that morning.

ATALANTA: What is he doing?

ORPHEUS: Who?

NARRATOR: As Medea had said they would, warriors began rising from the rows—metal helmets showing first, followed by fearsome torsos and brandished swords. There were hundreds of them. Jason turned to face them—rock in hand. He threw it into their midst.

The deathless warriors fell upon one another—slashing and hacking until all of their bodies littered the ground.

Medea breathed a secret sigh of relief as Jason turned to face the king victorious.

JASON: *(winded)* Your majesty, I have completed this task. I must ask for the Fleece.

NARRATOR: Shaking, the old king rose—fire in his eyes.

ÆETES: *(hoarsely, but loudly)* You shall have no fleece.

NARRATOR: Jason's heart sank.

ATALANTA: *(angrily)* I don't believe it! Cheaters!

MEDEA: *(coldly)* This man has *obviously* cheated. He will receive no prize.

NARRATOR: Jason started to object, but he saw a glimmer in Medea's eye. She had anticipated this. So, by his command, the Greeks allowed the situation to pass. The king and his court returned to the palace, and the Argonauts slunk back to their ship.

Medea was already there when they returned.

ATALANTA: What does this witch want?

JASON: Atalanta, silence. It was she who helped me to live today.

MEDEA: Prepare your men to sail upon our return.

JASON: But the Fleece!

MEDEA: Exactly. We're going to get it.

NARRATOR: She led Jason swiftly across the plain toward a distant grove of scraggly trees.

MEDEA: The Fleece is there.

JASON: There? Out in the open?

MEDEA: There is no need to hide it. It is guarded by a giant serpent—one who would love to sharpen his teeth with the bones of adventurers like you. Now, quickly.

NARRATOR: They entered the grove of Ares. Jason saw the serpent first—a mountain of green scales coiled around an ancient, gnarled tree. Then he saw the Fleece—the Golden Fleece—the object of all his travels. It hung on a branch, as if it had been forgotten there, shining like the sun. Every ordeal he had passed to behold such a thing was suddenly worth it. This was a treasure worth dying for.

MEDEA: I have fed the snake a powerful drug. Now I only need to lead him to sleep.

NARRATOR: Medea raised her arms into the air. Jason expected her to utter a spell, but instead, she started to sing. It was the strangest song he had ever heard. Mixed into the melody, he heard the voices of those he had once known—Chiron, his mother, his father—and other voices, voices he had not yet heard but someday would—his children, his wife . . .

Medea had stopped singing.

MEDEA: Now, my love, it is yours to take.

NARRATOR: Jason gave Medea a questioning look, but did not falter. He walked forward and climbed the side of the slumbering serpent. From this height, he was able to reach to the branch on which the Fleece hung, and he touched it, the treasure of kings.

MEDEA: Jason, time to flee.

NARRATOR: The Argonauts were making the final preparations to leave when they saw Medea and Jason's figures swiftly covering the ground toward them. But another group of men with flashing shields was heading toward the boat as well—warriors from the palace.

MEDEA: Faster! My brother comes with troops! My father has discovered my treachery!

ATALANTA: Jason approaches! Ready the ship!

NARRATOR: Jason reached the boat and quickly jumped inside. He turned to help Medea in as well, but she was not there. She was running swiftly toward the approaching soldiers.

MEDEA: Brother! I can explain! Stop your march! A truce!

NARRATOR: The Colchian soldiers halted when they saw the princess. A lone man came forward to meet with Medea—her brother, the prince. When he drew near to her, a knife glinted in the sun, drawn from under her robe. They all gasped as she drove it into his throat.

Before Jason could react, he felt Medea beside him.

MEDEA: That should keep them for a while. Let's go.

NARRATOR: And so, with the fresh corpse of Medea's brother lying in the sun, the Argonauts pushed away from Colchis with their prize.

Jason pulled out the Fleece, and everyone stared. Medea flashed him a coy grin. He shuddered. This was a woman who had just murdered her own brother.

The trip home was filled with many perils, but the Argonauts had Medea. Time and time again, she saved them from certain death—all for the love of her Jason.

When they reached the shores of Jason's kingdom, it was time for him to say goodbye to his most trusted companions, those with whom he had shared the journey of a lifetime.

JASON: Goodbye, Atalanta. I never could have made it without you.

ATALANTA: I know. But you weren't too bad yourself.

JASON: And Orpheus, your songs are truly the greatest in the world. I hope someday you find some happiness.

ORPHEUS: I'm not going to hold my breath.

JASON: Now, I must go face cousin Pelias myself. I have my prize. Thanks to you. Farewell.

NARRATOR: Atalanta and Orpheus sauntered into the distance—and into legend. Jason never saw or heard from them again. He and Medea now turned toward the castle. She reached and grabbed his hand and pulled him close to her. Inside, he recoiled.

MEDEA: Love, you owe this man nothing. You have proved yourself to all by merely getting the Fleece. He will not give you his kingdom freely. It's too dangerous to appear before him. Let me play a trick upon him. He deserves such a trick for what he did to you, and he will get his due reward.

NARRATOR: Jason agreed to let Medea deal with the king. Swathed in her sorceress garb, Medea requested an audience before the king. Pelias had grown even older and fatter. His days were slipping by him. In his presence she declared herself a sorceress, one who had discovered the spell of eternal life. To demonstrate, she brought forth a gray sheep, withered with age. She took her knife, cut it apart, and threw it into her bubbling cauldron. Chanting and dancing, Medea circled the pot, and to the amazement of all the court, a newborn lamb sprang forth from the rising smoke of the spell.

PELIAS: Witch, you work your spell well! This rite must be performed on me!

NARRATOR: Medea instructed the daughters of Pelias, dressed in ceremonial black, to cut their father apart with knives, bit by bit, and place these pieces in the cauldron. Medea chanted as his dying cries filled the throne room. When the grisly task was done, every eye was on the boiling pot. But no young king sprang forth.

MEDEA: *(spitting)* So passes an evil king. *(evil laugh)*

NARRATOR: The entire court gasped. Medea's eyes flashed, and she disappeared in a cloud of smoke. When Jason learned what Medea had done, he was horrified. This was not what the way a king should regain his kingdom. Chiron would be ashamed. This girl had cursed him.

JASON: Woman, you have shamed me. Why did you do such an evil thing?

MEDEA: To prove my love. Now, you must prove yours. You must marry me.

JASON: I have promised that I will do so, but I will not take back this kingdom. It was taken through witchcraft and deceit. I want nothing to do with it.

NARRATOR: So the two fled the kingdom Jason had journeyed so far to reclaim and came to a new kingdom. There he pledged himself to Medea, but they did not marry. She bore him two sons. He had heard them laughing long ago in Medea's song. As he grew older, they were the one tiny bit of happiness in his life.

He often thought of old Chiron and his great adventure for the Golden Fleece. The Fleece hung as a relic now in his meeting hall, along with the remains of the Argo, suspended from the ceiling. But they were meaningless now. Where was the young man who once dreamt great dreams? How had this woman poisoned him?

Then, one day, the king of his new realm came to visit and with him he brought his beautiful daughter. He had heard of Jason's great deeds and his forgotten kingdom. He deemed him to be a worthy match for his radiant girl.

Jason looked into her eyes. In them, he saw hope. This was his love, not the black-hearted creature who shared his bed. He felt young again, and rashly, he pledged to be her husband.

Up on Olympus, Hera mourned.

HERA: Oh, Jason, had I known what trouble I would bring you, I would have never asked for the arrows of love. Now, this witch will take her revenge and ruin the beautiful hero I have created. I will remember you, Jason, as you once were—shining and young. Great was your rise, great will be your fall.

NARRATOR: When Medea heard of the engagement, she was infuriated. The magic of Eros had grown thin. Love no longer controlled her heart. Hatred lived there instead.

MEDEA: *(crazy)* Deceiver! After all I have done for him! All that I have gone through! I have borne him sons! I have forsaken my dead father, killed my own brother, left my home—for what? For what? I shall poison his bride and erase all happiness from his life!

NARRATOR: In her madness, she took a royal gown and sewed it with a poison so that anyone who wore it would be consumed in flame. She sent it as an anonymous wedding present to Jason's fiancé. She then took her two young sons into a closed room—dagger in her hand. Their innocent minds thought nothing was wrong.

MEDEA: I will destroy everything he has ever loved. I have given them life, and I can take it from them.

NARRATOR: The coldness of her heart became the coldness of her hand as she put the dagger to her own sons.

Screaming in anger, their blood on her gown, she ran to the roof. There she conjured herself a chariot pulled by two dragons, and jumping inside, she laughed insanely, for her revenge was completed.

MEDEA: (crazed laugh)

NARRATOR: The chariot took to the sky, and she was taken out of Jason's life forever.

The news came to Jason all at once. His bride-to-be had been consumed in flames, as was her father in an effort to save her. His children were murdered. His mad-witch wife had fled to the skies. He was numb. He wanted to cry, but he could not. He stumbled into his meeting hall where the remnants of his once great ship, the Argo, hung suspended from the ceiling. All of his life, all of his adventures had come to this. How had he been so foolish? Through a window he could see the sky. The stars were just beginning to appear. He saw his old master forming in them.

JASON: (sobbing) Master, why? I don't want to live. Gods above, take me from this world!

NARRATOR: As if in answer to his prayer, he heard a dry rope crack. He closed his eyes and smiled. Hera had heard his final cry.

With a great groan, the skeleton of the Argo crashed down upon him, and in that moment, he was free. Free from the pain of the world, free from grief. All was blackness around him. He saw a great black river, and on the far side, the silhouette of his old master, beckoning him home.

DISCUSS

- Who was ultimately responsible for Jason's downfall? Explain.
- How would Jason have fared without his helpers? Explain.
- Jason is crushed by the remains of the Argo. How, in the modern world, does a career or reputation sometimes destroy a person?

ANALYZE

Legendary filmmaker Alfred Hitchcock developed the term *MacGuffin* to describe the object within a story that drives the action forward. The MacGuffin is something that the characters in the story want or search for: It could be money, a jewel, government secrets, or even the Holy Grail. It can even turn out to be completely inconsequential, but as long as the characters are willing to sacrifice anything to obtain it, the MacGuffin serves its purpose. In the myth of Jason, the Golden Fleece serves as the MacGuffin, as it is the object the Argonauts journey for, yet ultimately its only purpose in the story is to prompt the quest.

FUN FACT

Greek mythology contains only two witches—one is Circe, the enchantress who delays Odysseus on his journey home, and the other is Medea. Interestingly, Circe is actually Medea's aunt, as she is the sister of King Æetes. Although most witches in European fairy tales appear as old hags, Medea and Circe are young and beautiful. The magic practiced by Greek witches comes from potions and rituals, rather than spoken spells. One etymologist theorized that the word *medicine* actually derived from Medea's name.

VIEW

View either *Jason and the Argonauts* (1963) or *Jason and the Argonauts* (2000) and compare it to the original myth. The first is a feature film that contains stop-motion monsters by legendary special effects artist Ray Harryhausen. The second is a 3-hour made-for-TV miniseries.

Creature Feature: Golden Ram, Golden Fleece

A fleece (the wooly hide of a ram) may seem like an odd object to quest after—no matter how much gold is laid over it—but like most magical objects, the Golden Fleece has an interesting back-story. A powerful Greek king, tricked by his new wife and a crooked oracle, agreed to sacrifice his own children to prevent a widespread famine. As the king led his children, a boy named Phrixus and a girl named Helle, to their own execution, there appeared to the children a golden ram, a magical beast sent by Hermes to rescue them. Phrixus and Helle jumped upon the ram's back, and it took to the sky, bearing them forever away from their father and wicked stepmother. They flew far to the east, and as they passed over the sea, Helle lost her grip on the ram's golden wool and fell down into the sea. The Hellespont, the strait where she drowned, was named for her. The ram set Phrixus down in the country of Colchis, a kingdom beyond the Black Sea. As the gods demanded, the boy skinned the magical beast and presented its fleece to the young king of that country, King Æetes, in thanks for giving him a new home. The king hung the fleece from a tree in the sacred grove of Ares and guarded it with an enormous serpent that never slept.

Creature Feature: Chiron and the Centaurs

Centaurs were half-man, half-horse creatures known for their savage behavior—murder and rape being two of their favorite pastimes. Chiron, a wise centaur renowned throughout Greece for training heroes, was an exception to his race. The reason for this was his raising. Apollo and Artemis, the twin gods, found him as an orphaned "colt" and raised him up to be wise and caring. His most famous pupils were Jason (leader of the Argonauts), Achilles (Greece's greatest warrior), Aesculapius (a legendary healer), and Actaeon (a renowned hunter). After his death, Zeus transformed Chiron into a constellation in recognition for his many good deeds.

The Harpies

Harpies were foul-smelling creatures with the head of a woman and the body of a bird. They were frequently referred to as the "Hounds of Zeus," as the god used them to punish offending mortals. Today a woman who is rude and shrill is referred to as a *harpy*.

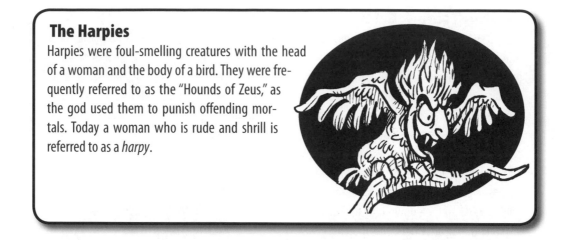

Teamwork: The Argonauts, the Original Super-Group

The Argonauts do not have a multimillion-dollar movie franchise like the *X-Men* do, but they might deserve one. After all, the Argonauts were the original super-group—a collection of previously established heroes who joined forces to complete a common goal. Even though the ancient Greek heroes do not have secret identities or the ability to shoot laser beams out of their eyes, they are still the ancient equivalent of modern superheroes. (The sons of Boreas, the North Wind, who were present on Jason's voyage in the original myth, *were* able to fly—which is getting closer. Plus, Heracles did have some amazing super-strength, not to mention some Incredible Hulk-like rages.) Heroes teaming up is an idea that sells, and the enduring myth of Jason tells us it has been selling for nearly 3,000 years.

Even powerful heroes realize the importance of teamwork. By the time the Argo sailed, the Greek heroes had already achieved some amazing individual feats: Atalanta hunted the Calydonian Boar, Orpheus descended into the Underworld, and Heracles completed 12 impossible labors. Yet when they signed up to accompany Jason on his mission to Colchis, they put their egos to the side and accepted the role of a team member—which was probably not easy for such widely renowned heroes. They all accepted the leadership of Jason, an inexperienced young man, for one simple reason: It was his quest, not theirs.

Even a legendary team like the Argonauts would be worthless without a good leader. Over the course of the story, Jason proves himself to be as much a hero as the rest of his companions by his resolve and determination to reach his goal. There is a saying concerning leadership: "In order to be a good leader, you must be a good follower." Jason asks others for advice, takes their suggestions, and uses their strengths—coupled with his own—to achieve success. Leaders should never be too proud to accept the help of others.

The Quest for the Golden Fleece was a heroic catch-all for storytellers. Because it was a group expedition, more and more heroes were added to the impressive list of members. (In the version of the story found in this book, that list has been shorted considerably for the sake of clarity.) The *Dioscuri* twins, Castor and Polydeuces, the brothers of the infamous Helen of Sparta, were famous warriors in their own rite. Also the Boreads, the sons of the North Wind Boreas, used their flying powers to battle the Harpies. Peleus, the father of Achilles, was there as well—not nearly famous as his son would become, but a hero nevertheless. Theseus, the hero who killed the Minotaur, appears on some versions of the roster; he was probably an afterthought—because almost all of the other heroes were along for the ride, why not him, too?

In spite of all of this heroic prowess, it is not the accompanying heroes (or even Jason, for that matter) who really determine the mission's success. The Colchian witch they add to their group, the deadly beautiful daughter of a king, is the true key to their success. She made it possible for Jason to obtain the Golden Fleece, she murdered her own brother to ensure their escape, and she stopped a giant bronze giant, Talos, from crushing their ship as they sailed by his island. When the Argonauts return safely to Greece and the Argonauts disband, Jason had seemingly forgotten that he had forged an even smaller team—a team of two— just Medea and himself. Ultimately, he betrayed *that* team and suffered a brutal revenge.

DISCUSS
- Teamwork is a buzzword in society today. Is it really as important as it is made out to be? Explain.
- What are some instances where teamwork would not be important? Explain.
- Some criticize Jason as being a very *un*heroic, ineffective leader. Do you agree with this? Explain.

ANALYZE
Comic books such as the *Justice League*, *Teen Titans*, and *The Avengers* combine established superheroes into crime-fighting teams—similar to what happens in the story of the Golden Fleece. Why is it interesting to read about superheroes working together rather than individually? Explain.

Atalanta

Atalanta is the only female hero in Greek mythology. As a baby she was abandoned in the wilderness by her kingly father, who had been hoping for a son, but was saved from death by a passing she-bear that nursed her as its own cub. A band of hunters later took her in, raised her, and trained her to love the hunt. Atalanta gained fame during the hunt for the Calydonian Boar, a gigantic boar that was terrorizing the Greek city-state of Calydon. During the hunt, she earned the love of Prince Meleager of Calydon, but she was sworn to virginity in the tradition of the huntress-goddess Artemis. The hunters were successful in killing the boar, but when Prince Meleager's uncles refused to give Atalanta the honor of the kill, he slew them. In retribution, the prince was murdered by his own mother. Atalanta mourned his death but went on to many more adventures—including her trip on the Argo.

Sailing the Wine-Dark Sea

The sea was a place that the Greeks knew very well, and because the Greeks were a sea-faring people, sea voyages play a large part in their myths. Homer used the adjective *wine-dark* to describe the color of the sea, which is odd because most Mediterranean waters are beautifully blue. The most famous sea voyage is the *Odyssey*, Homer's account of Odysseus' 10-year journey home from the war at Troy, while Jason and his journey for the Golden Fleece is a close second. Historians have used details found in the myths, as well as archeological and historical records, to gain an accurate picture of what sailing was like for the characters of Greek mythology.

The type of ship used by the heroes of Greek mythology is called a Bronze Age galley. The ship was probably built of pine because Greece was well-forested in those days and pine was abundant. Painted on most bows were a pair of eyes, above which rose a figurehead, a carving of a mortal or god. Everywhere else the hull was blackened from the pitch that sealed it. Ships in Greek mythology are labeled as *black* because of the pitch used. Each ship was equipped with sails, but relied mainly on oar power. Some ships of the time could seat 25 men on one side. Fortunately for those rowing, the ships were designed with a narrow hull and built for speed. The rowing was very physically demanding, and sailors probably rowed in shifts, letting half the men rest while the others rowed to keep a fresh reserve of manpower. The pilot, standing on the stern of the ship, maneuvered the steering oar to guide the vessel. Sailors stowed their gear—shields, spears, and swords—under the galley benches. Just in case they were attacked, weapons would be at the ready. The supply of grain would be kept in leather bags; water and wine would be stored in jars or skin bottles.

The Greeks knew the sea was a dangerous place. The second-most-feared god behind Zeus was Poseidon. The god of the blue mane was labeled the Earth-shaker for a good reason: With a swirl of his trident he could summon storms and sink ships without batting an eye. The Greeks were cautious sailors. Rather than striking out over open sea, like the Vikings frequently did, Greek sailors preferred to sail close to the coastline and, in many cases, island-hop their way across the sea. If at all possible, the ship would beach each night or at least anchor in a safe cove. The men would go ashore, refill their water jars, make their fire for a meal, and sleep out in the open. If they were lucky, they might find a nearby cave to take shelter in. Of course, by going ashore they ran the risk of being ambushed by local villagers, who could slit their throats and make off with what provisions they had. Another advantage of ships sticking close to the coast was that, at the sight of an approaching storm, the sailors could beach the ship and stay ashore until it had passed. On the occasions when night-sailing was imperative, sailors navigated by the stars.

Although the portions of the sea nearest Greece were familiar to sailors, the further one journeyed to the east or west, the more unfamiliar the territory became. Stories about deadly obstacles and fearsome monsters waiting to snap up ships kept sailors close to home. Faraway places such as Colchis on the far side of the Black Sea were almost imaginary— way beyond the known world. Only heroes ventured to these far reaches of the sea and lived to tell about it.

Heracles: The True Story

The Greeks revered Heracles (called Hercules by the Romans) as their greatest hero. He accomplished almost every great deed there was to do. He once held up the weight of the sky, he founded the Olympics, he created the Milky Way, and when it was all over, he became a god. His is quite the résumé.

It is said that when Zeus fathered Heracles, he set out to make the greatest hero of all time. From the moment baby Heracles entered the world, he was a focus of Hera's hatred. The goddess hated any child who was the result of her husband's numerous affairs, and she decided to destroy Heracles while he was still in the cradle. Two deadly snakes, conjured by Hera, slithered into the crib where the baby lay. But Heracles was no ordinary baby. Taking the snakes into his chubby hands and laughing at their attempts to escape, Heracles twisted and choked the life from them. This was his first heroic deed.

Alcmena, the mother of Heracles, discovered the dead snakes and took them as a sign that the gods wanted her baby dead. Fearing for her own life if she stood in their way, Alcmena abandoned her son in the countryside. There, the starving Heracles would have died if Athena, the Goddess of Wisdom (his half-sister), had not found him. In order to prevent his death, Athena saw he would need divine milk. Only Hera, a mother herself, could help, but she would never nurse the infant she was trying to destroy. So Athena devised a trick.

Asking the Queen of Olympus to join her in a walk, Athena led Hera through the forest to the very spot where Heracles lay. Hera, not recognizing the baby (she thought he had died by snakebite as planned), took pity and began to nurse him. At once the goddess realized that she had been tricked: This baby was no normal mortal child. When she tried to remove him, Heracles clamped down upon her breast. Hera cried out, and when she finally succeeded in yanking the child away, milk sprayed across the heavens. This event explains the misty path seen in the night sky called the Milky Way. Outraged, Hera turned to destroy the baby once and for all, but Athena had spirited him safely back to his relieved mother.

Heracles grew up and started to make a name for himself. In one of his early deeds, he defeated the Lion of Nemea, whose skin could not be pierced. Because weapons were no good against the beast, Heracles strangled it to death. Afterward, as a reminder of just how powerful he was, Heracles wore the lion's skin as a cloak. The King of Nemea was so impressed with Heracles that he asked him to spend the night with each of his 50 daughters. In one night Heracles gave the king 50 new grandsons, all imbued with their father's heroic might.

After many adventures in his younger days, Heracles decided to settle down by marrying a princess and starting a family. But Hera, who had time and time again failed in destroying him, saw a perfect chance to ruin his heroic career. She cast a spell of madness over Heracles, a bloodfrenzy. In a blind, murderous rage, Heracles murdered his wife and sons. When he returned to his right mind, he saw his new family dead at his feet and their blood upon his hands.

The hero was devastated, yet he did not commit suicide as Hera had hoped. Instead Heracles journeyed to Delphi to speak to the Oracle, who alone could tell him how to receive forgiveness for his horrible crime. Her words were not comforting: Heracles had committed the ultimate sin; therefore, his punishment would be an arduous string of nearly impossible feats. He would swear to serve the corrupt King Eurystheus, a tyrant known his cruel-heartedness, and complete without question whatever 12 tasks the king asked him to do. If he refused or failed, Heracles would be cursed by the gods forever.

The strongman did as the Oracle commanded, giving himself over to the will of the wicked king. Eurystheus relished his job as punisher and, receiving divine inspiration from Hera, sent the hero on every doomed mission he could. But to his growing amazement, Heracles returned from each journey successful. In fact, it was during these 12 labors (as they came to be called) that Heracles became even more famous than before. Infuriated by the hero's many successes, Eurystheus chose for the final deed a task he thought for sure no mortal could ever achieve. He commanded Heracles to descend to the Underworld and bring back Cerberus, the three-headed hell-hound.

Heracles did not bat an eye. He forged into the depths of Hades and returned, dragging the enormous hound into the King's hall. Terrified at the sight of the beast's foaming jaws, Eurystheus scurried inside the large urn that sat beside his throne and weakly declared that the 12 labors had been completed as promised. Heracles had proved he was the greatest of all heroes and cleared his named for good.

In an attempt to return to a normal life, the hero remarried. He lived happily for a number of years until his wife, Deianira, began to fear that he was in love with another woman. To rekindle his passion, she presented her husband with a cloak she had sprinkled with a love potion, or so she thought. Unfortunately, the centaur who gave her the love potion had tricked her, and it was actually a flesh-eating poison.

As soon as Heracles wrapped the cloak around him, it began to burn away his skin. He cried out and tried to pull it loose, but the cloak had already grafted itself to his body and bits of flesh came with it. Deianira fled in terror and hanged herself in shame. In unendurable torment Heracles, sure that his defeat had come, presented his legendary bow and arrow to a trusted companion and commanded that a funeral pyre be built.

When the fire was prepared, Heracles laid down upon it—ending his life and his suffering. The spirit of Heracles began to descend into the Underworld, but Zeus, watching his son's final moments from on high, stopped its descent, summoning it instead to Olympus. Zeus declared that Heracles, in return for his many brave deeds, would not die as a mortal man but would become a god of Olympus. All of the gods gathered there rejoiced (even Hera, who could no longer resist the hero's charm). Appearing in his new godly form, Heracles was married to Hebe, the Goddess of Youth, and has lived on Olympus ever since.

DISCUSS
- In which ways is Heracles a good role model? In which ways is he not? Explain.
- Which modern day superhero would be Heracles' equivalent?

VIEW
Watch Disney's *Hercules*. How have the events of the story changed? Do you think these changes are necessary? Explain.

Medea: Victim or Villain?

Medea emerges from Greek mythology as one of its most despicable characters. She has quite a rap sheet. She's guilty of both *filicide* (the murder of her sons) and *fratricide* (not only does she murder her brother

in the original myth, but also cuts him into tiny pieces), the assassination of two kings (the evil King Pelias, Jason's cousin, and King Creon, Jason's would-be father-in-law), and the fiery destruction of one princess (Jason's fiancé, the princess Glauce) with a poisoned dress. It is hard to feel sorry for such a cold-blooded murderer, but does she deserve some pity?

The Greek playwright Euripides thought so, and his tragedy *Medea* put the Colchian witch at center stage, allowing her to plead her own case. Had *she* not been wronged? She gave up everything for Jason—only to have him betray her. In the play Medea's actions are still cruel, but we are a given a clear look at her thought process. Weighing the consequences of such a brutal revenge against her own emotions, Medea is given complexity and reality. Here is a powerful woman, for good or for evil, who is able to perform the unthinkable. Under Euripides' touch she is no longer a one-dimensional villain. She is alive, wounded, brutal, and savage. Her choices show us what a person is capable of when conscience has been eroded away by hurt. During a time when women were kept confined to the home, Euripides created a Medea who was every Greek man's worst nightmare: a powerful, liberated, and dangerous wife.

The Roman poet Ovid, inspired by Euripides' play, gave Medea a voice as well. His *Heroides* are letter-like poems written from the points of view of mythical female characters. In the following letter, Medea voices her frustration to Jason.

"Medea to Jason"

And yet I, a Colchian princess, had time for you, I recall,
when you came begging me to use my magic to help you. . . .
Why was I all too smitten with your golden locks, your good looks,
and that sweet-talking charm of your tongue?
I betrayed my father, gave up my kingdom and country.
My reward? I am allowed to live in exile. . . .

[then] you had the gall to say, "Take your leave of [my] house."
So ordered, I vacated the house, accompanied by our two sons and
that ever-faithful companion, my love for you.
Then suddenly I heard the sound of Hymen's wedding song. . . .
I was stricken with fear, but did not think such an outrage was pos-
    sible.
Yet my heart was all encased in ice. . . .
Right then our younger boy . . .
said, "Come here, Mom! There's a parade, and dad—Jason—is out
    front
leading it. He's dressed in gold, driving a team of horses!"
Right then and there I ripped my dress and beat my breast,
and my cheeks were not safe from my fingernails.
I felt the urge to plunge into the middle of the crowd,
to fling that crown off her nicely coiffed hair. . . .
I have lost my kingdom, country, and home, and now I have been
abandoned by my husband, who was everything to me. . . .
A mistress now embraces the limbs I once saved,
and she enjoys the fruits of my labor.
Perhaps, while you flaunt yourself in front of your stupid wife
and speak the words her biased ears want to hear,
you will invent new slurs against my looks and behavior.
Let her laugh and take pleasure in my faults. . . .
She *will* weep, in flames that will exceed the heat of my passion.
So long as iron, flames, and magical poisons are at my disposal,
no enemy of Medea will go unpunished. . . .
Where my anger leads, I shall follow. Perhaps I'll regret my actions.
But right now I regret having protected a traitorous husband.
Let this be the concern of the god that now stokes my heart.
Be sure, though, something truly momentous is stirring in my soul.
    (Brunet et al., 2004, p. 323)

Medea is not weak—and refuses to be weak. She strikes a blow
against the man who has wronged her and destroys the life they have
made together. In her own mind she has justified these actions, but what
price has she paid for revenge?

Hera, Jason's Heavenly Helper

In the story of Jason and the Argonauts, Hera takes on an unfamiliar
role for herself. Typically when the goddess appears in a myth, she is the

DISCUSS

- Is Medea a victim, a villain, or both? Explain.
- Why is it easier for storytellers to use one-dimensional villains instead of well-rounded ones?
- Some have described Medea as manly because of her bravery and assertiveness compared to Jason's cowardice and passiveness. Do you think this is a good description? Explain.

WRITE

Imagine Medea is put on trial for the murder of her children, the princess Glauce, and King Creon. Write a case for the prosecution or the defense. Share your case with the rest of the class.

antagonist. In the story of the Trojan War, she is out to destroy Troy. In the story of Heracles, she is that hero's greatest adversary. Therefore, it is strange to see a normally spiteful character in the role of divine bene-factress.

In this book's version of the story, Hera's only reason for helping Jason is the fact that he is *not* a son of Zeus. (The exact phrase she uses is "the putrid offspring of your insatiable loins." You may have to get a dictionary out to decipher that phrase, but it is worth it.) Almost all heroes claim to be the illegitimate children of Zeus. She hopes to prove to her husband that his genetic contribution is not what makes these heroes great. Any mortal can be a hero with the right kind of backing. Hera gives her backing to Jason, who is a heroic rarity—the son of two mortals.

Yet, in the original myth, there is another explanation for Hera's generosity. While Jason is journeying to confront his cousin, he encounters an old woman on the bank of a river. The old woman asks him to bear her across the river on his back, as it is too swift for her to cross. Jason agrees, and when he has delivered her safely to the other side, she reveals herself to be Hera, Queen of Olympus. As it turns out, she has been poking about in her human disguise looking for displays of mortal nobility. In return for his kindness, she uses all of her power to help him achieve his quest.

No matter what motivated Hera to help Jason, this myth definitely proves that she is one Olympian that you want on your side.

DISCUSS

• Which qualities of Hera make her a good helper? Do the same qualities make her a formidable adversary? Explain.

Eros (Roman: Cupid)

In most myths, Eros appears as a winged child, complete with chubby, cherubic features. This is the image most modern people associate with Cupid. In some tales, Eros appears as a winged teenager. He is the son of Aphrodite and the archer of love. His father's identity is sketchy. Some say his father is Ares; others say Hephaestus. One story of Creation states that Eros is not the son of any god, but an elemental force that existed in the darkness before the world began. Two types of arrows can come from Eros. One type causes intense infatuation, an attraction that is usually sexual in nature. From this we get our words *erotic* and *erogenous*. The other type, instead of softening the heart, hardens it against all emotion. True to the nature of Love, Eros is mischievous. He may strike you with the arrow of love, but send the arrow of hard-heartedness into your beloved. The Greeks frequently showed him as wearing a blindfold, hence the saying, "Love is blind."

CHAPTER 4
Heart and Soul

EROS AND PSYCHE

Cast

Eros *The young god of love*

Psyche *A beautiful mortal princess*

Aphrodite *Goddess of love and beauty*

King *Psyche's father*

Sister One *Psyche's conceited sister*

Sister Two *Psyche's other conceited sister*

Zephyr/Voice *The West Wind*

Servant *An invisible servant*

NARRATOR: In a far, mountainous kingdom, a king had three daughters. Although his eldest two were as beautiful as humanly possible, the third and youngest, Psyche, seemed to radiate an immortal glory. She seemed to be a goddess among women. Many said she was as beautiful as Aphrodite herself. In fact, those who had once flocked to Aphrodite's shrine began to pay homage to the mortal princess instead, and so began Psyche's troubles.

APHRODITE: *(angrily)* Eros! Eros!

NARRATOR: In the billowy halls of Olympus, the Goddess of Love and Beauty paced the floor, calling for her archer son. Aphrodite's immortal features could never lose their youthfulness, but something aged and cracked was starting to show through. The god Eros hovered into the room.

EROS: Mother! What's the matter?

APHRODITE: It's about time! I've been yelling for nearly 5 minutes.

EROS: *(sarcastically)* Sorry to keep you waiting. I was on yet another one of your little missions.

APHRODITE: Did you shoot the arrow like I asked you?

EROS: Yes, yes. She loves him, but he finds her absolutely repulsive. Just like you requested.

APHRODITE: Good! I'm sending you out again—immediately. Some stupid mortal princess has been bad for business, and I want you to fix her wagon.

EROS: She has a wagon?

APHRODITE: Don't be smart! You can't imagine the stress in my life. Do you have any idea what it's like to be an aging Goddess of Beauty?

EROS: No, but I can imagine being an annoyed god of love.

APHRODITE: *(ignoring him)* There are *thousands* of women down there—all of them trying to get the better of *me!*

EROS: Good grief. You look exactly the same as you did the day you were born.

APHRODITE: Exactly. Over time men grow tired of the same delicate features . . . porcelain skin, ruby red lips. From the moment I sprang from the sea foam, I was praised. They flocked about me to admire my glory. "How radiant is Aphrodite," they said. "The sun barely compares to her glow."

NARRATOR: Eros rolled his eyes at his mother's trip down memory lane.

APHRODITE: *Now* what do they say? Every time some ugly little sow comes along, they starting praising her with, "Why, she's as glorious as Aphrodite!" What insolence! Oh, yes, my son—men have changed. They have forgotten their goddess, but I *will* remind them and destroy anyone who gets in my way!

EROS: Sooo . . . Did you call me in here just to rant, or were you going to give me some details on my assignment?

APHRODITE: *(angrily)* This upstart princess whose beauty—*allegedly*—equals my own, she must be ruined.

EROS: *(sigh)* Let me check my contract. Is this in my job description? I thought I was supposed to use my arrows to bring love, not pain.

APHRODITE: Ha! Love *is* pain. You're bound to figure that out soon enough. Now, fly down to Earth. Psyche is her name.

EROS: What should I do once I find her?

APHRODITE: Cause her to fall in love with the vilest man you can find—someone completely hideous. Ha! Look for a satyr. Or a shepherd. They're usually grotesque. That will shame her! She will be the laughingstock of her kingdom. Perfect. Perfect. And once she's fooled away her beauty on a lowly shepherd, no one will ever speak of her again! *(evil laugh)*

EROS: All right. He's off. Eros, the god of gloom and doom.

APHRODITE: *(absentmindedly)* Be careful, darling. Remember, Mother loves you.

EROS: Uh-huh.

NARRATOR: Eros eased quickly down through the night sky. The stars winked out at him, socketed in the dark air. Eros considered himself to be a romantic god, more romantic than some, at least, but he wondered if *he* would ever find love, real love—not the cheap stuff he doled out with his flimsy arrows. Would he ever cease to be his mother's lackey and be worthy in his own right? The stars did not reply, and he flew on.

Far below, the object of his pursuit, the princess Psyche, was wearily returning to her room, which she shared with her two older sisters. It had been a tiring day. A crowd of would-be suitors had amassed before the gate early that morning, and she had spent hours being bombarded by proposal after proposal. Upon Psyche's entrance, her two sisters looked up from their weaving.

SISTER ONE: *(snottily)* My, my. Look who it is. Our darling little sister.

SISTER TWO: *(snottily)* Have you finished greeting all of your admirers?

PSYCHE: *(tiredly)* I didn't *ask* them to come.

SISTER ONE: Of course you didn't. That's the beauty of it all. They just showed up. Like flies to . . . beauty, or is it something else?

SISTER TWO: *(sarcastically)* It's sad to think that no one will want *us trolls* after seeing a prize such as you.

SISTER ONE: But think, when they take Psyche to Olympus and make her one of the goddesses, we'll be able to go visit her! What excitement!

SISTER TWO: A fantastic idea, sister. *(cruel laughing)*

PSYCHE: *(angrily)* You two are just jealous.

SISTER ONE: *(angrily)* Jealous of what? You being auctioned off like a piece of meat?

SISTER TWO: Don't think your looks will bring you happiness, dear. Father will marry you off to the first old king who offers him a good price.

PSYCHE: *(defensively)* He would never do that!

SISTER ONE: It is *you* who should envy *us*—at least we dog-faces won't be miserable the rest of our days.

NARRATOR: Psyche's eyes filled with tears, and she threw herself onto her bed.

SISTER TWO: Well, goodnight, sister. Don't cry too much, or you'll ruin those beautiful eyes of yours.

NARRATOR: Shortly after, Eros entered Psyche's chambers. He had come to see this beauty for himself before he cursed her with one of his arrows. The god—invisible to human eyes— floated above her.

EROS: *(to himself)* Why does she weep and hide her face?

NARRATOR: Psyche raised her head from the cushions to dry her eyes. At the sight of the girl's face, Eros felt his guts tighten into a knot, and a feeling he'd never known before radiated throughout his body. At once, his mission was forgotten. His only desire was to console this gorgeous creature. He started to materialize, to make himself known, but then he remembered . . .

EROS: *(despairingly)* I am a god. She is a mortal. We could never be together. Mother would drive her to madness—or worse.

NARRATOR: To his surprise, Eros felt his own heart breaking. How many times had he broken the hearts of others? Now he knew how much pain he had caused. He was suddenly sure of one thing: He could cause this lovely maiden no more hurt. He dissolved into the night, his task abandoned.

EROS: *(angrily)* I won't do Mother's dirty work anymore!

NARRATOR: Despair coursed through him. He had seen the love of his life, but she could never be his.

EROS: *(to himself)* Wait a minute! Could it work? I'll ask Apollo. He'll speak the truth.

NARRATOR: The course of the young god's flight veered toward Olympus. His cousin, Apollo, the God of Light, received him there, and together they hatched a brilliant scheme—one that would allow Eros to have his love.

A week later, Psyche's father, the elderly king, burst into his children's chamber room distraught. As the old man fell to his knees, his three daughters ran to him.

KING: *(in pain)* Woe and grief! Daughters! Come to me at once!

SISTER ONE: *(shocked)* Father! What has happened?

KING: *(through tears)* Oh, gods! The Oracle of Apollo has spoken a terrible prophecy! Zeus, help me! I can barely utter the words.

SISTER TWO: What is it? What is it?

KING: The Oracle has spoken. Olympus is furious. My daughter has set herself up to be as beautiful as the goddesses—an unforgiveable sin. And unless we wish our kingdom to be destroyed, we must take Psyche to the holy mountain . . . and . . . and . . .

SISTER ONE: And what, father?

KING: *He* will come to her . . . to be her husband.

SISTER TWO: Who, father? Who will come?

KING: A terrible beast! A winged serpent! Oh, my daughter. Forgive me. I cannot resist the will of the gods. They will destroy us if we disobey.

NARRATOR: Psyche saw her sisters staring at her anxiously. They were not as thrilled as she had expected them to be.

PSYCHE: *(numbly)* Then I guess I have no choice. I must go . . . to be the bride of the beast.

NARRATOR: Dawn broke, and wailing was heard in the streets of the kingdom. Black cloths were draped from every balcony. The word had spread quickly throughout the night: The beloved princess Psyche was to be sacrificed to the gods. A solemn precession led the princess up the mountain. As for the sacrifice herself, her spirit had left her. She prepared herself for nothingness.

PSYCHE: *(numbly)* At least an end will come.

NARRATOR: Even though everyone lamented her death, no one was brave enough to go against the will of the gods. They left her there—alone on the mountain to await her monstrous bridegroom. Psyche sat silently upon a rock and watched the black procession make its way back down the mountain path. A thin rain began to fall. She wrapped her wet robes around her and closed her eyes. A faraway sound reached her ears— wind—growing louder and louder, until it was almost upon her. Surely it must be her serpent husband come to claim his bride.

VOICE: *(wind whooshing)* Come.

NARRATOR: An unseen force lifted her from the rock and into the air. She timidly opened her eyes. Ahead the clouds had parted. Perched atop a spindly peak, shining like a jewel, was a glorious palace.

PSYCHE: *(gasp)* This is the home of a serpent?

NARRATOR: She dared to look over her shoulder. To her shock, it was no winged beast that carried her, but a bearded little man.

PSYCHE: You aren't a snake!

ZEPHYR: *(insulted)* Of course I'm not, you dumb girl. I'm Zephyr, the West Wind.

PSYCHE: They told me a giant serpent was coming to take me away.

ZEPHYR: Don't be stupid.

PSYCHE: Are *you* to be my husband?

ZEPHYR: Good gods, no. The last thing *I* need is a wife. I'm free! Free as, well, the wind. The master of that golden hall there is a friend of mine, and I owe him a favor or two. He'll be your husband.

PSYCHE: Is *he* a winged serpent?

ZEPHYR: Are you fixated on snakes for some reason? I've heard my friend there called plenty of names, but never that. I'm to take you to his house, and then he'll be along shortly. You'll find the servants of the palace ready to accommodate your every need. They're not winged serpents either; they're spirits. You do know what a *spirit* is, don't you?

PSYCHE: *(defensively)* Yes.

ZEPHYR: Good. I was beginning to think you were a *complete* idiot.

NARRATOR: The West Wind swooped down low and set Psyche neatly upon the front step of the palace.

ZEPHYR: All ashore. Now, when your husband shows up, don't talk him to death with all those stupid questions of yours. If you can't say anything smart, don't say anything at all. I don't want to have to come back here when he realizes what a ninny he married. If you'll excuse me, it's hurricane season.

NARRATOR: The little man dissolved into a faint breeze and blew away. Psyche turned to face the palace doors. With the slightest pressure from her fingers, they swung open, and behind them stretched a long, hushed hall. An unexpected voice at her shoulder caused her to jump.

SERVANT: Welcome, mistress.

NARRATOR: Seeing only air to the side, she waited for the voice to speak again.

SERVANT: We are here, although you cannot see us. We are the spirits of the house. We serve the master—your husband.

PSYCHE: *(confused)* How … how nice … to meet you.

SERVANT: The master has commanded us to give to you whatever you may require.

PSYCHE: I see. Tell me, what kind of being is he?

SERVANT: Oh, he is the kindest of masters.

PSYCHE: Can you tell me what he looks like?

SERVANT: As we are invisible to you, *he* is invisible to us. His goodness is all that we see.

PSYCHE: Oh.

SERVANT: Is there anything you desire?

PSYCHE: Well, yes. I guess I could use a bath. And perhaps some dinner?

SERVANT: It is already prepared. The master will arrive tonight—in darkness.

NARRATOR: Psyche quickly acclimated herself to her otherworldly surroundings. The voices spoke calmly to her, and objects floated of their own accord, lifted by invisible hands.

PSYCHE: *(to herself)* Is this really happening? Or did I go mad back there on the mountaintop, and this is all a hallucination?

SERVANT: Your chamber is prepared. The master will arrive shortly.

NARRATOR: As night fell, the phantom guided her to the sleeping chambers. There she lay down to await her mysterious husband. Sleep—as if another spell of the house—overcame her.

She awoke much later. The room was pitch black, and she felt that someone or some*thing* was very near.

PSYCHE: *(frightened)* Who is there?

EROS: *(lovingly)* Your husband.

NARRATOR: Psyche started as the voice spoke in her ear. She felt his touch upon her arm.

EROS: Do not be afraid.

PSYCHE: Show yourself!

EROS: *(sadly)* I cannot.

PSYCHE: I don't understand. If you don't want me to be afraid, then you should show yourself. I have left my home and my family to come here, and yet I'm forbidden to see my husband's face?

EROS: You can never gaze upon me, Psyche. Your love is all I desire, and you would never truly love me if you were to see my true nature.

PSYCHE: How can you know that? Not knowing is worse than any appearance could be!

EROS: I shall keep you here, and we shall spend each night as husband and wife. But when the day comes, I must be gone from your sight.

PSYCHE: *(angrily)* It's unfair! If you make me a prisoner here, you must at least give me some right . . .

EROS: This is the way that it must be. You must learn to live with this curse as I have. Trust me, Psyche.

NARRATOR: So Psyche's life began its mysterious routine. She would spend her days idly, always attended by the spirits of the house. In the blackness of midnight, her husband would return to her and caress her in that hour but then disappear by the dawn. By some other enchantment, even as they touched, she could never tell his true form. It shifted beneath her fingers, refusing to be identified. He loved her true enough, and over time, the absence of his appearance ceased to concern her. Whatever her husband truly was, giant serpent or bodiless spirit, Psyche quickly grew to return his love. Though she had her nightly companion, Psyche's days were lonely affairs. She often thought of the father and two sisters she had left behind.

PSYCHE: Husband, can I ask you a question?

EROS: What is it, my love?

PSYCHE: I miss my family. Other wives have their families over for a visit. I would like to do the same.

EROS: You are not like other wives.

PSYCHE: But they're my family . . . I miss them. Surely you can understand. I need some human companionship.

EROS: It's not a good idea, Psyche, but, because I love you, I will have Zephyr bring them here. They may only stay for a day, and then they must return home.

PSYCHE: Thank you! Oh, thank you!

NARRATOR: The next day Psyche waited on the front step of the palace anxiously. At last she saw Zephyr approaching from afar—bearing three bodies in his arms.

SISTERS ONE & TWO: Ahhhhh!

ZEPHYR: Be quiet already! I never thought I'd be missing the annoying questions of your sister!

PSYCHE: Zephyr, please be careful! They're my family.

ZEPHYR: Of course they are. I told the fools that everything would be okay. I've been at this for thousands of years, and I've never dropped anyone yet—unless it was on purpose.

NARRATOR: The West Wind deposited Psyche's family in a heap before her feet.

ZEPHYR: Good riddance! And tell your husband that Zephyr's maximum occupancy is one! I think I pulled something hauling these three!

PSYCHE: Thank you, Zephyr.

ZEPHYR: (grumble, grumble)

NARRATOR: As the little old man disappeared, Psyche helped her sisters and father to their feet.

KING: I can't believe it! Psyche, you're alive! We were walking in the garden, and the mightiest wind caught us up into the air. We thought we were dead!

NARRATOR: Her father paused.

KING: But wait a minute. Are we dead? Is this . . .

PSYCHE: (overjoyed) No, father. This is where I have lived these many months! I asked for the West Wind to bring you here for a visit. I'm so glad to see you all again.

NARRATOR: Psyche led them into the glittering passageways of the palace. Her frazzled sisters eyed the luxury of her home with jealousy.

PSYCHE: We'll have a feast to celebrate your visit!

SISTER ONE: A feast? *Who* will prepare it?

PSYCHE: The servants, of course.

SISTER TWO: Servants? I see no servants.

PSYCHE: Well, it's complicated. There are many servants here. I can't even say how many—you can't actually see them.

SISTER ONE: (in disbelief) Hmmmm. You can't see them?

SISTER TWO: (snickering) That is a problem.

PSYCHE: No, you don't understand. Please. Don't think I'm crazy. I'm really not.

SISTER ONE: Is your husband here . . . or is he invisible as well?

PSYCHE: (hurt) You're mocking me now.

KING: Psyche, look at this from our point of view. This is all so strange. We thought we would never see you again, but here you are in this mysterious palace where everything seems to be under a spell.

PSYCHE: I can't explain it either, father.

SISTER TWO: What about your husband? Perhaps he can explain it to us.

PSYCHE: I'm afraid that's out of the question.

SISTER ONE: Out of the question? Psyche, dear. We're not afraid. Bring the beast forward. We're dying to meet him.

SISTER TWO: We're sure his hideousness must have been exaggerated.

PSYCHE: He's not hideous. I mean . . .

SISTER ONE: If he's not hideous, then there can be no objection to his meeting us.

PSYCHE: It's just that . . .

SISTER TWO: Psyche, we're *not* judgmental people. If your husband is ugly, just come out and say it.

PSYCHE: I . . . I just don't know.

KING: What do you mean, my dear?

NARRATOR: Her answer came in a rush of sobs.

PSYCHE: (crying) I have never seen him—and I can never see him. He comes at night, and I cannot look upon his face. Oh gods, I *am* married to a beast.

NARRATOR: The two sisters looked at one another slyly as they moved to Psyche's side to comfort her.

SISTER ONE: (soothingly) Such pain, sweet one. He is causing you so much pain.

SISTER TWO: What a stupid rule! Not seeing your own husband! How can he do this to you?

PSYCHE: Oh, it's not so bad . . . I just . . .

SISTER ONE: Not so bad? It's a crime!

SISTER TWO: He *must* be hiding something.

PSYCHE: No, he's kind—and gentle.

SISTER ONE: That's what he wants you to think.

SISTER TWO: There is only one way to make this agony stop, sweet sister.

SISTER ONE: End the mystery.

SISTER TWO: Yes. You must look upon his face.

PSYCHE: No, I cannot. I have sworn not to. I will be banished.

SISTER ONE: How could he banish one who loves him so deeply? It's obviously a trick to keep you in ignorance.

PSYCHE: No.

SISTER TWO: If he is a beast, you must escape immediately.

PSYCHE: But how can I?

NARRATOR: Her sister pulled a gleaming knife from the folds of her cloak.

SISTER ONE: The world is a dangerous place. I carry one of these with me always. Now I give it to you, my beloved sister. It may save you from your fate.

PSYCHE: You can't be serious. He's my husband.

SISTER TWO: What kind of husband? An animal who keeps you in a cage?

PSYCHE: He loves me!

SISTER TWO: What a way to show it!

SISTER ONE: Look, if he is a man, then you may live your life happily. But if he *is* a monster, you must kill him—and flee—before he does the same to you.

PSYCHE: *(weakly)* I can't!

SISTER ONE: Don't shame our family, sister. I will have no blood-relation of mine being the concubine of a demon. Do you want that for yourself?

NARRATOR: Psyche shook her head in sorrow.

KING: It's for the best, dear. Come home to us. I miss our walks in the garden.

NARRATOR: By the time Zephyr returned to carry her family back to their kingdom, cold resolve had frozen Psyche's heart. She must see her husband's face—at any cost.

ZEPHYR: *(grunting)* Have you gotten heavier since this morning? That's it. No more favors. I don't care what the little jerk does to me. Zephyr is getting out of the transportation business.

(whooshing sound)

SISTER TWO: *(yelling)* Remember, Psyche, the truth will set you free!

SISTER ONE: *(yelling)* Good luck!

NARRATOR: With the knife gripped tightly in her hand and a tear rolling down her cheek, Psyche bid her family goodbye. Once they had disappeared over the mountaintops, Psyche went to her chamber and perched on the edge of her bed. She stared at the little lamp that had always sat on the bedside table yet had never been lit. Her knuckles grew white around the knife handle. Tonight would be the night. The sun finished its journey across the sky—and darkness engulfed her.

EROS: Psyche, my love.

NARRATOR: He was there—her phantom mate. Tonight she remained silent, cold, and unyielding. When she finally felt that he had succumbed to sleep, she stood and took the lamp in her trembling hands. She lit its flame and—holding her blade ready to strike—turned its light upon the form of her lover. What she saw caused her to gasp. Gracefully asleep in the half-empty bed was the most perfect youth she had ever seen. Golden curls built around the handsome features of a god—his eyes closed in the serene sleep of love.

PSYCHE: Oh, forgive me, my darling.

NARRATOR: As she moved to snuff her lamp, a tiny bit of oil fell from it and landed upon his perfect shoulder. His golden lashes flew open; his eyes moved from knife, to lamp, to Psyche.

EROS: *(shocked)* Psyche! What are you doing?

NARRATOR: Psyche's weapon fell from her hand.

EROS: *(hurt)* Is this all I mean to you? I told you never to look! Why did you not trust me? You betrayed me.

PSYCHE: I . . .

EROS: *(growing angry)* What if I had been a beast? Would you have driven the knife through my heart?

PSYCHE: No! It's not like that!

EROS: *(enraged)* Silence! You have broken our agreement! The spell is undone! This palace will fade away, and you will be alone once again! But I suppose that is what you wanted, wasn't it?

PSYCHE: No!

EROS: Foolish girl. Love cannot live where there is no trust. You have ruined the one thing in life that has brought me true happiness. Go. Go back to your people. I can bear the sight of you no longer!

PSYCHE: Wait. I can undo it.

NARRATOR: He turned away.

EROS: There is nothing you can do now. Go back to your mortal world, and forget that you once loved Eros, the immortal son of Aphrodite, the doomed god of love.

NARRATOR: With these words the lamp snuffed out— and the world with it. Psyche cried out and clutched blindly at nothing. Eros was gone. It may have been hours or seconds before the shining chariot of the sun rose above the peaks, but on the barren mountaintop no golden walls reflected its radiance. The palace was gone . . . evaporated. And where it had once stood sat a broken girl, her face hot with tears.

DISCUSS

- Are Psyche's sisters typical siblings? Explain.
- Are Eros' restrictions on Psyche fair? Explain.
- Is Eros deserving of love, or does he deserve to be heartbroken? Explain.
- How is Aphrodite's characterization ironic?
- What has this story had to say about love so far?

ANALYZE

This myth displays many motifs (repeated story elements) that would later appear in many fairy tales. Do you notice any fairy tale elements in "Eros and Psyche"? Explain.

The Four Winds

Greek mythology personified the wind as four different gods. The rough North Wind, Boreas, was an angry, cold wind who once abducted an Athenian princess to be his wife. Because of this, the Athenians considered him to be a relative, and when the Persian King Xerxes threatened Athens with a fleet of ships, the Athenians called on Boreas for help. The North Wind responded and stirred up a storm that sank the Persian ships. In modern terms *boreal* means "northern," which gave rise to the Aurora Borealis ("northern dawn") along with the Roman goddess of the dawn, Aurora. Eurus was the East Wind and was considered unlucky. Notus was the South Wind who brought heat and storms. Zephyr was the West Wind, a favorite of the Greeks, for he was considered the herald of spring. He was also considered to be the gentlest of the four winds, which is why a gentle wind is today called a *zephyr*. Like Boreas, Zephyr was the father of famous stallions—the horses of Achilles who could, of course, run like the wind.

The Nature of Love: Heart and Soul

Which is more powerful, the heart or the mind? Each controls a powerful capability, the ability to *love* and the ability to *think*. These two capabilities drive everything that we as humans do. If you had to give up one of these, which would you choose? If you were all mind and no heart, you would be a robot, devoid of emotions. Yet if you were all heart and no mind, you would be a bleeding heart—a senseless, emotional wreck. Either way, you would be just half a person.

Stoics were ancient philosophers who prided themselves on their ability to suppress their emotions and rely solely on their intellect. They believed that in order to function at maximum potential, people should rely only on brainpower and not let their emotions cloud the issue. *Hedonists* were the opposite. They believed that whatever your urge or emotion, you should act on it—regardless of the consequences. According to them, thinking should not figure into the equation. Basically, if it feels good, do it. Both philosophic groups got their start in classical Greece.

There are problems with both of these extremes. If you refuse to grieve over the death of a close family member, you might be considered heartless. But if you are so emotional that you cannot bring yourself to

DISCUSS

- Which is more powerful, the heart or the mind? Explain.
- Can you think of a person, living or dead, who was a *stoic* or a *hedonist*?
- Why is it a good idea to achieve a balance between the two?
- Some adults criticize "young love" because they feel it relies too strongly on the heart and not enough on the mind. Do you think this is true? Explain.

FUN FACT

Just as we associate certain emotions with certain organs (love with the heart, thought with the brain), it was once believed that the spleen was the source of anger and the liver was a source of courage and other strong passions. This gave rise to two idioms: "Vent your spleen" means to get rid of your anger and "lily-livered" is a word to describe someone who has a white, bloodless liver—a complete coward.

PERFORM

Write a dialogue between two teenagers, one who is a *stoic* and one who is a *hedonist*. Act out your dialogue for your classmates.

Continued on page 93

attend the funeral, you might be considered disrespectful. A healthy personality achieves a balance between the two. Your mind wins out in some matters, your heart in others.

Now moving on to love.

How do the heart and mind figure into love? Love is not usually an intellectual process. If love was based solely on facts, you could simply enter your stats, your interests, and your likes and dislikes into a computer, and you would be matched you up with the perfect companion in a matter of seconds. Blind dates would be much more successful than they are now if this process actually worked. But the heart has to have input too. Love is a feeling, so it is naturally attributed to the heart. Yet if a person relies solely on his or her heart and fails to consult the mind, tragedy can ensue. Two people may be passionately in love but have fundamentally different values. If they don't *think* about these differences, they may face a troubled relationship.

The Greeks showed us both concepts of a *stoic* and a *hedonist*, but they also had a tale for those who believed more in balance. It was a story about Eros, a Greek god whose name meant *love*, and Psyche, a mortal girl whose name meant *soul* or *mind*. As you read the story of Eros and Psyche, think about the nature of love. What comment does this story make on the subject? How will you live your life? By mind, by heart, or by a combination of the two?

Eros: Angry Teenager, or Cupid: Naked Baby?

The Greeks pictured Eros as a teenage boy, who in some representations appeared with wings. In his myth with Psyche it is obvious that Eros is not a child, but a young man seeking love for himself. This portrayal of the god goes against almost all other portrayals of his character. Eros is often shown to be mischievous, rude, and not to be trusted under any circumstances. Rather than using his arrows to bring love, he usually brings about pain and despair. In many stories he gets some sick thrill out of making some god or mortal fall in love with someone else who does not return the sentiment. In fact, some myth-makers tell how Eros actually had two types of arrows in his quiver: one for inspiring love, the other for hardening the heart against love. The second type he used just as often as the first. (Some connect the word *Eros* with *arrows*—usually because the god's name is pronounced incorrectly—yet there is no connection between the two words.)

The type of love that Eros inspired was not considered to be a long-lasting variety. It was *erotic*, meaning mainly sexual and immediate. A modern term for this type of love is *lust*, and words like *erotic* and *erogenous*, words that deal with lust, have their roots in Eros' name. Eros' nature also showed the cynicism that many Greeks must have felt toward love: It usually leads to pain and despair than to happily ever after.

The Romans modified the image of Eros as teenager by reimagining the god (whom they renamed Cupid) as a young child with wings. Cupid's arrows still had the same effect as Eros' did, but his actions seemed more innocent because they were coming from a chubby infant-god, who was not yet old enough to understand love for himself. Painters in the Renaissance, as they were rediscovering the classical myths as a source of material, latched onto this chubby baby image and decorated their paintings with cutesy flying Cupids. Eventually the image of Cupid became confused with the images of Christian angels, and now there are pictures of cute, winged babies on cathedral walls, calendars, greeting cards, you name it. It appears that Cupid's arrow has struck society.

Love Conquers All

The myth of Eros and Psyche did not end with Psyche alone on the mountaintop. She decided that she must get back her love. Because Eros had revealed his true identity to her, Psyche persuaded Zephyr to carry her to Olympus, where the she begged an audience with the merciless Aphrodite. (If you remember, Aphrodite's hatred for Psyche is what caused her and Eros to meet in the first place.) The goddess' anger toward Psyche had not cooled; in fact, it only increased after Eros returned to Olympus at the point of death from the oil burn he had suffered from Psyche's lamp. The girl begged to see her sick lover, but Aphrodite refused, declaring that the only way Psyche could undo the pain caused to Eros would be to complete three perilous tasks. The girl agreed.

For Psyche's first task, Aphrodite made a pile of various seeds all mixed together and commanded Psyche to sort them out by separating each kind into its own pile by the end of the night. Psyche found the task to be impossible; the seeds were too tiny and her fingers too large. She was on the verge of giving up when she heard a small voice speaking to her. It was an ant. The insect volunteered the services of his whole hill, and a thousand ants worked through the night sorting the seeds into separate piles. When Aphrodite returned at dawn and saw that Psyche had finished her first task, she was furious.

Continued from page 92

ANALYZE

In his poem "Psyche and the Candle," Archibald MacLeish (1892–1982) analyzes the paradox of Love: "Love is a bird in a fist:/To hold it hides it, to look at it lets it go . . . /Either you keep it forever with fist closed/Or let it fling." He ends his poem with the paradox still unsolved: "There is no answer other to this mystery." Even though neither Psyche nor Eros is mentioned in his poem, what does its theme have to do with the myth?

WRITE

Write your own poem about the nature of love. It can even begin with the phrase "Love is . . ."

DISCUSS
• Which image do you like best—teenage Eros or chubby Cupid? Explain.

For her second task, the goddess commanded Psyche to fetch some wool from the back of a flock of golden sheep. The catch: These were man-eating sheep, and Psyche was sure to die if she tried to touch them. Defeated she sat down by the stream that flowed through the sheep's pasture, and as she contemplated drowning herself, a reed began to speak to her. It told her to wait until the sheep came down to drink from the stream: Every day many tufts of their wool became entangled in the riverside brambles. When the sheep were gone, she could collect as much wool as she needed. The girl did this, and when Aphrodite reappeared, seeing Psyche holding handfuls of golden fleece, she could not believe it.

For the girl's final task, Aphrodite sent her to a place she thought she would never return from: the Underworld. She commanded Psyche to visit Queen Persephone in Hades in order to demand that she put a bit of her immortal beauty in a box. Psyche journeyed to the entrance to the Underworld, but had no idea how she would navigate the depths. Once again in despair, she climbed a high tower in order to jump off. Before she could, the tower began to speak to her—telling her how to manage the dangers of the Underworld.

Psyche began her descent into Hades. To get past the three-headed guard dog Cerberus, the girl tossed a cake to the side of the path. As Cerberus—who apparently had a sweet tooth—bounded after the cake, Psyche slipped by. When she reached the Styx, Charon the boatman took the coins that the tower had told her to hide in her mouth and ferried her across the river. Standing before King Hades and Queen Persephone at last, Psyche pleaded her case. Her quest for love moved Persephone's heart, and she gave the girl a bit of beauty trapped in a box. On her journey back to the surface, Psyche entertained the foolish idea of stealing some of the beauty for herself, so that she could impress Eros even more when she was reunited with him. She decided to open the box just a crack and let a bit out. When she did so, all of the beauty escaped, and Psyche fell to the ground in a faint.

The face of Eros was hovering over her when she regained consciousness. His wound had healed, he had learned of her quest to win him back, and, better yet, he had forgiven her for not trusting him. Because gods and mortals cannot marry, Eros carried Psyche to Olympus to ask Zeus what could be done. Aphrodite appeared as well, railing at the girl and her ungrateful son. Zeus had the perfect solution: No, a mortal could not marry a god, but Psyche had proven herself to be very heroic. Therefore, he would make her a goddess. The couple was overjoyed. Hebe brought forth the Olympian cup, and Psyche drank the nectar of the gods and became one of the immortals. Eros and Psyche were married and lived happily ever after on Olympus.

DISCUSS
- What do you think of the ending of this myth? Does it fit with the first half? Explain.

DISCUSS
- Does this scene seem to fit with Psyche's character? Explain.

Sisterly Love

In a scene deleted from this book's version of the myth, Psyche's cruel sisters meet a horrible death. Because her sisters tricked her into disobeying her husband's orders, Psyche decided to play a trick on them. Before attempting to get Eros back, she went to visit her sisters and, amid tears, told them Eros' true identity and how he banished her from his palace. She made up a second story: Eros commanded Psyche to send his sisters to him, and he would choose one of them to be his wife in Psyche's place. All they had to do was to jump off the cliff near their home, and the West Wind would bear them up to Eros' palace. Overjoyed, the sisters ran to the nearby cliff and jumped over its edge. Psyche had her revenge.

Psyche and the Beast

The myth of Eros and Psyche has often been cited as an inspiration for the fairy tale "Beauty and the Beast" because of the many similarities between the two stories. Belle, the fairy tale heroine (sometimes called Beauty), is the youngest and most beautiful of three sisters whose cowardly father agrees to marry her to a hideous beast when he is caught picking roses in the garden of the creature's castle. Once married to the beast, Belle (always attended by invisible servants) grows to love him in spite of his hideous appearance. After several months, she begs the beast for permission to visit her family; he reluctantly agrees, provided she returns within a week. Once Belle is back with her family, her older sisters become jealous at the notion of their sister living in a castle—even if it is with a beast. They rub onion in their eyes and go to Belle crying, saying they will die of grief if she leaves them again. Goodhearted Belle decides to stay away longer than she promises. At last she returns to the beast's castle and finds him dying of a broken heart because she did not honor their agreement. Belle declares her love for him, and he transforms into a handsome prince, which has been his true form all along.

Types of Love

The Greeks had three separate words that all translate into English as "love." *Philia*, which literally means "friendship," is the type of love

DISCUSS
- What are some common elements between Eros and Psyche and "Beauty and the Beast"?
- Do both stories have the same message concerning love? Explain.
- How are Psyche and Belle similar?
- How are the supporting characters (the father and sisters) similar?

ANALYZE

Modern commentators have viewed "Beauty and the Beast" in a new light. They propose that the fairy tale was invented to encourage girls, specifically new wives, to look past the beastly habits of their husbands and love them in spite of rude, hurtful, or even unfaithful behavior. What do you think of this theory? How does it apply to "Eros and Psyche" as well?

between friends or family. *Agape* is a general love, a love-your-neighbor type of love. (For this reason it is the most commonly used form of love found in the New Testament.) Finally, there is *eros,* love defined by sexual attraction. The Greeks viewed this type of love as sent by the gods (through Eros himself), so many of them had no reason to resist it. Many of the philosophers, on the other hand, spoke out against it. Man should not be controlled by sexual urges, they said. The mind must master them.

Psyche is also a Greek word with an important meaning. It means "soul," "self" (more modernly translated), and "mind." Philosophers believed that the soul was the driving force behind mankind's decisions and should not allow emotions to rule it.

Myth as Allegory

An allegory is a story told to teach a lesson or illustrate an idea. Each character within the story actually represents a larger idea or theme, and the plot of the story leads to a deeper understanding of something outside the story. Two modern examples are C. S. Lewis' Christian allegory *The Lion, the Witch, and the Wardrobe* and George Orwell's allegorical satire of Communist Russia, *Animal Farm.* Some mythologists think that the Greek myths are complicated allegories.

DISCUSS
• Think of the other myths you have read. Could any of them be allegorical? Explain.

To apply this approach to the Greek myths would be to say that Zeus represents "power," Ares represents "war," Athena represents "intelligence," and so on, and then try to determine some deeper meaning behind the stories by analyzing their events. Most of the myths do not make neat allegories, but many ancient Greek philosophers tried to view them this way. Many of them did not believe in the literal truth of the myths, yet they still saw value in them if used as allegories. If the myths did begin as allegories, the original meanings behind many of the stories have been lost throughout the years.

The myth of Eros and Psyche does seem like it could be an allegory. Eros is an obvious symbol for love, and Psyche, a Greek word that means "soul," represents the soul or mind. As Psyche goes through her various trials to win back Eros, she is on a quest for love. Many times she thinks of quitting or ending her life, yet through perseverance she overcomes many obstacles, and finally Psyche (mind) and Eros (heart) become one.

Merciless Aphrodite

Most people would expect the Goddess of Love to be a bit more *loving* than the hateful and vindictive shrew she is in the Eros and Psyche myth. This ode to love (or as she is called here, Merciless Aphrodite) paints a similarly unflattering picture of the goddess and the emotion she symbolizes. It is taken from one of the ancient Greek playwright Sophocles' most famous plays, *Antigone*.

Love, unconquerable . . .
Even the pure immortals cannot escape you,
And mortal man, in his one day's dusk,
Trembles before your glory . . .
A girl's glance working the will of heaven:
Pleasure to her alone who mocks us,
Merciless Aphrodite. (Sophocles, 442 BC/1977, p. 224)

DISCUSS

- What does Sophocles mean when he speaks of man's "one day's dusk"?
- Why is this a negative portrayal of love?
- Another ancient Greek playwright, Euripides, said this of love: "He is not a lover who does not love forever." Do you agree? Explain.
- The British poet Alfred, Lord Tennyson penned this famous quote about love: "'Tis better to have loved and lost than never to have loved at all." Do you agree? Explain.

CHAPTER 5

Self-Love (Vanity)

NARCISSUS AND ECHO

Cast

Girl One *One of Narcissus' admirers*
Girl Two *One of Narcissus' admirers*
Girl Three *One of Narcissus' admirers*

Narcissus *Handsomest youth*
Echo *Chatty nymph*
Nymph *Woodland nymph*
Hera *Queen of Heaven*

NARRATOR: Narcissus was the most beautiful boy who ever lived. It was said that his mother was a woodland nymph and his father a river god, yet Narcissus was born mortal. His only godlike quality was his unparalleled looks. Wherever he went, girls flocked to him in droves. Although they cried, begged, and pleaded to be his, the boy would have none of them.

GIRL ONE: *(excitedly)* Narcissus! Over here! Here!

GIRL THREE: Out of my way! He's mine! He's mine!

GIRL TWO: *(scream)* I touched his hand! I really touched his hand!

NARCISSUS: *(sigh)* Calm yourselves! What are you? Women or beasts? Give Narcissus some peace and quiet!

GIRL THREE: *(crazy)* Please! Make me your wife!

NARCISSUS: *(haughtily)* Ha! That's a laugh. Just take a look at yourselves! Obviously none of you are worthy of Narcissus. When I meet one whose beauty equals my own, then—and only then—will I love.

NARRATOR: At this, the girls wilted.

NARCISSUS: But with such impossible standards, why get my hopes up?

NARRATOR: In the region where Narcissus dwelt, there also lived a band of woodland nymphs. One in particular, a dimwitted and chatty nymph named Echo, happened to hear of Narcissus' legendary beauty one day.

ECHO: *(rapidly)* Narcissus is his name. They say he's a complete dreamboat—what does that mean anyway—dreamboat—anyway they say he's to die for—in fact, several girls already have—died that is—they committed suicide just to get his attention—can you imagine? — committing suicide just to get some attention? —sounds pretty pathetic to me—I've never liked anyone that much—although I did have a thing for Apollo a while back—but who am I kidding? —I'm a nymph! I have a thing for everyone!

NARRATOR: Echo was bending the ear of one of her nymph sisters. The nymph took a rare opportunity to interject.

NYMPH: *(interrupting)* Fascinating! By the way, Echo, will you do me a favor?

ECHO: A favor? —oh, that sounds serious—just last week Artemis herself asked me to do her a favor—we were having the most lovely chat, but she suddenly got a leg cramp, so she asked me to go fetch her brother, Apollo—y'know, the god of medicine—when I came back, she must have gotten better, because she was gone—but you know—

NYMPH: *(interrupting)* Great. I'm kind of in a hurry. I'm supposed to be meeting a . . . um, friend . . . here in a minute.

ECHO: Well, that's so sweet—that reminds me of a friend I used to have—she was my best friend growing up—did I ever tell you about her? —she was a naiad, so she was bit wet behind the ears, if you know what I mean—

NYMPH: *(angrily)* Stop! *(nicely)* I mean . . . I haven't finished yet, dear. My friend's wife doesn't know we're meeting, so if she happens this way, maybe you could distract her.

ECHO: Sure—that would be great—I mean, are you two planning some kind of surprise party for his wife or something? —I love surprises—there was this one time when I found all of my friends hiding from me, and when I asked why, they said they were throwing me a surprise party—but the strange part was it wasn't even my birthday or anything—

NYMPH: That's nice. Well, my friend is waiting. Just remember: If his wife shows up, distract her.

ECHO: Distract her? —well, I can tell you one thing, I'm probably not very good at stalling people—I mean, what am I supposed to say? —I'm not very good at coming up with stuff right off the top of my head—

NYMPH: *(gritting her teeth)* You're doing pretty well right now! Just talk to her, Echo! Keep her entertained! Welcome her to our woods!

ECHO: Oh well, I can sure handle that all right—I mean, if our woods had an official greeter, I think it would be me—most people say that I have a infectious personality—or did they say infected?—I can't remember—my memory's just not what it used to be—I was telling—

NYMPH: Gotta run! Bye! *(under her breath)* Idiot!

NARRATOR: Her sister nymph disappeared into the underbrush.

ECHO: *(quietly)* Well, okay. Seems like everyone's in a hurry. No time to talk. Hurry. Hurry. Hurry.

NARRATOR: Echo smiled to herself and sat down upon by the edge of a small, clear stream. She leaned over the rippling water, and her face reflected back.

ECHO: At least I always have you to listen. Talking to yourself is better than not talking at all.

NARRATOR: Her mind soon returned to her mission.

ECHO: *(to herself)* I wonder who her mysterious married friend is? —surely it's not this Narcissus everyone's been talking about—no, no, you simpleton, it couldn't be him—he's not married—plus he's sworn to only love the one who's beauty equals his own—tee hee—I wonder—

NARRATOR: She returned to her reflection. After staring into her own eyes for a time, she broke the surface with a slap of her hand.

ECHO: Nah. Probably not. But a nymph can dream, can't she?

NARRATOR: Little did Echo know that the nymph's visitor was Zeus himself, on yet another one of his extramarital escapades. And the wife that the nymph had mentioned was none other than his vindictive queen, Hera.

Echo had just fallen silent when she noticed the leaves of the trees vibrating about her.

ECHO: I wonder what that is. You know, it could be an earthquake. The last time Poseidon caused one of those, I remember a whole—

NARRATOR: The leaves shook themselves free from the trees and were caught up in a ferocious whirlwind. In the midst of this, there appeared a feminine form.

HERA: *(booming)* Where is he?

NARRATOR: The form of Hera solidified, and before the nymph could react, the angry Queen of Heaven was stalking toward Echo.

HERA: You there! Answer when you're spoken to!

ECHO: Oh, you were talking to me! I'm sorry—I really didn't know for a second—in fact I was kind of taken aback by that dramatic entrance of yours—do you do that all the time or only when you're going to surprise parties—

HERA: Cut the chit-chat! Obviously you're not her, but I bet you know where she is!

ECHO: So you're looking for a she now—that's funny—when you first showed up, I thought you said he—I've always had a hearing impediment though, so it's no wonder—by the way, I'm Echo, and it's very nice to know that I'm not her—whoever that is—because you seem very intense about finding this mystery woman and this he you keep talking about—say, you're one of the goddesses aren't you?—don't tell me—I'm good with faces—Aphrodite—you're Aphrodite, aren't you?

NARRATOR: Hera's anger had been slowly boiling; now it exploded in a burst of rage.

HERA: (roaring) Silence! I would do the world a favor and cut out your prattling tongue, but as you might have noticed, I'm kind of in a hurry!

NARRATOR: Echo closed her mouth sheepishly.

HERA: I am looking for Zeus. Perhaps you've heard of him? He is my husband. Now I know he's around here somewhere, frolicking in the fencerows with one of your little hare-brained hussies.

ECHO: Oooh—I must say I have seen your husband—let me congratulate you for marrying so well—I have my own eye on a high-born lad as well—so that must mean that you are Hera, Queen of Heaven—I forgot to curtsy—you must think I am the rudest nymph who ever lived—

NARRATOR: Hera's eyes were growing red, filled with flames of hatred.

ECHO: I thought I saw Zeus once—only from a distance—but then my friend told me that it was only a cloud—but you know I could have sworn it was him—he's

the one with the big beard, right? —sometimes I get you all confused—if you've seen one god, you've seen them all, that's what I say—

HERA: (violent scream)

NARRATOR: The barren trees burst into flames. Hera stalked forward and grabbed the suddenly frightened nymph by the wrist.

HERA: Either you tell me where they are, or you're going to be a worthless pile of ashes.

ECHO: My—my—my—I am so sorry—I apologize my queen—they're here—or somewhere close by—I—I—just get so nervous—and I can't stop talking.

NARRATOR: There was a flash of light away through the trees, and Hera's gaze jerked toward it. A shining light shot heavenward, leaving behind a cloud-like trail.

HERA: There he goes! There he goes! I knew it! He will pay for this! He will rue the day that he ever—

ECHO: Well, that's great, your majesty—you know I'm so happy that I could help—I always say it's better to help people than—

HERA: (crazy) Help? I was going to catch him red-handed. I wanted him to watch while I ground his little playmate into fertilizer, but you, you kept me from it with that wagging tongue of yours!

ECHO: You know, I can tell you're upset with me, but I think it's always best to get a good night's sleep before you make any hasty decisions—I mean, you definitely don't want to do anything you regret—like this one time my uncle—

HERA: You don't learn, do you? Fine! So one floozy has flown the coop, but you'll make a fine replacement.

NARRATOR: The nymph began to back away.

HERA: Because you are so fond of the sound of your own voice, you, Echo, are forever cursed. You always wanted the last word, well, now you'll have it! (evil laugh)

NARRATOR: Hera snapped her fingers, wiped her hands clean, and gazed coolly at the nymph.

HERA: No need to thank me for sparing your life. And for future reference—stay away from my husband.

NARRATOR: Then she was gone. Echo couldn't believe it. She had been sure that Hera would kill her, but here she was—alive—but still cursed. Whatever that meant.

There was a rustling in the brush, and her nymph sister appeared looking quite frightened.

NYMPH: Thanks for stalling her, Echo. We heard her yelling. What did she do to you?

ECHO: To you. To you.

NARRATOR: Echo brought her fingers to her lips. They had acted without her control. She had meant to say so much more.

NYMPH: What? I don't understand. I heard her yell something about being cursed.

ECHO: Cursed. Cursed.

NARRATOR: Huge tears formed in Echo's eyes. Then her sister nymph understood.

NYMPH: Oh, Echo. I'm so sorry for you.

ECHO: For you. For you.

NARRATOR: Echo hid her face with her hands and ran from the grove.

NYMPH: Echo, where are you going?

NARRATOR: As she ran, she covered her mouth. She did not wish to answer. But her lips moved of their own will.

ECHO: *(crying)* Going. Going.

NARRATOR: Her voice was lost forever.

From that time on, Echo lived apart from the other nymphs. She couldn't stand the sight of them. They were so frivolous and carefree as she had once been. Now she only wanted to be alone in her misery. But one day as she sat by the damp cave she now called her home, she heard a voice not far off—the voice of a young man.

NARCISSUS: Let's see those hags find Narcissus out here. It's almost a crime for such looks to be here—in the middle of woods—where no one can see their glory. An absolute waste. But look, even nature is not more beautiful than Narcissus.

ECHO: *(to herself)* Narcissus! Narcissus!

NARRATOR: She crept to the mouth of her cave to get a glimpse of the legendary boy. Once she beheld his golden face, her cold heart was revived. He was everything the legends said: a mortal beauty with no rival.

NARCISSUS: Look on me, Nature. See that the gods have created something truly perfect in Narcissus—something that is completely worthy of a world's share of love.

ECHO: *(dreamily)* Love! Love!

NARRATOR: Narcissus was marching away proudly, addressing the forest around him, so Echo fell silently into step behind him. A new hope had entered her heart. How many had failed to entice this boy? Maybe she was the one who would at last be his match. She would have no words to profess her love, but true love needs no words, she told herself.

(snap of a twig)

NARCISSUS: *(loudly)* Who dares interrupt the walk of Narcissus? If you've come for a glimpse of my beauty, take it and be on with your miserable little life. I said, is someone here?

NARRATOR: Echo stepped around the bend in the path and beamed proudly.

ECHO: *(loudly)* Here! Here!

NARRATOR: The boy stared at her in annoyance.

NARCISSUS: All right. You've had your look, now be on your way.

NARRATOR: Echo lowered her outstretched arms.

NARCISSUS: *(hatefully)* Well, what do you want? A souvenir? A lock of the hair of Narcissus? I don't think so. The only hand that will ever touch my hair will be the hand of my wife.

NARRATOR: Echo folded her arms across her chest.

ECHO: Wife. Wife.

NARRATOR: Slowly—very slowly—the mouth of Narcissus curled into a smirk.

NARCISSUS: *(laughing)* I would rather die than give something like you power over me.

ECHO: *(weakly)* Power over me. Power over me.

NARCISSUS: Oh please. Don't sulk. You look bad enough as it is.

NARRATOR: The golden boy turned on his heel and shuddered.

NARCISSUS: Yikes.

NARRATOR: As she watched him disappear into the trees, Echo felt something inside of her crumbling. Though her lips could not speak the prayer, she formed the words in her mind. She prayed that some god, above or below, would make Narcissus come to know the same heartbreak she had felt.

Nemesis, the goddess of retribution, heard her prayer.

Narcissus continued through the forest and came at last to a secluded pool. Its waters were so clear, and its surface so completely undisturbed that nothing obscured its mirror-like surface.

NARCISSUS: Even Narcissus—a god among men—grows thirsty and must drink.

NARRATOR: The boy bent to the waters, but stopped short. There, just below the surface, was the most glorious creature he had ever seen. There was an odd feeling in his chest accompanied by a lightness of the mind.

NARCISSUS: *(breathlessly)* Who or what are you? You, who have at last made Narcissus feel love!

NARRATOR: He examined the flawless face intently. There they were—the very features he had imagined—the shining eyes, the pink lips, even the lustrous hair of his dreams.

NARCISSUS: Only I among all living things can rival your beauty, sweet one. Speak! What is the name that the gods have given to such splendor!

NARRATOR: His love did not answer, only stared back expectantly.

NARCISSUS: *(excitedly)* Don't be coy! Surely you are some goddess or some nymph! Speak! You have nothing to fear!

NARRATOR: No reply.

NARCISSUS: Please! You must tell me your name! I will die if I do not hear it!

NARRATOR: Nothing.

NARCISSUS: What prevents you from speaking? Are you under some spell? Trapped in this magical pool? Come! Let your love Narcissus free you from this prison!

NARRATOR: He reached into the pool—searching for the form to match the face—but he had disturbed the surface.

NARCISSUS: *(panicking)* No! Don't go! I will die if you leave me! *(calming)* There! There! You are returning. You looked scared before. You did not want to leave me either, did you?

NARRATOR: The boy reseated himself beside the pool.

NARCISSUS: So, my love, you are trapped in a pool. What does that matter to me while I can still gaze upon your beautiful face? I will sit here by your side as long as my life endures.

NARRATOR: There Narcissus sat, day after day, admiring his love, never suspecting its true identity. At length his stomach cried out for food and his throat for water, but he would not leave his love—even for a moment—and he would never again dare to break the surface of her mystical pool.

NARCISSUS: *(weakly)* I would rather die than leave you, my love.

NARRATOR: Then the head of Narcissus fell forward upon his chest and his final word escaped his lips:

NARCISSUS: Farewell.

NARRATOR: Only Echo the nymph, watching from the woods behind, was there to witness the death she had prayed to bring about.

ECHO: Farewell. Farewell.

NARRATOR: The soul of Narcissus slipped down into the Underworld. As he rode across the Styx in the grim craft of Charon the boatman, Narcissus could not help glancing in the black waters at his side, searching for one last glimpse of his one and only love.

On the bank where Narcissus died, there sprang from the ground a beautiful flower—a flower that still bears his name.

As for Echo, she returned to her cave. She regretted the prayer that had ended the life of her love. Her regret began to eat her away. She wandered deeper and deeper and faded into the shadows. Her bones became stone, her sinewy arms reached up and joined the rocky roof of the cave, and her legs hardened into the floor. All that remained was her voice.

So even to this day, when man journeys to where darkness and stone rule, he can still hear Echo stealing his voice and making it her own.

DISCUSS

- Does Narcissus get what he deserves? Does Echo? Explain.
- What elements in this myth help explain events in nature?
- In Greek society male beauty was highly prized. If this story were set in your society, would Narcissus be a man or a woman?
- Some psychologists claim that all people should have a "healthy" level of narcissism. Do you think this is true? Explain.

FUN FACT

Narcissus was the name of a Roman athlete in the 2nd century A.D., who was the personal fighting trainer of the Roman Emperor Commodus. Commodus loved the brutal gladiator fights of the Coliseum and fought in several events himself—an unheard of act for a Roman Emperor. Narcissus gained lasting fame when he assassinated Commodus by strangling him in his bedchamber. This Narcissus was the partial inspiration for the character of Maximus in Ridley Scott's epic film *Gladiator* (2000).

Reflections: The Dangers of Self-Love

Narcissus is a famous myth-character for two reasons. First, even though there are plenty of bizarre mythological love stories to be found (e.g., Oedipus loves his mother, the Queen of Crete loves a bull), Narcissus is the only character to ever fall passionately in love with himself. Secondly, the adjective formed from his name, *narcissistic,* is one used to describe those people who seem to be in love with themselves. (You know who I'm talking about. If you don't, you might be one of them.)

Now, in everyday life, people might casually say, "So-and-so is in love with himself," but they do not mean it literally. The person in question has not been sending himself flowers or taking himself on moonlit gondola rides. Falling passionately and romantically in love with yourself is something that just does not happen too often. Instead, they just mean that this person thinks a lot of himself.

Narcissism has been described as self-love that shuts out all other loves. It keeps people from experiencing other type of loves that *could* bring them happiness, and instead they focus their love back on themselves—often with destructive results. There are many types of narcissism, but two general categories are *cerebral* and *somatic.* Those who are cerebral narcissists derive their excessive pride from their intellect and their academic achievements. Those who are somatic narcissists derive their excessive pride from their appearance, their physical beauty, and their ability to attract admirers. Whichever type of narcissism narcissists suffer from, they are *completely* focused on themselves. People might throw the word *narcissistic* around, but it is not the same thing as just being cocky or stuck up. Narcissism is serious business. Some people actually *believe* that they are the center of the universe, and that is a dangerous belief—for them *and* everyone else involved.

Looking at the other side of the coin, there are people who need a little more self-love in their lives. While the narcissists are busy thinking they cannot do anything wrong, there are people out there thinking they cannot do any right. This is from a lack of self-esteem. So where is the dividing line? Having too little self-esteem can lead to depression or suicide, while too much can lead to hurtful, destructive behavior and warped sense of reality. When does too much self-esteem turn into narcissism? Perhaps it is best to heed one of the mottos engraved above the doorway to the Delphic Oracle: "Everything in Moderation." Love yourself, but not too much. And how can you regulate this? The Delphic Oracle has an answer for that, too. "Know Thyself" is the second motto carved there.

All Is Vanity by C. Allan Gilbert

Myths as Examinations of Human Nature

Many Greek myths use storytelling to explain truths about human nature by exposing flaws that we all possess. (Do not take the *human* in human nature too literally. More often than not, it is the gods who are demonstrating human flaws.) Who can say that he or she has never been vain like Narcissus or foolish like Echo? In order to make the criticism as clear as possible, the characters always take these flaws to extremes—Narcissus is *incredibly* vain, and Echo is *incredibly* foolish. The myths also warn the audience to avoid the behaviors that lead the characters into so much trouble. Echo, who prattles on endlessly, loses her voice. Narcissus, who callously breaks the heart of everyone else, accidentally breaks his own. By reading about the fates of these fictional characters, the audience learns from the characters' mistakes but is spared the pain of going through the situation themselves. This one of the many great uses of literature.

Out of the many character flaws outlined by the myths, the most common is hubris. Over the years hubris, which used to be a generic word for crime, came to mean "overweening or excessive pride." Most Greek tragedies—plays that tell of the downfall of a noble character—preach against the dangers of putting oneself above the gods, the most extreme case of hubris.

Time and time again, characters in Greek mythology suffer because of their pride. Narcissus' excessive pride comes from his looks, and eventually those he has callously wronged call on the gods to cut him down to size. The Greek goddess Nemesis is just the god for the job. Nemesis was inescapable—she always got her man (or woman as the case may be.) She was the personification of divine retribution, a force that made those who committed the crime of hubris wish they had never been born.

DISCUSS
- How does Narcissus commit the crime of hubris?
- What other myths show truths about human nature? Explain.

Oh, What a Tangled Web She Weaves!

Another myth-character found guilty of the crime of hubris was a weaver named Arachne, who boasted that her weaving was even better than that of the goddess Athena, the patron of domestic arts. Athena, not to be trash talked by an upstart mortal, appeared to Arachne and challenged her to a contest—a weave-off. Arachne cockily agreed, and the two flew to their weaving. The goddess Athena presented the tapestry that she had woven, and it was truly a divine specimen. Yet in some miraculous way, within the tapestry that Arachne wove, the craftsmanship was finer and the colors more vivid than in the goddess' work. Athena, forgetting that she was the Goddess of Wisdom, went berserk and moved to strike down the mortal weaver. Before the goddess could do her in, Arachne denied Athena the pleasure and hanged herself. Death is not necessarily the end to a goddess though. Athena restored Arachne to life and, inspired by her fondness for hanging, transformed her into a grotesque creature with hairy legs, a bulbous body, and hundreds of beady eyes—the very first spider. To this day *arachnids,* the children of Arachne, are still the best weavers around.

Other Flower Children

As mentioned in the first chapter, myths often explain occurrences in nature. Narcissus is one of many myth-characters whose death explains the birth of a certain type of tree or flower. Although you may not have heard of the Narcissus flower (as the Greeks call it), you have probably heard of the daffodil, which is the North American equivalent. The Greeks could tell that the daffodil sprang from Narcissus because the flower bends down, as if admiring its reflection in the water. If you have ever seen a daffodil, you might have noticed its droop.

Hyacinthus was another boy who became a flower after his death. He was the beloved friend of the god Apollo, who accidentally fractured his skull with a forcefully thrown discus while the two were showing off. To partially remedy the fact that he had just killed his friend, Apollo caused Hyacinthus to transform into the Hyacinth, a flower that bears his name.

The nymph Daphne, possibly hearing what a dangerous god Apollo was to befriend, ran away when the god approached her with romantic proposals. Rather than be his lover, she transformed herself into a tree called the laurel. Apollo honored the beauty of the nymph by weaving her leaves into his hair. You have probably seen a picture of an ancient Greek or Roman man wearing a crown of leaves on his head; this is a ring of laurel leaves, signifying that this person is especially honored. In ancient Greece, laurels crowns were presented to the winners of both athletic and artistic contests. In modern times this tradition is kept alive through the position of *laureate,* an honorary title bestowed upon a gifted artist, such as the poet laureate of the United States.

Adonis was a boy who was loved by the goddess Aphrodite. When Ares learned of the affair, he became insanely jealous, because he was involved in a long-standing affair with Aphrodite as well. Vowing to get rid of his rival, Ares transformed himself into a boar and attacked Adonis while he was out hunting. Aphrodite found her love dying, gored by the boar's tusks. To honor his memory, she caused a tiny, red flower to spring up from each drop of his precious blood.

CHAPTER 6
Wisdom vs. Intelligence

DAEDALUS AND ICARUS

Cast

Daedalus *Famous inventor*

Icarus *His young son*
Minos *King of Crete*

NARRATOR: For 18 years, the inventor Daedalus had lived on the island of Crete and served the Bull-King Minos. In the king's service, Daedalus had designed fast ships that allowed Crete to subdue the mainland city-states, a beautiful dancing floor for the princess, and, his greatest creation of all, the Labyrinth—a subterranean maze filled with twisting passageways, sudden drop-offs, and every kind of perilous trap. At its center lived the Minotaur, the half-man, half-bull creature that Minos had imprisoned there. Yet Daedalus gradually realized that he, too, was trapped. With every new invention he became more and more valuable to the king, who would never allow him to leave Crete alive.

DAEDALUS: All of my genius—all of my skill—and still I am helpless.

NARRATOR: Daedalus was making his way back to his workshop built atop the cliffs of Crete, a lodging that he shared with his son Icarus. He heard his son's cries as he neared his home. Icarus would be 7 next spring. How many years had he wasted in the service of this tyrant?

ICARUS: *(happily)* Father!

DAEDALUS: How will I tell Icarus? He'll never see our homeland. He'll never see Greece.

ICARUS: Father, what did the king say? Did he say we can sail for the mainland?

DAEDALUS: I'm afraid not, Icarus. We can never leave this island.

ICARUS: Why not?

DAEDALUS: Because King Minos is strong, and your old father is weak.

ICARUS: We could steal a ship!

DAEDALUS: Are you kidding? Minos controls the seas, and I helped him. I'm trapped in a web of my own making.

ICARUS: There must be *some* way.

DAEDALUS: Icarus, it's impossible! It's just better to accept it now than later.

NARRATOR: The next few days brought a terrible melancholy on Daedalus. He gazed listlessly around his cluttered workshop. It was filled with useless wonders and trinkets. The Labyrinth had been his masterwork, but it had ultimately trapped even him.

ICARUS: Father, what's wrong? Why don't you come out to the cliffs with me? Play your pipes! It will make you feel better.

NARRATOR: Daedalus looked up and smiled at his son.

DAEDALUS: At least we are together, Icarus. Just let me grab my pipes.

NARRATOR: Overlooking the sheer drop to the sea, father and son seated themselves on a pair of rocks. Overhead the gulls were soaring in the breeze.

ICARUS: Look at the birds, father! Why can't we fly like them?

DAEDALUS: *(laugh)* That is not the way the gods intended it. Oh, but if we could, we would be gone from this cursed island.

NARRATOR: The inventor paused and thoughtfully examined his shepherd's pipe.

DAEDALUS: *(breathlessly)* Is it possible?

NARRATOR: He stared at the pattern of the pipe-reeds, each one longer than the one before. He glanced to the birds wheeling above. He saw the same pattern there in the elegant curvature of their wings.

ICARUS: *(yelling)* Look at me, father! Look at me!

NARRATOR: Icarus jumped up from his rock, his arms widespread, mimicking the wheeling of the birds overhead.

DAEDALUS: Quick, Icarus! Back to the house!

NARRATOR: Once there Daedalus dug furiously through the piles of supplies that littered his shop. He found several lengths of string—some for him and some for Icarus.

DAEDALUS: *(excitedly)* Tie this! Tie the end like this—into a loop.

ICARUS: What for, father?

DAEDALUS: To snare the gulls.

ICARUS: Why?

DAEDALUS: Just do as I say!

NARRATOR: Daedalus gleefully knotted a loop in his string.

DAEDALUS: Do you have yours? Good! Now back to the cliffs!

NARRATOR: Back on the cliffs, father and son laid their makeshift snares and baited them for the gulls.

DAEDALUS: Easy, son. Wait until they have eaten almost all the bait and suspect nothing and *then* pull the string tight. Only when they take off again will they realize that they are snared.

NARRATOR: They caught gull after gull. Daedalus knocked each on the head with a rock and placed the bodies into a large sack at his side. After a while, Daedalus noticed that Icarus was no longer springing his snares.

DAEDALUS: What's the matter, son?

ICARUS: I'm tired of this game.

DAEDALUS: It's not a game, Icarus. This is how we're going to escape this island.

ICARUS: I feel sorry for the birds. Why must they die?

DAEDALUS: Every creature dies eventually, Icarus. Now is simply their time. See how some of the birds never give our traps a second glance?

ICARUS: Yes?

DAEDALUS: Those are the *wise* birds. Only the foolish birds, the ones that are too curious for their own good, come close enough for us to catch. We are teaching them a lesson.

ICARUS: But they're dying—just for one little mistake.

DAEDALUS: It's the way of the world.

NARRATOR: The sack was bulging now. Daedalus hoisted it over his shoulder and carried it back to their workshop. He heated a great jar of water and boiled every gull body to loosen the feathers.

DAEDALUS: After the bodies are boiled, the feathers will pull free—like so. Start plucking! We should have enough feathers here for my plan.

NARRATOR: Icarus plucked and said nothing. Daedalus worked late into the night, fashioning frames from green limbs that resembled the wings of birds. Using melted wax, he attached the gull feathers to these frames. He built two leather harnesses and attached to these his newly made wings. When Icarus awoke, he stared in amazement at his father who now wore an impressive wingspan.

ICARUS: You're going to fly, father! You're really going to fly!

DAEDALUS: Yes, Icarus. And you will too.

NARRATOR: Only then did Icarus notice a second pair of wings, one much smaller and made for a boy just his size, sitting on the workshop floor.

ICARUS: *(excitedly)* This is going to be great!

DAEDALUS: But first a test.

NARRATOR: They made their way to the cliff-side, where the breeze was blowing swiftly out to the sea.

DAEDALUS: I will need the up-draft of a fall from the cliff. If I fail, Icarus, never forget your old father.

NARRATOR: The boy nodded. Daedalus paced backward from the cliff's edge, gauging the distance carefully. Then with great speed, he ran toward the precipice. When he reached the edge, he jumped forward—out onto the breeze—and plummeted out of sight.

ICARUS: Father!

NARRATOR: The boy ran to the edge, expecting to see his father's body dashed to pieces on the rocks below.

DAEDALUS: Woo-hoo! Woo-hoo!

NARRATOR: Daedalus swooped up from the waves, soaring on the breeze.

ICARUS: You did it! You really did it!

DAEDALUS: Look at me, Icarus! Look at me!

NARRATOR: He looped up and around, up over Icarus' head, and with several settling flaps, landed neatly in front of his son.

ICARUS: Me next! Me next!

DAEDALUS: Of course, son! Of course! We'll leave immediately! No further test is needed. My invention is a success! Wouldn't it be great to see the look on old Minos' face when he realizes we have escaped? Ha-ha! He may control the seas, but no man controls the skies!

NARRATOR: Icarus tore back to the workshop and quickly returned with his own miniature set of wings. He began strapping them on.

ICARUS: I can't wait to fly like you did, father! What was it like?

DAEDALUS: Exhilarating, son! I felt like one of the gods!

NARRATOR: Icarus flapped his own wings for a test and then aimed himself toward the cliff's edge.

ICARUS: Here I go!

DAEDALUS: Icarus! Wait!

NARRATOR: Daedalus lunged forward and seized the boy's arm.

DAEDALUS: No! I am an adult, and you are just a boy. Don't rush ahead foolishly before thinking. What I have just done was a calculated flight! There are things I must tell you first.

ICARUS: Why? I can't wait to fly!

DAEDALUS: Listen to me! If you fly too close to the ocean's spray, the water will wet down your feathers. They will grow too heavy, and you will fall into the ocean and drown. If you fly too high, the heat of the sun will melt the wax that holds the wings together. So, please, son, fly a moderate pitch, or you will be in great danger.

ICARUS: No loopty-loops or anything?

DAEDALUS: No.

ICARUS: I'm not stupid. I watched you. I know what to do now.

DAEDALUS: Promise me, Icarus.

ICARUS: *(grudgingly)* I promise.

NARRATOR: The aged father wrapped his winged arms around his son.

DAEDALUS: Now, let us leave this place for good—before Minos' guards spot us here. Icarus, you will go first, but don't fly too far ahead. Head straight north, toward the mainland.

ICARUS: Got it!

NARRATOR: The youth bolted toward the cliff's edge, wings spread. As soon as he had disappeared over the side, Daedalus began his own take-off.

Soon father and son were soaring on the salty sea breeze.

ICARUS: Father! This is greater than I ever imagined! Look at this!

NARRATOR: The boy twirled about in the sky.

DAEDALUS: Icarus, be careful! This isn't a game! You promised!

ICARUS: What? I can't hear you! Hurry up, father. I'll beat you there if you're not careful!

NARRATOR: The old inventor beat his wings furiously to catch up with his son, but Icarus easily outstripped him.

DAEDALUS: *(shouting)* Icarus! You're flying too fast—and too high! Icarus!

ICARUS: This is great! This must be how the gods feel!

NARRATOR: Icarus looked back over his shoulder. His father was far below and far behind. Then the boy looked up. The sun was much too close—its heat was bearing down upon him. Sweat was dripping from his brow.

ICARUS: *(scared)* Father?

NARRATOR: Something hot and sticky was running down both his arms. He flapped them furiously to shake it loose. When he did, feathers flew in all directions. They had come loose. To his horror, Icarus began to fall!

ICARUS: No! Father!

DAEDALUS: *(yelling)* Icarus!

NARRATOR: Daedalus saw his son spiraling down toward the sea, a trail of feathers in his wake. He turned his head just as Icarus crashed into the brine.

DAEDALUS: *(weeping)* My son. My son.

NARRATOR: Time and time again, the old man swooped as low as he dared over the spot where his son had fallen, yet he never saw any trace of the boy. Finally he gave up hope and, despairing, continued his flight toward Athens.

Many sailors later reported seeing a large bird in the sky that day, a bird with its head hung low, who only barely saved itself from plunging into the sea when the wind brought it low. They said it had the strangest cry—like a man whose heart was broken.

DISCUSS

- What is the difference between *wisdom* and *intelligence*?
- Why is it so hard for children to listen to their parents?
- Is Daedalus a good father? Explain.

DRAW

Draw a diagram of what you believe the Labyrinth looked like.

WRITE

Modernize the story of Daedalus and Icarus.

Minos and the Minotaur

In his time, King Minos was the most powerful king in the regions surrounding Greece. His superior navy, commanded from his island kingdom of Crete, kept the mainland city-states in constant terror. It was rumored that beneath his palace at Knossos there was a baffling maze called the Labyrinth. Through the many corridors and passageways roamed a frightening beast, part-bull, part-man. Those who displeased Minos were dropped into the Labyrinth and made a quick meal for the Minotaur, "The Bull of Minos." Even though King Minos used the Minotaur as an agent of fear, it was also one of his darkest secrets. When Minos ascended the throne, he begged Poseidon, the sea-god, to give the Cretans a demonstration of divine favor. Poseidon complied and sent a pristinely white bull out of the sea. Minos was to sacrifice the bull back to the sea-god in order to thank him for his blessing.

The Cretans had a long history of bull-worship—to them it was a sacred animal—and this bull was the best specimen Minos had ever seen. He simply could not sacrifice it; instead he substituted an inferior bull in its place—hoping that Poseidon would be fooled. The sea-god was not fooled, and in retribution he cursed Minos' wife, Pasiphaë, with a maddening lust. The object of her lust was none other than the bull from the sea.

About this time Daedalus, an Athenian exile, arrived in Crete and quickly became a court favorite because of his brilliant inventions. Queen Pasiphaë went to the inventor in secret and begged him to devise a way to bring her and her love together. Goaded by the offer of riches, Daedalus designed a cow-like structure that the queen could hide within and through this disguise meet with the bull. This unnatural union produced the Minotaur.

When Minos saw the creature his wife had delivered, he was disgusted. He called Daedalus to him—and rather than punishing the inventor for his part in this sordid affair, commissioned him to build an enormous maze beneath the palace—filled with tricks and traps that could contain the horrific creature. Minos would use the Minotaur to strike fear into the hearts of his enemies.

Wisdom Versus Intelligence

It is easy to look at the story of Icarus and think of how you would do things differently. What kind of idiot blatantly ignores instructions from such a wise father? But do not start casting stones too quickly. Think about *your* parents. Have you ever disregarded their advice only to later find out they were right? Almost everyone has. Every day, sons and daughters disobey parents who have much more wisdom than they do. This statement might cause you to pause. Are your parents *wiser* than you are? *Yes.* Does this mean that they are *smarter* than you are? *Not necessarily.* This is because there is a difference between wisdom and intelligence.

Wisdom seems to come with age. There is an etymological (word history) connection between the words *wisdom* and *wizard*. The stereotypical *wizard* is very *wise* and very *old*. Wisdom means accumulated learning, and the way that people learn best is by doing. Elderly people have done a lot in their time—each wrinkle and gray hair exists for a reason. They have lived life; they have made their mistakes, and even though the bruises have faded, the lessons learned remain.

Intelligence is the ability to learn and reason. But most of the time, you cannot learn something from a situation until you have gone through it. Adults telling children that the stove is hot will not keep them from touching it. Children will have to touch it themselves before they *know* it is hot. No pain, no gain. Or to change up the words, *know* pain, *know* gain. Human experience is one of the best teachers around, and even though not all lesson are painful ones, some are learned in such a hard way that there is no second chance. Life isn't a video game. There's no *Reset* or *Redo* button. *Game over.*

Everyone has had an "Icarus moment," where parental directions were ignored and things went badly. If you are reading this, you might have experienced yours and lived to tell about it. The myth of Icarus is a serious one: Young people are not immortal, no matter how much they feel so. The world is a dangerous place, and *wisdom* teaches that. Sometimes it is a lesson learned the hard way.

Most young adults find it hard to listen to their parents. Yet as they grow older (and give life a shot on their own), they realize that their parents were actually smarter than they thought. They realize that their parents' *wisdom* is not an insult of their own *intelligence.* In a Ken Burns (2002) documentary, Mark Twain put it this way: "When I was a boy of 14, my father was so ignorant I could hardly stand to have the old man around. But when I got to be 21, I was astonished at how much he had learned in 7 years." Even though he is being humorous, Twain realized that it was *he* who had done the learning, not his father. He had gotten older and wiser.

DISCUSS
- Describe an Icarus moment in your own life when your parents offered wisdom but you did not listen.
- Are there situations where *parents* should listen to their *children*? Explain.

Myths as Warnings

One function of myths in ancient societies was to act as warnings. Some tales came with what we would call the "moral of the story." Even though these morals were unstated, they were outlined clearly enough in the story for the listener to catch on. More often than not, myths warned of *hubris*, or pride. Other myths warned against the minor and major taboos of Greek society: incest, murder, rude conduct in the home of a host, neglecting the burial of a dead body, and bestiality. The myth of Minos gives us two warnings: First, do not disregard the edicts of the gods, or your wife will lust after a bull. Secondly, do not engage in bestiality, or your son will be half-man, half-bull. It seems somewhat silly to us now, but these warnings were an integral part in the formation of the myths.

In this story, Icarus' act of hubris was comparing himself to the gods—a comparison that always brings plenty of pain to those who make it. He's also incredibly careless. Not only does he completely disregard his father's instructions, but he also ignores the danger of his situation—placing himself above mortal consequences. It is only when the wax is dripping down his arms that he realizes that he is doomed. Up until that point, he forgets that he is mortal.

In ancient Rome, when a general returned from battle victorious, an enormous parade was often conducted in his honor. As he rode triumphantly through the adoring crowd with all of Rome shouting his praises, it was his servant's job, riding in the chariot behind him, to whisper "*memento mori*" in his master's ear—"Remember: Thou Art Mortal." This served as reminder to the general, in spite of his enormous success, to not place himself on the level of the gods. Today, Fortune may be smiling on him. Tomorrow, maybe not.

Mythology is filled with characters who get a little too full of themselves and rashly compare themselves to the gods. The gods, not taking this lightly, appear and remind these characters of the pecking order—destroying or transforming them in a flash of divine fury.

In Detail: The Fall of Icarus

The Roman poet Ovid, renowned for his dramatic storytelling ability, provides us with the best account of Icarus' fall.

And as a bird who drifts down from her nest
Instructs her young to follow her in flight,
So Daedalus flapped wings to guide his son.
Far off, below them, some stray fisherman,
Attention startled from his bending rod,
Or a bland shepherd resting on his crook,
Or a dazed farmer leaning on his plough,
Glanced up to see the pair float through the sky.
And, taking them for gods, stood still in wonder. . . .
By this time Icarus began to feel the joy
Of beating wings in air and steered his course
Beyond the father's lead: all the wide sky
Was there to tempt him as he steered toward heaven.
Meanwhile the heat of sun struck at his back
And where his wings were joined, sweet-smelling fluid
Ran hot that once was wax. His naked arms
Whirled into wind; his lips, still calling out
His father's name, were gulfed in the dark sea.
And the unlucky man, no longer father,
Cried, "Icarus, where are you, Icarus,
Where are you hiding, Icarus, from me?"
Then as he called again, his eyes discovered
The boy's torn wings washed on the climbing waves.
He damned his art, his wretched cleverness,
Rescued the body and placed it in a tomb,
And where it lies the land's called Icarus.
As Daedalus put his ill-starred son to earth,
A talking partridge in a swamp near by
Glanced up at him and with a cheerful noise
The creature clapped its wings. And this moment
The partridge was a new bird come to earth—
And a reminder, Daedalus, of crime. (Ovid, 8/1958, p. 205)

Immediately after his description of Icarus' fall, Ovid segues into his next story—a dark tale from Daedalus' past.

The Inventor's Apprentice

Long before Daedalus made his journey across the sea to Crete, he gained fame in Athens as an inventor. It is said that Daedalus was the first to invent the tools of carpentry and with them created statues that walked as humans do. His workshop was on the Acropolis, the high hill of Athens, and when his reputation was cemented, his sister sent her son, Perdix, to be apprenticed to him. She hoped Daedalus' genius would rub off on the boy; after all, Perdix had always dreamed of being an inventor. Daedalus grudgingly agreed, as long as the boy did not get in the way. He tried to ignore the boy as much as possible, giving him menial tasks like running to the marketplace, boiling water, and stoking the fires.

One day Daedalus and Perdix were visiting the Athenian seashore, and Perdix discovered the skeleton of a fish half-buried in the sand. He excitedly showed his find to his uncle, who grumbled and shooed the boy away. An idea had awoken in Perdix's mind. Watching his uncle work had sharpened his own ingenuity, and within the spine and ribs of the fish, he saw his first invention. Because Daedalus barely acknowledged his existence, it was not hard for the boy to hide his project from his uncle. Perdix patterned the shape of the fish's ribs in a sheet of tin and attached a makeshift handle to one end. When he pulled the invention across a wooden surface, the metal teeth dug in. He had invented the first saw.

Eventually, Perdix caught Daedalus' attention long enough to unveil his inventions. Not only had the boy made a saw, but also a compass for drawing perfect circles. Daedalus was flabbergasted. Here was a boy he had passed off as a complete imbecile showing him the most perfect inventions he had ever seen. Along with astonishment, something else was hiding in Daedalus' heart: He feared that the genius of this boy would match or even surpass his, that Perdix's inventions would become world-famous instead of his own. Barely knowing what he was doing, Daedalus grabbed the boy and, despite his pleas for mercy, hurled him out the high window of the workshop. Many in the streets below looked up as they heard the commotion and saw the young boy falling to his death and Daedalus' shadowy figure in the window. An outraged mob of witnesses stormed the workshop and dragged Daedalus before the king. Because Daedalus had done so much for Athens, the king did not execute Daedalus but banished him from Athens forever.

Those who went to search for the body of the boy could find no trace of it. It had disappeared. In fact, the goddess Athena had transformed the boy as he fell into a new type of bird, the perdix. According to the Greeks, the perdix remembers its fall from the high Acropolis, and because of this, never builds a high nest like other birds; it is completely content to stay safe and sound on the ground. In English, the perdix is called the partridge.

DISCUSS

- What impact, if any, does the previous story of Daedalus and Perdix have on the story of Daedalus and Icarus? Explain.
- Do you feel less sorry for Daedalus after finding out he is a murderer? Explain.
- How is the myth of Perdix another example of myth explaining nature?

Unearthing the Palace of Minos

When British archeologist Sir Arthur Evans unearthed the remains of a Bronze Age palace on the island of Crete, it was quickly associated with the legendary King Minos. Evans named the culture that he discovered *Minoan* after Minos. The site became known as "the palace of Knossos," and the ruins discovered there reflect the ancient legend of the Labyrinth. In fact, the term *palace* gives off a false impression, for it's not a single structure built as the home of royalty, but a tight cluster of interconnected buildings that served a variety of purposes and housed people from every level of society. Of the hundreds of rooms, some are very obviously royal quarters, some appear to be workshops, and some were designed for religious practices. The layout of the "palace"—many rooms connected by narrow hallways that curve sharply and intersect with one other in a way that confuses a logical sense of direction—probably gave rise to the Labyrinth legend. The term *labyrinth* is a Minoan, not Greek, word meaning "place of the double-axe." Some believe that the double-axe (or battle axe, as some might call it) was used in Minoan sacrifices.

One of the most amazing discoveries was the artwork of the palace, which gives even more insight into the culture. Frescoes decorate the passageway walls (which have a disorienting effect on those who pass through them). These paintings show a society devoted to the divinity of the bull—as the Minos legend suggests. The most famous image shows three youths performing a sacred bull-jumping ceremony. In the painting, a young girl holds the horns of a large bull as a youth leaps nimbly across its back, and another young girl waits behind to assist with his landing. It is believed that acrobatic, bull-jumping feats such as this one (kind of an ancient rodeo) were common entertainment on Crete. Other paintings depict a man (probably a priest) wearing a bull's mask, an image that could have inspired the Minotaur myth. Some speculate this was the king or a priest enacting a ritual as the divine bull-god. (Ceremonies performed in this way could have given rise to the myth of Pasiphaë and the bull.) One of the most splendid artifacts is a vessel shaped like the head and horns of a black bull used for the pouring of libations (liquid sacrifices).

At some point the Minoan civilization was destroyed (possibly by a volcanic eruption) and the Minoan kings lost the power they had over the sea. Later Athens would arise as one of the greatest naval powers in the Mediterranean. The fall of Crete and the rise of Athens is reflected in the myth of Theseus' defeat of the Minotaur, and like most others, this myth contains the echoes of historical truth.

Landscape With the Fall of Icarus, by Pieter Breughel the Elder, 1558

Paintings, Poems, and Progressive Rock

Throughout the centuries, artists have tried to capture the Fall of Icarus in various media, using the subject matter of Icarus to comment on youthful impetuousness and the brevity of life. For this activity you will analyze three types of media: artwork, poetry, and song.

Go to the Web Gallery of Art (http://www.wga.hu) and analyze the following paintings: "Landscape With the Fall of Icarus" by Hans Bol (1534–1593) and "Landscape With the Fall of Icarus" (c. 1588) by Pieter Brueghel the Elder. Although the paintings have the same title and originate from the same time period, they have different themes. What is the difference between the two paintings?

Now read an excerpt from a poem by the Anglo-American poet W. H. Auden (1907–1973), "Musee des Beaux Arts," which comments on "Landscape With the Fall of Icarus" by Brueghel:

About suffering they were never wrong,
The Old Masters; how well, they understood
Its human position; how it takes place
While someone else is eating or opening a window or just walking
    dully along;

DISCUSS
- What is the poem trying to say about Icarus' death?
- The poem is a comment on the second painting that you viewed. How are the poem and the painting connected?

. . .

In Breughel's Icarus, for instance: how everything turns away
Quite leisurely from the disaster; the ploughman may
Have heard the splash, the forsaken cry,
But for him it was not an important failure; the sun shone
As it had to on the white legs disappearing into the green
Water; and the expensive delicate ship that must have seen
Something amazing, a boy falling out of the sky,
had somewhere to get to and sailed calmly on. (Auden, 1938/1979,
     lines 1–4, 14–21)

Finally, listen to the song "Dust in the Wind" by the band Kansas. Connect the theme of the song to both the painting by Brueghel and the poem by Auden.

DISCUSS
- What is the connecting theme between the painting, the poem, and the song?
- Can the various forms of art achieve the same purpose?
- Which do you find the most effective? Explain.

Theseus and the Minotaur

The Athenian hero Theseus is the warrior who finally put an end to Minos' monster. Theseus grew up unaware that he was actually the son of a king. His mother showed him an enormous boulder and told him that the secret to his father's identity lay beneath it. When he was strong enough to move the boulder, she would tell him who his father was. Theseus trained throughout his teenage years, and at the age of 16, he at last lifted the boulder. Beneath it were a pair of old sandals and a well-crafted sword. These, his mother told him, belonged to his father, Aegeus, the King of Athens. Theseus at once set off to be reunited with his father at Athens.

When Theseus arrived, he found Athens in the midst of a dark time. Every 9 years, the Athenians were forced to select from their children seven boys and seven girls to send to Crete—sacrifices to King Minos and his Minotaur. The next round of sacrifices was due, and the king was powerless to stop it. There was also a rumor that the woman whom he had recently married was actually a witch. Theseus gained entrance to the palace, but kept his true identity a secret.

The new queen was, in fact, the witch Medea, who had fled to Athens after murdering the king and princess of Corinth. She invited Theseus to a banquet, and because she had divined that he was actually Aegeus' son, convinced the old king that Theseus must be an agent of his enemies. Aegeus offered Theseus a poisoned drink, but when Theseus rose to propose a toast, he recognized the boy's sword as his own. He knocked the drink from Theseus' hands and banished Medea for trying to murder his true son.

The reunion between father and son did not last for long. Theseus declared that he felt it his mission to go with the sacrificial youths to Crete and put a stop to this grisly tribute. Aegeus reluctantly agreed, but he begged Theseus to let him know from afar if he was successful. The ship that carried the sacrifices would leave Athens with black sails. If he returned alive, Aegeus pleaded, Theseus should change the sails to white so that Aegeus could know his son's fate from far off. Theseus agreed.

Theseus was let in among the sacrifices and journeyed along with them to Crete. When the prisoners were brought into the court of King Minos, Theseus confronted the king bravely. King Minos' daughter, Ariadne, saw Theseus' bravery and fell in love with the handsome Athenian. That night—the night before the prisoners would be fed to the Minotaur—she met Theseus in his cell and promised to help him kill the beast if he would promise to take her back to Athens and make her his wife. Theseus agreed.

Daedalus had told Ariadne the secrets of the Labyrinth. She, in turn, told these to Theseus. She gave him a sword and—in one version of the story—a magical crown of light to guide his path. She tied one end of a spool of string to the entrance of the Labyrinth and gave the Theseus the other end. Using this he could find his way back after killing the Minotaur. Theseus thanked her for her help and disappeared into the depths of the maze.

In the middle of the Labyrinth, Theseus wrestled with the Minotaur and slew it. In some stories he did this with his sword. In others, he killed the creature with his bare hands. He returned to Ariadne, they freed the other prisoners, and sailed away from Crete under the cover of night, but not before drilling holes in the hulls of Minos' fastest ships. Along the way the crew stopped on the island of Naxos for a rest, and while Ariadne slept in the shade, Theseus ordered everyone back on the boat. He left the girl who had saved him alone on an island to die. When at last the cliffs of

DISCUSS
- What is heroic about Theseus? What is unheroic?
- What could have been a possible motivation for Theseus leaving Ariadne on the island?

MYTH-WORD

The sea where Aegeus jumped to his death is called the Aegean Sea today because of this myth.

Athens came into sight, Theseus saw his father standing on the heights—watching for his son to come back to him. To his horror he saw his father jump forward and fall the length of the cliffs. Then he remembered: He had forgotten to change his sails from black to white.

Archimedes (c. 287–212 BC): A Real-Life Daedalus

The writers of Greek mythology imagined Daedalus as an inventor whose abilities could never be rivaled—a visionary who could think a thing and then bring it into existence. In many ways, Daedalus is similar to a real-life Greek, one who lived in the city of Syracuse on the island of Sicily, and had a similar relationship to its king as Daedalus had to Minos. Just as King Minos commissioned Daedalus to build the Labyrinth, the King of Syracuse put the brilliant mind of the inventor Archimedes to work.

Archimedes was first and foremost a mathematician. He successfully calculated the geometrical relationship between a sphere placed inside a cylinder of the same height and width: The sphere has 2/3 the volume and surface area of the cylinder. He also calculated the relationship between the diameter of a circle and its circumference, also known as π.

In a famous story, the King of Syracuse approached Archimedes with a problem: The king had commissioned a solid gold crown to be made, but he suspected that the crown-maker had used a combination of silver and gold in order to cheat him. After the king asked Archimedes to prove that the crown was not solid gold, the mathematician was perplexed. How could he prove such a thing without actually destroying the crown? Later when Archimedes was climbing into his brimming bath, he noticed how the addition of his body to the water caused it to overflow. He immediately knew how he could prove whether the crown was solid gold. He jumped out of his bath and, running naked through the streets of Syracuse, shouted, "Eureka! Eureka!"—which in Greek means "I have found it!" He ran all the way to the king to tell him that he could determine if the crown was solid gold without destroying it. By placing it in water and measuring the amount of water displaced, and then repeating the experiment with a block of gold that equaled the amount given to the craftsman in order to make the crown, Archimedes determined that because the density of the crown was indeed lighter than the amount of gold, the crown was not solid gold.

In another story, the mathematician impressed the king by rigging a fully loaded, three-masted ship up to a series of pulleys. Then, with only the small effort of working the controls, Archimedes was able to raise the ship and move it along the land just as if it were sailing on the sea. Archimedes boasted, "Give me a place to stand on, and I will move the Earth" (Anderson & Stephenson, 1999, p. 42). Upon seeing this, the king marveled at it and begged Archimedes to design battle engines that could defend the seaside city from invaders. The inventor honored this request. Although Archimedes invented "peaceful" inventions such as the screw pump (or the Archimedes Screw—a spiral within a cylinder that can elevate water from one level to another for irrigation), the majority of his recorded inventions were created for warfare.

When the mighty Roman military decided to crush Syracuse by sea, they learned the hard way how one brilliant mind can pose an incredible obstacle. Archimedes invented huge catapults and stone-throwers that were accurate enough to sink many Roman ships from a great distance. When the surviving ships had made it close enough to be out of the range of the larger weapons, Archimedes unveiled a series of smaller catapults and stone-throwers—perfect for closer distances—and continued to sink ships. Some Roman ships oared close to the city cliffs and began to erect ladders in order to scale them. This only gave Archimedes occasion to show the attackers his next deadly invention: a crane that swung out over the cliff-walls, dropping a metal claw that clamped down on the bows of the ships. When the ropes attached to the claw began to retract, the cranes pulled the ships up into mid-air. The soldiers on the ships clung on for dear life, as the claws dashed their vessels back into the water. Some accounts of this battle even say that Archimedes invented a heat-ray— a series of mirrors that was able to focus the sun's rays on approaching ships to such an intensity that they burst into flames. Whether or not the heat-ray was actually true (or just a colorful addition as most historians think), the war engines of Archimedes effectively demonstrated mind over matter.

The Romans had the last laugh. Because their sea attack had been completely obliterated by Archimedes' arsenal of deadly gadgets, they decided to surround the city, blockade its port, and starve its citizens into submission. When at last the Romans made a successful offensive against the besieged city, a Roman soldier found Archimedes squatting in the road. The old mathematician was muttering to himself while he drew a diagram in the dirt. The soldier ordered him to surrender and come along quietly. When Archimedes refused, the soldier killed him on the spot. "Do not disturb my circles!" are often said to have been Archimedes' last words.

DISCUSS

- What are some of the similarities between the real-life Archimedes and the legendary Daedalus?
- Legends can grow up around real-life people. Do the exploits of Archimedes sound realistic or more like legend? Explain.

ANALYZE

Who are some of the other great inventors of history? What personal characteristics helped develop their innovative spirit? What purpose do inventors serve in society?

FUN FACT

Historians noted that Archimedes worked so intensely that he sometimes forgot to eat, sleep, or bathe. Now *that* is a workaholic.

CHAPTER 7
Greed

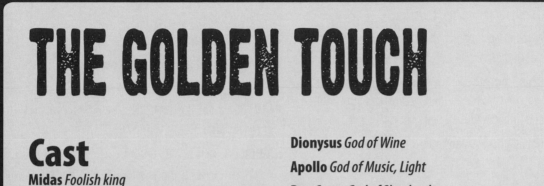

THE GOLDEN TOUCH

Cast

Midas *Foolish king*

Plautus *Slave to Midas*

Silenus *Drunken old satyr*

Donkey *His donkey*

Dionysus *God of Wine*

Apollo *God of Music, Light*

Pan *Satyr, God of Shepherds*

Voice *Female voice*

NARRATOR: There once lived a very rich and very foolish king in Phrygia named Midas. He spent his days hatching ridiculous schemes to make himself even richer than he already was. For most of these schemes, he enlisted the help of his infinitely intelligent and mostly faithful slave, Plautus.

MIDAS: Plautus, it's official: I simply *must* have more money!

PLAUTUS: Master, why do you want more money? You have a humongous palace, a 200-acre rose garden, and more fountains than you can shake a stick at.

MIDAS: Yes, but there are kings out there who have bigger palaces, bigger rose gardens, and more fountains than you can shake an even bigger stick at.

PLAUTUS: (*sigh*) I heard a new philosophy about wealth just the other day: Apparently, you have to *spend* money to *make* money.

MIDAS: Ha! That's the stupidest thing I've ever heard. You might as well say, "It's better to give than receive."

PLAUTUS: (*sarcastically*) Blasphemy.

MIDAS: Think of the richest kings in Greece. What do they have that I don't have?

PLAUTUS: More money?

MIDAS: (*annoyed*) What else?

PLAUTUS: Ships. Armies. Good looks. Talent.

MIDAS: (*angrily*) That's enough.

PLAUTUS: Intelligence. A filled-out beard—not that patchy thing of yours.

MIDAS: Enough!

PLAUTUS: People skills. Fashion sense. Gods for parents.

MIDAS: Wait! That's it!

PLAUTUS: What? Fashion sense?

MIDAS: No, you fool! All of the greatest kings have been descended from the gods! All I need to do is prove I'm a descendant of the gods.

PLAUTUS: And you'll automatically be richer?

MIDAS: Exactly. I'm bound to be.

PLAUTUS: Forget it! Don't you remember that rumor going around about your mother?

MIDAS: (*angrily*) My mother didn't have a beard! It was more like fuzz.

PLAUTUS: More fuzz than you have, but, no, Your Thickness—the rumor *you* tried to start.

MIDAS: It wasn't so far-fetched. Lots of kings are descendants of goddesses.

PLAUTUS: Not from Athena, they aren't. Maybe if you hadn't claimed the Almighty Virgin Goddess as your mother, more people would have believed you.

MIDAS: I get all of the A-gods mixed up. I meant to say Aphrodite.

PLAUTUS: Well, there's no problem believing *she* had children.

MIDAS: Maybe this time I could say I'm the son of Zeus?

PLAUTUS: Who isn't?

MIDAS: What about Apollo?

PLAUTUS: Too good looking. Not believable. How about Hephaestus? *(pause)* But, you know, the trick isn't to fool your subjects. You'd have to trick the gods into believing they had accidentally sired you before they would start heaping divine favor on you.

MIDAS: Great idea! Besides, how hard could it be to trick a god?

PLAUTUS: Wouldn't try it, master. Remember my former master, Tantalus? He thought he'd get in good with the gods if he murdered his own children and served them up as a stew.

MIDAS: Brilliant! Why didn't think of that? If only I had children. *(thinking)* I wonder if I could buy some . . .

PLAUTUS: It didn't work. The gods cursed him forever.

MIDAS: Why'd he waste perfectly good children on the deal then?

PLAUTUS: Bad communication. He asked me what the gods liked to eat, and I told him *nectar*. He thought I said *Nestor*. So then he figured if they liked to chew on an old guy like Nestor, they'd really go for some young, juicy flesh.

NARRATOR: The conversation between master and slave was interrupted by a commotion: loud, drunken singing accompanied by even worse lyre playing.

SILENUS: *(offstage, drunken singing)* Take it down and pass it around . . .

DONKEY: *(offstage)* Hee-haw! Hee-haw!

MIDAS: What's that racket? It's coming from the rose garden!

PLAUTUS: I hope it isn't Orpheus again. I was depressed for weeks after his last visit.

NARRATOR: They rushed out into the garden to investigate. What they saw there astonished them: A fat, white-bearded goat-man had capsized in the closest bed of roses. His tiny hooves waved helplessly in the air as he continued his singing and playing.

MIDAS: *(angrily)* Who are you? Why are you lying in my rose bed?

SILENUS: *(drunkenly)* Forty-two skins of wine in the hall, forty-two skins of wine—

MIDAS: He's drunk!

NARRATOR: The second party, a flea-bitten donkey, was making the most of the situation by biting the heads off the nearby roses.

DONKEY: Hee-haw! Hee-haw!

MIDAS: Ah! My babies! *(angrily)* Who is this—*freak*?

PLAUTUS: Wait a minute, master.

NARRATOR: Plautus pulled a scroll from his tunic and examined it furiously.

MIDAS: Plautus, get that donkey out of my flowerbeds! I hate donkeys! They look so buck-toothed and stupid! Shoo! Shoo!

PLAUTUS: Just a second, master.

MIDAS: And just look at that fat goat-man crushing my prize roses!

PLAUTUS: Please, Your Ignorance. They prefer the term *satyr*.

MIDAS: Whatever he is, have him arrested at once!

NARRATOR: The slave raised his head from his scroll triumphantly.

PLAUTUS: Yes! I knew I'd seen him before! He's right here in *Who's Who of Olympus.*

MIDAS: They make goat-men gods now?

PLAUTUS: *Satyr.* And he's not a god. His name is Silenus. *(reading)* Often seen riding his donkey from one festivity to another when he is too drunk to walk. Interests: wine, drinking—drinking is underlined. Looks like he's the tutor and foster father of one of the gods—let me see here—Dionysus!

MIDAS: *(trying to remember)* Dionysus. Dionysus. Is he the one with the limp?

PLAUTUS: No, the god of wine. He's new. The Greeks just invented him a few months ago.

MIDAS: God of wine, eh? Not the *best* god to forge a connection with, but oh well. *(yelling)* Mr. Solaris!

PLAUTUS: *(hissing)* Silenus!

NARRATOR: Plautus rushed forward to raise the old goat-man to his feet.

SILENUS: *(drunkenly)* Ugh! Where am I?

MIDAS: You are in the gardens of Midas, my friend. Those are also *my* roses, too, that you're making quite a mess of.

SILENUS: No need to yell! Who did you say your name was? What month is it?

MIDAS: *(loudly)* I am King Midas. We'd like to offer you— and your nasty donkey—some food and shelter.

SILENUS: No thank you! I am *lost*! I went to a party, and I was supposed to be back by July. It isn't July, is it?

MIDAS: We will help you get home. Come along, my inebriated friend! Can we offer you some food—or maybe something to drink?

SILENUS: Drink! I thought you'd never ask!

MIDAS: *(to Plautus)* Get that donkey out of my garden before it makes a real mess.

DONKEY: *(hacking)*

NARRATOR: The donkey regurgitated its botanical breakfast.

PLAUTUS: Too late.

NARRATOR: Once the old satyr and his donkey were seated at the royal table partaking of even more wine, Plautus whispered to his master.

PLAUTUS: This may work to our advantage. If Silenus is lost, there might be some reward for finding him.

MIDAS: Don't be stupid. Who would pay money to find an old, liver-damaged goat-man?

PLAUTUS: Maybe his foster son? Dionysus?

MIDAS: Ah, yes. Him. The god of goats.

PLAUTUS: No, wine.

MIDAS: That's what I meant. So how can we contact Dio-noodle?

PLAUTUS: *Dionysus!* Don't you remember when Orpheus visited here?

MIDAS: Do I ever! I couldn't get those sappy songs out of my head for weeks.

PLAUTUS: Exactly.

MIDAS: Weren't they all about death and despair and despairing over death?

PLAUTUS: Mainly. But there was one—a chant for summoning Dionysus. Orpheus was one of Dionysus' converts, you know. Let's see if I can remember it.

NARRATOR: Plautus scribbled furiously on a roll of parchment.

MIDAS: Plautus, I had no idea you could write!

PLAUTUS: I had no idea *you* could read. Just say the words!

MIDAS: *(chanting)*

Ivy-wreathed god of ripest grape

God of curly hair and shaven nape

Shrouded in thy purple cape

Now appear to me a humble ape

(speaking) I don't care for that last line—

NARRATOR: A rumbling shook the palace. The large, decorative wine bowl in the midst of the table began to vibrate, and a godly head and torso emerged from the dark liquid within. Full clusters of grapes hung from the wine-god's temples.

DIONYSUS: *(grandly)* Behold! I am Dionysus!

SILENUS: *(really drunk)* Whoa! What a trick! Do it again!

DIONYSUS: Silenus! I've been looking everywhere for you. When did you wander off?

SILENUS: I'm not surely right, meboy. Around March, I think. Has the party died down yet? These folks here found me and offered me hospit—they offered me hospit—they offered me food and drink. But I only took them up on the drink. *(drunken laugh)*

NARRATOR: Dionysus turned toward Midas, who began bowing profusely.

MIDAS: It's true, your most holiness. I am Midas—a kind, but *poor*, king.

DIONYSUS: Poor? Are you kidding? Look at this table. And this pillared hall. Not to mention this gilded wine bowl I'm currently swimming in.

MIDAS: Well, yes. I admit this hall is nice, but the rest of my home is very meager indeed. I'm a poor country king.

NARRATOR: The god dipped his finger into the wine that surrounded him and tasted it.

DIONYSUS: Good year. Expensive stuff.

MIDAS: It was a gift! Usually we drink plain old water here and eat . . . um . . . sand.

NARRATOR: Dionysus turned to Plautus.

DIONYSUS: Who are you?

PLAUTUS: His slave, your highness.

DIONYSUS: One of how many?

PLAUTUS: One-hundred-and-three.

DIONYSUS: Ha! I knew it. I assume, Midas, that you are fishing for some kind of reward.

MIDAS: Heh. Heh. I would hate to ask for one, but I have so many children, so many mouths to feed, and my wife is in poor health.

DIONYSUS: Where is she then?

PLAUTUS: Dead.

MIDAS: Heh. Heh. Dead. The poorest health a body can be in, right?

DIONYSUS: *(sigh)* Very well. Even though you're the biggest buffoon I've ever met, and I sincerely doubt you have any true financial need, I *am* grateful that you have found my old schoolmaster here. So I will grant you one wish.

MIDAS: Oh, thank you for this one wish, most noble god of . . . of . . .

PLAUTUS: *(whispering)* Wine!

MIDAS: *(whispering)* I'm not wishing for wine! I have my own vineyard!

DIONYSUS: If you need time to—

MIDAS: *(excitedly)* I wish everything I touch would turn to gold!

DIONYSUS: —think about it.

PLAUTUS: Zeus save us all!

DIONYSUS: Interesting. All right, Midas. You have made your one and *only* wish.

(chanting)

By the waters of the River Styx and the power of Dionysus

The touch of gold I give to thee, king of mortals, Midas.

If this wish future years cause you to regret

The waters of swift Pactolus may undo it yet.

(speaking) It is granted. Now, we will take our leave. Come, Silenus.

SILENUS: Zzzzzzzzzzzzzz.

DIONYSUS: *(sigh)*

NARRATOR: The god reached out and grabbed the old satyr and his donkey by the scruff and pulled them back into the wine bowl after him.

PLAUTUS: What a waste! Of all the stupid wishes you could have made, why did it have to be that one?

NARRATOR: But Midas did not hear his slave. He was staring in wonder at his hand, which had now taken on a golden sheen.

MIDAS: Don't you know what this means? I have can have all the gold—all the gold I desire! Imagine it! Golden floors! Golden walls! Golden everything!

NARRATOR: The king laid his hand upon the table, and it instantly transformed into gold.

MIDAS: Fantastic!

PLAUTUS: *(sarcastically)* Yeah, fantastic, but you're not the one who has to move it.

NARRATOR: He ran from object to object in the palace, touching it gleefully like a child. He whooped when each item assumed a golden shine. Plautus followed him about the palace, shaking his head in disbelief.

PLAUTUS: The cooks have set the table for dinner, Your Giddiness.

MIDAS: Don't be stupid! I can't think about food right now. There's so much gold to make!

PLAUTUS: But you'll want to keep your strength up. It's going to be a long night of gold-making!

MIDAS: Oh, fine. What a dumb kill-joy you are, Plautus. Can't you let an old king have a bit of fun?

NARRATOR: He jauntily pulled a chair up to the feast, grabbed an apple from the spread, and sank his teeth into it—or tried to.

MIDAS: *(cry of pain)* Ahhhhhh! My toof! My toof!

PLAUTUS: See? You've cursed yourself, you soft-headed old fool!

NARRATOR: Midas picked his tooth up from the table from where it had fallen and tenderly reinserted it into his gums.

MIDAS: No. Look. There. Good as new.

NARRATOR: He flashed Plautus a smile. A golden tooth gleamed out amid the others.

MIDAS: There's no problem at all. I don't need to feed myself anyway. *You* can feed me.

PLAUTUS: *(sarcastically)* What a pleasure, Your Freakishness.

MIDAS: Give me some of that wine.

NARRATOR: Plautus tipped the cup to the king's lips. No sooner had the king taken a swallow, then he fell from his chair and rolled about on the floor, grasping his throat in pain.

MIDAS: *(hoarsely)* Ahhhhhhh! My throat! My throat!

NARRATOR: Plautus looked down at the wine still left it in the cup. It was still liquid—yet gold in color and steaming.

PLAUTUS: Molten gold!

NARRATOR: The king continued to wail.

MIDAS: My bowels! My bowels!

NARRATOR: Several excruciating hours later, the molten gold had finally passed through the king's system.

MIDAS: This is all *your* fault, Plautus! You should have stopped me from making such a foolish wish!

PLAUTUS: Look at it this way: Who else can say that they have a golden kidney stone?

MIDAS: But now I'm going to starve to death!

PLAUTUS: You'll be the richest dead guy around.

MIDAS: You have to help me! There has to be a way to get rid of this curse!

NARRATOR: The slave pulled out his scroll once again and examined it.

PLAUTUS: Apparently, only the same god can remove a curse once it has been given.

MIDAS: What if Dio-what's-his-name won't return?

PLAUTUS: Then I suggest *not* picking your nose—or anything else for that matter.

NARRATOR: In a panic, Midas clamored up onto the table and peered down into the wine bowl.

MIDAS: Hello! Wine-god! It's me—Midas. I need your help once again.

NARRATOR: A chipper, female voice replied.

VOICE: We're sorry. Your plea for assistance is very important to us, but Dionysus is not available right now. If you would like to leave a message—

MIDAS: No! There has to be some way to undo this!

PLAUTUS: Don't you remember what Dionysus said when he cast the spell?

MIDAS: Hocus pocus something . . .

PLAUTUS: No, no! The last line! What was it? I remember! *The waters of swift Pactolus may undo it yet.*

MIDAS: Patroclus! Of course! The beloved friend of Achilles. But he's dead, isn't he? And what waters would *he* have, anyway?

PLAUTUS: Not *Patroclus*! *Pactolus*! It's a river. Don't they teach you kings geography? Maybe if you wash yourself in that river, you will lose the Golden Touch.

MIDAS: What? Wait a minute. Who said I wanted to *lose* it?

PLAUTUS: You can't be serious.

MIDAS: Maybe I could just have it on weekends. It's really actually useful at times.

PLAUTUS: Master, give it up.

MIDAS: Very well.

NARRATOR: So king and slave made preparation to journey upland to the River Pactolus. After mounting two different donkeys, which both immediately turned to gold, Midas decided that the best solution was to walk to the River Pactolus. The king and his slave made the journey easily on foot—leaving a trail of golden grass in their wake.

MIDAS: I wish I'd never met Diomedes and that stupid old goat-man. I wish I'd made a better wish.

PLAUTUS: There's the river, master. Wash in there, and we'll see if my theory is right.

MIDAS: Life's funny, you know. One minute you have the Golden Touch. The next minute you don't.

PLAUTUS: (*sarcastically*) Hilarious. Wash up.

NARRATOR: The king knelt by the swift waters.

MIDAS: (*nearly in tears*) Goodbye, obscene amounts of gold.

NARRATOR: Midas plunged his hand into the water, which began to bubble and foam around it. When he removed his hand, the bottom of the river was shining: the rocks below had all been turned to gold.

PLAUTUS: Now try it, master. Touch something.

NARRATOR: Midas touched his hand to the grass. Nothing. It stayed grass—regular green grass.

MIDAS: (*laughing*) Who knew that the sight of plain old grass could make a man so happy?

PLAUTUS: (*philosophically*) Perhaps, master, this will teach you a lesson: The wealth of the world is not in gold. It's in nature—the beauty that the gods have created—the trees, the rivers, the sky.

MIDAS: (*pausing to think*) No. It's pretty much gold. But thanks for trying to make me feel better.

PLAUTUS: (*sigh*)

NARRATOR: As soon as they turned to go, a sudden burst of pipe-playing erupted from a stand of nearby trees.

MIDAS: Oh no. Surely that's not old Selenium again, is it?

PLAUTUS: No. I don't think so. This music sounds *good*. Perhaps we should investigate.

MIDAS: Hmph. Just because you've cured me of my curse doesn't mean you're making all the decisions now. I'm still the master, and you're the slave.

PLAUTUS: Yes, master. So are we investigating or what?

MIDAS: If you think it's a good idea, sure.

NARRATOR: The king and his slave walked toward the sound of the magnificent pipe-playing. In the midst of the stand of trees, there was a satyr playing his reed pipes, and seated directly across was the golden form of a god.

MIDAS: It's them again! Run for it!

PLAUTUS: No, no.

NARRATOR: Plautus produced his scroll.

PLAUTUS: It's Pan, the god of shepherds, and Apollo, god of music.

MIDAS: Oh, celebrities! Which one's Apollo—the pretty boy or the goat man? (*loudly*) Yoo-hoo! Hello, immortals. It's me—King Midas. Perhaps you've heard of me? The Midas Touch?

NARRATOR: The immortals stopped their pipe-playing.

PAN: Mortal, we are happy to see you. We were just having a contest.

MIDAS: What kind of contest, pray tell?

APOLLO: (*sarcastically*) An archery contest. What does it look like? A pipe-playing contest, you moron.

MIDAS: Ah! Fascinating. And how can I assist you?

PAN: We're in need of a judge.

MIDAS: And you were hoping *I*, King Midas, might be able to find you one.

APOLLO: No, fool. We want *you* to be the judge. Now sit down and shut up while we play.

NARRATOR: The gods returned to their music.

MIDAS: (*whispering*) Well, that Apollo certainly is full of himself, isn't he? Pretty rude if you ask me. I have half a mind to choose the goat-legged fellow.

PLAUTUS: Master, you *would have* half a mind if you did that. Apollo would be furious.

MIDAS: Bah. He's all talk.

PLAUTUS: I've heard stories of his anger. He's pretty trigger-happy with his bow and arrows.

MIDAS: I'm not afraid of him. Besides, goat-breath is doing much better anyhow.

PLAUTUS: Apollo is the god of music! He's the master of all instruments!

MIDAS: Exactly. He needs to be brought down a peg or two. (*loudly*) Ahem! Gentlemen, please. There is no need to play any longer. I have made my decision.

NARRATOR: The immortals lowered their pipes expectantly.

APOLLO: Let me warn you, Midas, offending me would have grave conse—

MIDAS: (*proudly*) I choose Pam!

APOLLO: —quences.

PLAUTUS: (*whispering*) It's *Pan*. Oh, forget it.

APOLLO: (*angrily*) What? You can't be serious! You choose this mangy little goat-man over me?

PAN: Um. We actually prefer the term *satyr*.

MIDAS: (*cockily*) You heard me, golden boy!

APOLLO: You ignoramus! I'll show you how the gods punish fools!

NARRATOR: The fiery anger of Apollo blazed forth and the clearing flashed with light.

APOLLO: There! Now all the world will know what a complete donkey-brain you are!

NARRATOR: The god disappeared.

MIDAS: Zeus Almighty, you were right about his fiery temper. But I'm alive! He didn't strike me down or anything!

NARRATOR: The slave sadly guided Midas' hands up to either side of his head. Two long, bristly ears had sprouted there.

MIDAS: (*shocked*) No! It can't be!

PLAUTUS: I'm afraid so, master. Donkey ears.

MIDAS: Oh! Woe is me! Hee-haw! Hee-haw!

NARRATOR: Midas covered his mouth in shock. Pan approached the king apologetically.

PAN: Tough break, Midas. Look on the bright side. It's not the end of the world. I'm a little goat man, and even *I* can still scare up a date or two on the weekends.

NARRATOR: He bowed and frolicked away, trilling on his reed pipes.

MIDAS: We've got to hide this somehow. I'll be the laughingstock of the whole kingdom. Maybe if I wear a very tall hat. What do you think?

PLAUTUS: We could wrap them in a turban, I guess.

MIDAS: Perfect. Then no one will ever know—except you, and *you'll* never tell a living soul.

PLAUTUS: Wait a minute. Why shouldn't I?

MIDAS: Because you love your kindly old master? Who has never beaten you unless it was for a really good reason?

PLAUTUS: Ha! Give me my freedom. *Then* I swear I will never tell another living soul.

MIDAS: Your freedom? But Plautus! What would I do? You know I can't function without you!

PLAUTUS: I didn't say I was leaving. You can put me on your staff—complete with a salary and everything.

MIDAS: *(shocked)* A salary! Why you . . . *(pause)* All right. You'll have your precious freedom.

PLAUTUS: Excellent. Now if you'll excuse me, before we head back, I'd like to have one more look at that golden river.

MIDAS: Fine. Just hurry. I'm starting to attract flies.

NARRATOR: As he walked to the river, Plautus had to cover his mouth to suppress his laughter. His foolish master now had the ears of a donkey. How could he keep a piece of juicy gossip like this secret forever? But he would have to: His freedom depended on it. He reached the edge of the river and knelt down on its banks. He made a little hole in the Earth there and leaned his lips down to it. Into that hole he whispered the whole story—every last bit. He ended with the best part.

PLAUTUS: Midas has the ears of a donkey.

NARRATOR: After he had fed these words into the hole, he covered them over with dirt, stood, and returned to where Midas waited.

PLAUTUS: Back to Phrygia! First thing's first: We need to see a hatter. Otherwise, you'll look completely *asinine*.

MIDAS: How true! Hee-haw. Hee-haw.

NARRATOR: Plautus never told another living soul the story of his former master. Yet from the hole he had dug on the banks of the River Pactolus, there grew a cluster of reeds, and whenever the wind blew through their stems, they whispered his words. Those who journeyed to see the river with the golden bottom heard this story carried in the night air, and through this, Midas at last gained his long-desired fame—as the most foolish of kings.

DISCUSS

- In this type of story, where a wish is granted by a supernatural force, the wish rarely has the desired result. Why do you think this is so? What are these stories trying to say about wishing for things?
- The slave Plautus is not part of the original Midas story. What does he add to the narrative? Explain.

ANALYZE

Read the story "The Monkey's Paw," which involves three wishes. Compare its events with the events in the myth of Midas. Even though the tones of the stories may vary, are the themes the same?

FUN FACT

The transfer of Midas' gift from himself to the River Pactolus helped explain why the actual river, located in modern Turkey, contains high amounts of precious mineral deposits.

The Morals of Money

There would be several good candidates if the myth of Midas needed a tidy moral tacked onto its ending. (A *moral* is a lesson that the reader is supposed to learn from the story.) The moral, "The best things in life are free" immediately comes to mind. There are some things that money simply cannot buy, and Midas learns this lesson the hard way. When a person is deprived of food and water—the very necessities of life—wealth means nothing. In a different variation of the myth, Midas accidentally transforms his young daughter—the light of his life—into a golden statue. After this incident the king sees clearly that the love of his daughter was a treasure that cost nothing. This also symbolizes the way in which wealth often damages personal and family relationships instead of improving them.

"Money can't buy happiness." After Dionysus grants his wish, Midas discovers that his imagined happiness is everything but. When deprived of the things that money cannot buy, wealth loses its meaning. It may be a depressing thought, but even money cannot save a person from pain, suffering, and eventually death. In yet another version of the Midas myth, rather than finding a way to rid himself of the Golden Touch, Midas instead commits suicide. This shows us the lonely and depressing side of riches and celebrity. There is a reason that millionaires and celebrities—people who seem to have it all—still take their own lives or retreat into a drug-induced haze. Although millions of people want to be them, they still feel alone.

"The love of money is the root of all evil." (This quote from the New Testament is often misquoted as simply, "Money is the root of all evil.") Midas also learns that greed, often defined as the love of money, only brings him evil results. Although he is slow to learn from his mistakes, an unselfish, generous act—the freeing of his slave, Plautus—brings good from his actions. In life, many people believe that money will solve problems. They picture and plan how their lives would be improved if they received a large inheritance or won the lottery. But it is also important to remember that many times a great amount of money causes more problems than it solves. It is estimated that one-third of lottery winners go bankrupt a few short years after collecting their winnings. Many regret winning the lottery at all—as it separated them from their family and friends.

"Too much of a good thing can be bad." With all of this depressing talk about the dangers of money, it should be said that money is not always bad. It puts a roof over your head and food on the table. It provides comfort and security. It is the goal of many young people to grow up to earn a good salary, so that they can live their lives comfortably and securely. Yet some people forget that money is a means to an end and focus their ambitions on the money itself—not the good things that can be bought with it. The problem with this is that very few people actually have *enough* money. Money is something that you always need *more* of. Not that you cannot buy what you need, not that you do not have enough already, but there is always more to be had—bigger things, more expensive things. Focusing on money makes you forget the things you wanted it for in the first place.

In his myth, Midas experiences these lessons (and a few more). Although this version of the myth is told for laughs, it could have been a tragedy. As you begin your own adulthood, think of what role money will play in your future plans. Will it be a means to an end? Or the end itself?

DISCUSS

- Discuss the saying, "It's lonely at the top." Do you believe this is true? Explain.
- Can you think of any examples of celebrities who still seem to be unhappy?
- What role should money play in a person's life?

Wishful Thinking

According to some mythologists, myths act as a form of wish fulfillment. The real world is limited, but in the myth world, the possibilities are endless. Human beings are full of dreams and secret wishes, and sometimes the only way these dreams can come true is through storytelling. For example, who has not—at least once—imagined what it would be like to fly like a bird? The myth of "Daedalus and Icarus" allows us to (through imagination) have that experience. Have you ever daydreamed of being a famous warrior? The *Iliad* provides its readers with a full-blown fantasy world where they can step into the famous sandals of warriors like Achilles and Hector. The myth of the Golden Touch has literal wish-fulfillment when Dionysus gives Midas the chance to have anything he wants, an opportunity most of us dream of. On a more somber note, the myth of Orpheus provides us with a common *what if*: What if a loved one could be brought back from the dead? Mythologists disagree whether these wishes are consciously (on purpose) inserted into the myths or if they subconsciously leak in. Regardless, it is interesting to see that the hopes and desires of people who lived roughly 3,000 years ago are not too different from our own.

DISCUSS

- If you had one wish, what would *you* wish for? Explain.
- Can you think of another example where a myth acted as a form of wish-fulfillment? Explain your answer.

Slavery in Greece

Although the slave Plautus who appeared in this play has an element of comedy about him, slavery in ancient Greece was no laughing matter. Slavery was a booming business in the ancient world. Slave traders typically captured slaves by raiding villages in "barbarian" nations and brought them to Greece to sell in the city marketplaces. Sometimes slaves were obtained by one Greek city-state conquering another and hauling away its women and children, while the conquered men were held for ransom or killed. Job duties for house slaves involved all kinds of household chores, and certain slaves in wealthy households were educated in order to be tutors for the master's children. Slaves owned by the city-state worked in factories, rowed on war ships, or dug for materials in narrow mine shafts. Many slaves were given freedom in their masters' wills, while some even managed to save enough of their own money buy their freedom. Slaves became so abundant in Greece that even the very poorest of families would still have one or two slaves to do odd jobs about the house. The extremely wealthy would easily own a hundred.

May the Farce Be With You

Although the ancient Greeks and Romans loved their tragedy, they also enjoyed good comedy. At the all day play competitions Athens hosted in honor of Dionysus, each competing playwright presented a series of four plays: three tragedies and a satyr play. Satyr plays were raunchy parodies of famous myths that used a chorus of satyrs to narrate the action. After sitting through three tragedies at a time (how many suicides can you stand?), the audience needed a break! Comedies, which were performed at separate festivals, were crowd favorites as well. Although satyr plays were crude versions of myths, comedies poked fun at everyday city life or satirized elements of society. In one of his comedies, the playwright Aristophanes mocked his contemporary Socrates, a famous thinker who epitomized the Athenian philosopher, by presenting him as an old fool. This style of comedy, which satirized society in order to produce a social or political message, is called Old Comedy. But out with the old and in with the new!

The Greek playwright Menander (c. 342–291 BC) and the Roman playwright Plautus (c. 254–184 BC) helped define a type of comedy called New Comedy. Unlike Old Comedy, New Comedy went for easy-going laughs by using situational comedy and stereotypical characters. New Comedy plots were fast-moving and generated their humor through puns, wordplay, and dirty jokes. These plays used conventions like mistaken identity, long-lost sons and daughters, thwarted love, maidens in distress, coincidental meetings, and happily-ever-after endings that are very familiar to modern audiences. The playwrights pulled from a stock of stereotypical characters that were familiar to Greek and Roman audiences: the prostitute with the heart of gold, the rich and greedy old man, the self-centered fop, the grumpy father opposed to true love, the manly military man who is only in love with himself, the innocent and naïve young girl, the slimy low-life, the honest-yet-dimwitted boy, and the wily slave. Many of these conventions were used in Shakespeare's time (the Bard based some of his plots on those of Plautus) and even show up in comedies today. (The closest genre of modern comedy to New Comedy is the *farce*.)

The stock character that Plautus favored and perfected was the wily slave. In many of Plautus' plays his slave characters eventually get the better of their masters and earn their freedom. This conception of the slave delighted ancient audiences because it played against their worldview. The idea of a slave being the most intelligent character in a play was a hilarious twist. It was also a bit of subtle subversion on the part of Plautus because playwrights and actors spent their lives nearly as penniless as slaves. The character Plautus in this version of the myth of Midas was added to this story as an homage to the spirit of New Comedy.

Comedy has greatly progressed since ancient times, and there are new terms in use to describe modern comedy (which we should we call "*Really* New Comedy"). The three commonly used terms for comedies today are *farce*, *parody*, and *satire*.

Midas' story plays out like a *farce*, a story told with broad comedic strokes and a pace that quickens as the story goes along. Farces use physical humor (slapstick), wordplay, and unrealistic situations to get laughs. Most sitcoms (situational comedies) on television are *farcical*. A second kind of comedy, *parody*, mocks another (typically serious) story or type of story. In order for parody to work, the audience must be familiar with the source material to get much of the humor. Films like *Blazing Saddles*, *Spaceballs*, and *Robin Hood: Men in Tights* parody three different types of film: westerns, sci-fi adventures, and Robin Hood swashbucklers, respectively. Although farces and parodies are just for fun, *satire* aims to bring out a change of opinion in its viewer concerning some social or political problem. The humor in satire is usually deadpan or ironic like the television news show *The Colbert Report* and the novel *The Adventures of Huckleberry Finn.*

No matter which type of comedy you prefer (Old Comedy, New Comedy, Really New Comedy), it is important to know that comedy is an art—one that has been developing for thousands of years.

Sympathy for the Donkey

Animals often are used to illustrate human qualities, and for many centuries, across many cultures, the donkey (or the ass) has been associated with ignorance. In many of Aesop's fables, the Greek storyteller used the donkey, a beast who commits ridiculous acts and is continually outwitted by the other animals, to symbolize human stupidity. In the Roman writer Apuleius' *The Golden Ass*, the foolish main character is transformed into a donkey by a witch and spends the rest of the story stumbling from one predicament to another—barely escaping with his life. In imitation of this story, the 19th-century Italian writer Carlo Collodi caused his famous puppet Pinocchio to suffer a similar transformation for his naughty behavior. And the myth of Midas that you have read is yet another story that contributes to the *association* (pun intended).

So what is it about the donkey that makes it such an object of ridicule? Is it the beast's strange features—long snout, comical ears, and goofy teeth? Or is it the beast's association with being stubborn, lazy, and good for nothing? Maybe the donkey should be given a break. After all, there are plenty of dumb animals in the world. Why have various cultures singled out the donkey as the dumbest of the animals?

A God Is Born

When the gods produced children with mortal partners, these children were always demi-gods—more than human, but still mortal offspring. Dionysus, the god of the vine, was an exception. His conception

DISCUSS
- Can you think of examples of each type of comedy—farce, parody, and satire—from literature, music, or film? Explain why each fits the definition.

VIEW
View the film *A Funny Thing Happened on the Way to the Forum* (1966), directed by Richard Lester. The story is set in ancient Rome, and the plot draws heavily from the works of Plautus. The film gives a hilarious look at what ancient New Comedy was like.

DISCUSS
- Animals often become the symbols of human characteristics. For example, the owl (because of its association with the goddess Athena) is known for its wisdom. What are some other examples?
- Why do animals act as good symbols of humanity?

FUN FACT
The Spanish word for donkey is *burro*, which means that the true name of the Mexican delicacy *burrito* is "little donkey." It is speculated that the name originated from the fact that a burrito somewhat resembles a donkey's ear.

occurred in the typical way: Zeus was having an affair with a mortal princess—this time a girl named Semele. Hera found out about the affair, as she usually did, and decided to destroy the princess in her typical fashion. (Up until this point, the story of Dionysus is about like every other story of this kind.) The way that Hera destroyed Semele was particularly sly. She appeared to the princess disguised as the girl's old nursemaid and began to whisper doubts into the girl's ear about the identity of her Olympian lover: Who was this new lover she had? How could she really know that he was a god? Maybe he was a mortal who was just taking advantage of her. Semele swore that he was really Zeus, but nursemaid-Hera said that the princess should demand proof from him. If he truly loved her, he should appear to her as he appears to his wife Hera on Olympus. Then she would know for sure.

Semele decided to follow her nursemaid's advice. After all, the princess was carrying the god's child. She needed to know the true nature of the father. The only problem with her request was that mortal eyes are not meant to behold the gods in their true form. This, of course, was all part of Hera's plan. When Zeus came once again to visit his mortal love, Semele made him swear by the Styx that he would grant her any wish. Completely enamored with the girl, Zeus agreed, but when she made her request, he begged her to reconsider. The god had no choice but to comply. His human disguise fell away and from behind this blazed forth his true divine form. The sight incinerated the mortal girl, but as her body crumbled away to ash, Zeus snatched free the baby that he sensed growing in her womb. He quickly made a gash in his own thigh and sewed the baby up inside. There the greatest of gods carried the child for 3 more months until it was brought to term and then delivered it. That child was Dionysus. Because of his time spent in Zeus' thigh, Dionysus was born a god, not a mortal, and stands alone as the only Olympian god who can boast having a mortal parent.

I Heard It Through the Grapevine

Dionysus, the god of wine, was a late addition to the Olympian pantheon, not to mention a controversial one. In Greece, a new religion sprang up around Dionysus—one that incorporated strange rituals in the middle of the forest, excessive drinking, bizarre sacrifices, and sex. His most fanatic followers were female and were labeled *maenads* or "mad women," which described their behavior once under the influence of too much wine. It was considered dangerous to encounter these women in their Dionysian frenzy. Animals and sometimes children were torn apart and eaten for their rituals. Because of the bizarre and violent behavior associated with the worship of this god, his religion was banned in many parts of Greece.

The myths surrounding Dionysus show how his worship was originally persecuted in Greece, but eventually came to be accepted. Myths tell how the young god journeyed from one city-state to another showing his divinity and demanding worship from the ancient kings. One king, Pentheus, denied Dionysus most vehemently and even tried to kill the god. In punishment, Pentheus, while he wandered through the forest, came upon a maenad ritual, one in which the king's mother and aunts were participating. The maenads—their minds clouded by a vision from Dionysus—perceived Pentheus to be a wild animal and ripped him limb from limb. In another story, a band of pirates kidnapped Dionysus, thinking he was a mortal prince, and hauled him onto their ship to hold for ransom. They were shocked, however, when vines began to grow over their vessel and twist up the sails. Dionysus freed himself from his bonds and transformed the pirates into a pack of dolphins, which helplessly flopped over the side of the ship into the sea.

The original myth of Midas references Dionysus and mentions the bard Orpheus spreading the religion to Phrygia where Midas ruled. In other myths, instead of converting kings to Dionysus' religion, Orpheus was actually opposed to the worship of Dionysus, and for this reason he was murdered by a band of maenads.

Eventually, Dionysus reached Olympus, and the Greeks incorporated him into the complicated network of gods that made up their religion. (In Athens, Dionysus became the patron god of the city-state's greatest creation, drama.) The persecution of Dionysus shows us that the worship of each Greek god probably began as a separate cult that was gradually incorporated into a larger religion. Because Dionysus was the last god to be admitted to Olympus, his myths are the only ones that show a god struggling for acceptance.

The Gordian Knot

The family of Midas was not always a royal family. Gordius, Midas' father, actually became king thanks to a strange prophecy. It had been a time of trouble in Phrygia; the region was without a king. An oracle prophesied that peace would return when the elders of the city-state made a king out of a commoner. The "chosen one" should be the first man they saw driving an ox cart toward the Temple of Zeus. A man named Gordius happened to be doing just that. After being made king, Gordius dedicated his ox cart to Zeus. The oxen yoke and the pole of the cart were joined in a strange knot, to which only Gordius knew the secret. This cart remained on display for centuries after the death of both Gordius and Midas with the knot still tied, and eventually a legend developed concerning it: Whoever was crafty enough to untie the knot would become the lord of Asia.

When Alexander the Great began a quest to conquer the known world (including Asia), he made a visit to the famous knot. After he pondered its construction and tried to think of a way to untie the knot, the young king grew frustrated, pulled out his sword, and slashed through the knot. Needless to say, Alexander became the lord of Asia.

CHAPTER 8

Mind Over Matter

IN THE CAVE OF CYCLOPS

Cast

Odysseus *King of Ithaca*

Shipmate One *One of Odysseus' men*

Shipmate Two *One of Odysseus' men*

Shipmate Three *One of Odysseus' men*

Shipmate Four *One of Odysseus' men*

Polyphemus *Cyclops*

Cyclops One *Brother of Polyphemus*

Cyclops Two *Brother of Polyphemus*

NARRATOR: After many adventures at sea, Odysseus and his men had moored their ship near a strange island. High on the hillside they could see a huge cave-mouth gaping in the side of the cliff. Some kind of crude pen had been built around the level area before the cave-mouth. From this pen they heard the bleating of sheep.

SHIPMATE ONE: Odysseus! Sheep! Whoever lives in that cave must have mutton and milk—and maybe even cheese.

(murmuring from all of Odysseus' men)

NARRATOR: Odysseus stroked his beard shrewdly.

ODYSSEUS: True. But living alone on this desolate island wouldn't do much for a person's social skills. Whoever lives there might be hostile.

SHIPMATE TWO: But mutton! Think about it, Odysseus! Real mutton!

ODYSSEUS: It is definitely tempting. Where is the wine that Maron gave us?

NARRATOR: The men dug in the ship's provisions and produced a huge skin of wine, its top tied with a golden cord.

ODYSSEUS: All right. We'll go. We'll take Maron's wine to barter with. There's nothing like a little wine to encourage friendly relations.

(laughs from everyone)

ODYSSEUS: Only a few of you come with me. We don't all want to go. A crowd might scare this fool shepherd out of his mind. He's got to be lonely—living alone on this rock with nothing but his sheep.

NARRATOR: The men debated excitedly amongst themselves—excited at the prospect of mutton, milk, and cheese. Their argument resulted in a few shoves, but at last the men cast lots to decide. Then Odysseus led the 12 winners up the hillside toward the mysterious cave.

ODYSSEUS: *(shouting)* Hello! Is anyone here? We are men from Ithaca! Friends!

NARRATOR: Only the bleating of the penned sheep was heard. Odysseus and his men passed into the gigantic mouth of the cave. When their eyes adjusted to the dimness within, they discovered that the cave was very high-roofed indeed, but did not go further than a couple of hundred feet before it ended in a blank wall. They also saw two more pens, one filled with sheep, and the entire floor was covered with a soft, flaky layer of sheep dung.

SHIPMATE THREE: This man is quite a shepherd!

SHIPMATE ONE: *(shouting)* Odysseus! Cheese!

NARRATOR: Along the cave wall there were piles of cheese and the devices used in its making. The men rushed forward to partake of the cheese and the nearby jars of milk.

ODYSSEUS: Wait, men! We are not barbarians. We will ask our host's permission first.

SHIPMATE TWO: *(worried)* What if he says no?

ODYSSEUS: What kind of fool would say no? We are his guests. Does he want to anger the gods? Even out here in the middle of the sea, men must respect the gods. Now be patient. He will be back soon enough. See? This pen has no sheep in it. He must have taken them out to graze.

SHIPMATE THREE: But look at these cheeses! The frothy milk!

ODYSSEUS: Fine. Eat. Our host will not care once I've explained our situation.

NARRATOR: While his men threw themselves upon these delicacies, Odysseus began to examine the cavern more closely. There was something strange about it. Everything within it seemed large—large bowls, large jars, a large hide lay over one portion of the dung-covered floor.

ODYSSEUS: This shepherd must be an extremely large man.

SHIPMATE ONE: Odysseus! I have an idea. Let's drive these sheep to our ship and make our getaway before the master of this house comes home.

ODYSSEUS: Have you lost your pride? Have 10 years of war turned you all into barbarians? We're Greeks—not a bunch of mannerless pirates.

SHIPMATE TWO: *(talking through a mouthful of cheese)* Bup we've stowen befowe.

ODYSSEUS: Think, simpleton! If he has this many sheep, what a wealthy man he must be! And if we steal his sheep, will he be willing to give us a present?

(bleating of sheep)

ODYSSEUS: Shh! Be quiet. Here he comes now. As usual, let me do the talking.

NARRATOR: The sound of an approaching herd neared the cave's entrance. The men turned—their mouths dripping with milk and stuffed with cheese—and nearly choked in their terror.

A herd of sheep was pouring into the cave's entrance, but the shock was the sight of the shepherd towering above them. The creature, strong in limb and clad in a large fur like the one that lined the floor, had to duck to make it into the cave. When he beheld his visitors, the one large eye in the midst of his forehead blinked in confusion.

SHIPMATE ONE: *(whispering)* Gods help us! A Cyclops! We must run.

ODYSSEUS: *(sharply)* Whatever you do, don't panic. Let me handle this. Hospitality is on our side. We are his guests.

POLYPHEMUS: *(growling)* Little men, what are you doing in my cave?

NARRATOR: Odysseus looked up—acting as if he had not noticed the giant standing there—and smiled.

ODYSSEUS: Oh, dear me! Where did you come from, sir? You gave me quite a start. We are sailors, and we stopped here on your island. We were just enjoying your hospitality here.

POLYPHEMUS: *That* is not for you! It's mine!

NARRATOR: He pointed toward the cheese and the milk. Odysseus' men began to shyly move away from its vicinity.

POLYPHEMUS: What are you? Dirty little pirates?

NARRATOR: The men were shaking in their sandals, but Odysseus remained calm.

ODYSSEUS: Pirates? Of course, not. We're soldiers sailing home from Troy. Now we're here on your doorstep, begging your hospitality, hoping that you will honor the gods' wishes, and give us gifts and lodging.

NARRATOR: As Odysseus spoke, the Cyclops braced his body against a huge stone that stood beside the cave-mouth. With enormous force he rolled it over the entrance.

(rumbling of a huge boulder)

ODYSSEUS: Remember, sir, Zeus guards all guests. Strangers are sacred.

POLYPHEMUS: Stranger, you must be a fool to waltz into my cave and tell *me* to fear the gods! We Cyclopes never blink at Zeus or any other blessed god. We are mighty sons of Poseidon, and we have more strength than all of the gods put together.

NARRATOR: But then the Cyclops' tone seemed to change suddenly.

POLYPHEMUS: *(coyly)* But tell me, friend, where did you moor your ship? Up the coast a way or close by?

NARRATOR: Odysseus saw the clever trap laid within this question.

ODYSSEUS: Our ship? No, no. Poseidon smashed my ship upon the rocks at the head of this island. Now it lies at the bottom of the sea. Luckily, my men and I escaped the turbulent waters and washed up on your shore.

POLYPHEMUS: Hmmmm.

NARRATOR: Without warning, the Cyclops lunged out, grabbing one of Odysseus' men in each hand.

SHIPMATE TWO: Ahhhhhhhh!

SHIPMATE THREE: Noooooo!

NARRATOR: With terrible speed, the Cyclops smashed the men against the hard walls, knocking them dead like pups. Something red oozed out of their heads as he ripped loose their limbs and gobbled them up, piece by piece. No bit of them was left behind.

Odysseus' remaining men pressed themselves against the back wall of the cavern.

SHIPMATE ONE: Oh, Zeus, save us from this monster!

SHIPMATE FOUR: May the gods avenge our shipmates.

POLYPHEMUS: *(loud belch)*

NARRATOR: The Cyclops grabbed up a huge jar of milk and guzzled it—washing down the human flesh. Then he reclined upon his bed of sheep dung and fell fast asleep.

POLYPHEMUS: *(loud snoring)*

SHIPMATE ONE: Now's our chance, Odysseus! Let's plunge our swords into his unholy heart!

SHIPMATE FOUR: No, let's go for the liver.

NARRATOR: Some of the men drew their swords and advanced. Odysseus threw out a hand of warning.

ODYSSEUS: Hold, men! Bottle up your anger, and think! If we kill this monster, we will die too. Only he is strong enough to move the boulder that blocks the way.

SHIPMATE ONE: Then we are doomed.

ODYSSEUS: Have courage. A solution will present itself. Have I not gotten us out of tougher scrapes than this?

NARRATOR: Odysseus and his men huddled against the back wall of the cave and watched the giant slumber peacefully until morning. Odysseus spent the night turning plan after plan over in his mind.

When at last morning arrived, the Cyclops yawned, stretched as he rose, and began to milk his sheep. He did all of this without giving Odysseus and his men a second glance, as if he had somehow forgotten about their presence in his home. Yet when he had finished these chores, his hands flew out again and two more men met a horrible fate.

POLYPHEMUS: *(laughing)* What a fine meal you've provided me, strangers! I was growing sick of milk and cheese.

NARRATOR: Pushing back the boulder from the door, the Cyclops drove a group of his penned sheep into the sunlight. As he slid the rock back in place behind him, he jeered at the men.

POLYPHEMUS: See you at dinnertime, sweet-meats!

SHIPMATE ONE: Gods! We must find a way to kill that monster!

SHIPMATE FOUR: What should we do, Odysseus? How will we escape?

ODYSSEUS: Surely Athena will give me a plan. Her wisdom has never failed me before.

NARRATOR: Odysseus sat down to think. He scanned the cave for something—anything—that he could use to defeat the giant. There were the wicker baskets that the Cyclops used to make his cheese, the piles of sheep dung, the jars of milk. Only one thing held any promise: an enormous club the Cyclops had fashioned from a tree. It lay against the side of one of the sheep pens. Odysseus drew nearer to examine it.

SHIPMATE ONE: Will we use his club against him?

SHIPMATE FOUR: Don't be foolish. It's as big as a ship's mast.

ODYSSEUS: Quiet! I'm trying to think.

NARRATOR: Odysseus drew his sword and hacked at the club. Wood chips flew easily from it.

ODYSSEUS: Yes! This will work! Draw your swords and do exactly as I say.

NARRATOR: Under the instruction of Odysseus, the men hacked at the club, planing it down into a thinner pole—one that would be more easily lifted. Odysseus himself fashioned the end, sharpening it into a deadly point.

ODYSSEUS: Now, hoist it up, lads. We'll sear the end in the fire to make it good and hard.

NARRATOR: Working together, Odysseus and his men accomplished this.

SHIPMATE FOUR: Won't the Cyclops see what we've done when he comes home?

ODYSSEUS: That's why we're going to hide it. Bury it beneath the dung here on the floor.

NARRATOR: When this was done, Odysseus rose with a pair of dice in his hands.

ODYSSEUS: Now we cast lots—to see who will be brave enough to wield this weapon with me.

NARRATOR: The lots were cast, and Odysseus breathed a sigh of relief, for the men they fell to were the very ones he himself would have chosen.

Soon the grating of the boulder announced the return of the Cyclops. He drove in his whole herd this time and closed the entrance behind him. The cave was full of sheep. When he had once again performed his chores, he caught hold of two more of Odysseus' men and ripped them into edible chunks.

POLYPHEMUS: Tastier and tastier you strangers become. *(burp)* What is this?

NARRATOR: Odysseus was advancing toward him, holding one of his huge bowls filled with a strange, dark liquid.

POLYPHEMUS: What is that?

ODYSSEUS: Here, Cyclops. Try this wine. Top off your banquet of human flesh. Even if you do not honor the commands of the gods, we do. Here is a gift to you—as our host.

POLYPHEMUS: Wine, huh?

NARRATOR: The giant snatched the bowl from Odysseus' arm and slurped its contents. He greedily smacked his lips and flung the bowl back at Odysseus, who had to duck to miss it.

POLYPHEMUS: More! Give me a heartier helping this time.

NARRATOR: Odysseus' men rushed with the skin of wine to fulfill his request.

ODYSSEUS: Of course, Your Greediness.

NARRATOR: The Cyclops guzzled two more bowlfuls.

POLYPHEMUS: This *is* a gift!

NARRATOR: As he continued to drink, his eye grew dull and his words slurred.

POLYPHEMUS: *(drunk)* Tell me your name, friend. *(hiccup)* Where did you get this delightful nectar of the gods?

ODYSSEUS: My name? You ask me my name?

NARRATOR: Odysseus paused for showmanship.

ODYSSEUS: My name is Nobody. That's my name—Nobody. So my mother called me, my father, and all my friends.

POLYPHEMUS: A strange name, but you men from far away are strange. Here is my gift to you, Nobody. I will eat Nobody *last* of all of his friends.

ODYSSEUS: You are too kind.

NARRATOR: There was time for no more conversation, for the drunken Cyclops slumped over onto his side. When his head hit the floor, he vomited—wine with little bits of human inside. Odysseus and his men covered their noses from the stench of rotted flesh.

ODYSSEUS: (hissing) He's out! No time to lose!

NARRATOR: The chosen men uncovered the sharpened pole, and Odysseus directed them to hold it in the glowing coals of the fire again to make it sure it would sear completely. Then, hoisting it high, they timidly made their way toward the sleeping giant's head. His one eyelid flickered for a moment.

SHIPMATE ONE: (whimper)

ODYSSEUS: Courage!

NARRATOR: The eyelid closed again, and Odysseus urged the men forward.

ODYSSEUS: Drive fast and hard, men. When you feel it penetrate, run and hide. He may kill us all in his madness if we do not. (shouting) Now!

NARRATOR: The men drove the point forward. The Cyclops barely had enough time to open his one groggy eye before the stake rammed into it. The eyeball burst, blood came boiling from around the point, the roots of the eye crackled, and a sickening sizzling sound filled the air.

POLYPHEMUS: (loud roar) Arrrrrrrrrg!

ODYSSEUS: It's done! Flee!

NARRATOR: The giant wrenched the stake from his eye and flung it against the wall. One hand tore at his now-empty socket, while the other frantically swept the floor for his unseen enemies.

POLYPHEMUS: (growling) My eye! My eye! Nobody has done this to me! Nobody shall pay for this!

NARRATOR: As the Cyclops roared, running from side to side within the cave, groping madly about, Odysseus' men covered their mouths to suppress their laughter.

ODYSSEUS: Not a sound, you fools! He's still dangerous. We're not out of danger yet.

POLYPHEMUS: Nobody! Hear my words! You and your miserable man-creatures might have blinded me—but my brothers live on this island as well. And you cannot escape *their* sight! They will heed my cries. They will come to my aid and crush your bones.

NARRATOR: The Cyclops fumbled for the boulder and rolled it away from the entrance. Then, falling upon his hands and knees in the threshold, he began to bellow:

POLYPHEMUS: Help, brothers! Come to the aid of your brother Polyphemus!

NARRATOR: From the nearby hillsides voices answered.

CYCLOPS ONE: (distantly) What is the matter, Polyphemus? It's the middle of the night.

POLYPHEMUS: An enemy has attacked me, brothers! Avenge me!

CYCLOPS TWO: (distantly) Who has wronged you?

POLYPHEMUS: Nobody—Nobody has tricked me. Nobody has harmed me. Nobody has taken my eye.

CYCLOPS ONE: (annoyed) You're having a bad dream. Go back to sleep.

CYCLOPS TWO: Yes. If nobody has harmed you, you have nothing to worry about. (laughing) Stupid Polyphemus.

NARRATOR: Odysseus could not help but smile at the ingenuity of his trick.

POLYPHEMUS: Fools! Fine, I will deal with these man-creatures myself.

NARRATOR: The Cyclops sat firmly down, blocking the entrance. He extended his hands, blindly feeling either side of the cave mouth.

POLYPHEMUS: There is only one way in and out of this cave. You will have to crawl over me to escape. And when you attempt it, I will have you!

NARRATOR: Odysseus drew his men close to him.

ODYSSEUS: (whispering) I have a plan for our escape. He will have to let the sheep out in the morning to graze. He probably plans to feel them as they walk by—to make sure they are sheep and not men. Cut some fibers from those robes over there and help me bind these sheep together.

NARRATOR: The men, who knew better than to question the mind of Odysseus, rushed to comply.

(bleating of sheep)

POLYPHEMUS: Quiet, my little ones. No need to be frightened. Soon these filthy man-creatures will be dead. Yes, then Polyphemus will have quite a feast.

NARRATOR: Three sheep were placed side by side and then lashed together. Odysseus and his men performed this task time and time again.

ODYSSEUS: One man will hang under the middle sheep. Then when the monster runs his hands over their fleece, he will not feel you.

SHIPMATE ONE: But Odysseus, we have no more rope. There's not enough for your sheep.

NARRATOR: Odysseus turned to the nearby pen. Within was a large ram, the leader of the flock, covered in billows of fleece.

ODYSSEUS: I will ride this one.

NARRATOR: By the time the rosy fingers of the dawn appeared in the sky, the sheep were bleating frantically. It was time for them to feed.

POLYPHEMUS: All right! All right, little ones! Come forward.

NARRATOR: The Cyclops rose from his spot, and the sheep—each tied to two others and bearing a man beneath—made their way between the giant's legs. As they passed, he ran his hand along their fluffy coats.

POLYPHEMUS: There you are. Yes. Yes.

I feel my sheep. But where is the ram? Usually he leads the flock!

NARRATOR: Clinging beneath the aged ram, Odysseus began to sweat. His weight was slowing the ram's pace. At last he came beneath the shadow of the Cyclops, and the enormous hand descended.

POLYPHEMUS: Here you are, old friend.

NARRATOR: The hand pressed down and stopped the ram's advance.

POLYPHEMUS: Why such a slow pace? In the old days, you led the flock.

ODYSSEUS: *(quietly)* Please, Athena. Spare me.

POLYPHEMUS: Are you depressed by that filthy man-creature who has taken your master's eye? If only you could speak, my ram, and tell me where that traitor is hiding, I would spill his brains for sure. Aye, that would do my heart good.

NARRATOR: His grip loosened, and the old ram continued its rambling gait out into the sunlight.

Odysseus saw that all of his men were free of their sheep. One man was sprinting down the hill toward the cape where the ship was moored.

ODYSSEUS: Men, let's drive these sheep to our ship. We will get our guest-gift after all.

NARRATOR: Those men who had remained at the boat had feared the worst for their comrades and were thrilled to see Odysseus returning. Yet they were shocked to see how few of the original company returned. The sheep were driven onto the boat, and Odysseus at last took his place at the helm.

ODYSSEUS: Pull away from the shore! There's plenty of time to tell the tale once we're away! Shove off!

NARRATOR: The cave was visible up the hillside—the ridiculous form of Polyphemus hunching just inside. Odysseus could not resist one final jab.

ODYSSEUS: *(bellowing)* Cyclops! Foolish Cyclops!

POLYPHEMUS: What? Nobody? It can't be!

NARRATOR: Polyphemus ran out of the cave, craning his neck to hear the voice once again.

ODYSSEUS: *(shouting)* What a blind fool! You tried to eat us up, but we escaped you. Zeus and all the gods have paid you back for your crimes, you piece of filth!

POLYPHEMUS: Nobody!

ODYSSEUS: Not Nobody, you fool! If anyone asks who has blinded you—what tiny man was able to defeat the mighty Cyclops—tell them it was Odysseus: *Odysseus, son of Laertes, who did it! (laughing)*

POLYPHEMUS: Grrrrrrrrr.

NARRATOR: At the sound of Odysseus' true name, the Cyclops' fury boiled over. He realized he had been had. Ripping loose a nearby hilltop, the Cyclops flung it toward the faraway sound of Odysseus' voice.

SHIPMATE ONE: Row! Row! Incoming!

(gigantic splash)

NARRATOR: The hilltop hit close—too close—and the spray nearly knocked the men to the deck.

ODYSSEUS: Enough. Let's go!

NARRATOR: Polyphemus fell to his knees and scratched the flesh of his face with his ragged fingernails.

DISCUSS

- How does Odysseus' pride get the better of him?
- What is Odysseus' greatest weapon? Explain.

WRITE

Rewrite this encounter from the Cyclops' point of view. Give Polyphemus a chance to explain his actions.

POLYPHEMUS: Father Poseidon! God of the sea-blue mane! Master of the Earthquake, hear my cry! Odysseus has blinded me! If Polyphemus is truly your son, grant me my wish—never let Odysseus, son of Laertes, see his home again.

NARRATOR: The ground below the Cyclops began to shake—an underground cry of rage—and the seas around Odysseus' ship churned.

ODYSSEUS: *(quietly)* What have I done?

NARRATOR: Despite the foreboding these words brought to Odysseus' mind, he turned to comfort his men. No curse could stand between them and Ithaca. The ship sailed on, and soon the moaning of the Cyclops was lost among the sounds of the sea.

Creature Feature: Cyclopes

A Cyclops is a one-eyed giant whose title literally means "wheel eye." The Cyclopes (sy-klo-peez), which refers to more than one Cyclops, were the first children of Uranus (Father Heaven) and Gaea (Mother Earth). The parents, deeming the Cyclopes too hideous to ever see the light of day, chained them in the deepest part of the Underworld to rot for eternity and set out to create their second batch of children, the Titans. When the Titans gave birth to the gods, and the gods revolted against them, Zeus came to the rescue of the Cyclopes and freed them from their subterranean prison. In thanks, the Cyclopes fashioned Zeus an almighty weapon—the thunderbolt. They also created a trident (three-pronged spear) for Poseidon and a helmet of invisibility for Hades. With these weapons at their disposal, Zeus and the gods defeated the Titans and banished them into the depths of the Earth where the Cyclopes had once been kept. Polyphemus and his brothers are lesser creatures than the original Cyclopes and claim Poseidon the sea-god as their father. It has been theorized that the Greeks developed the concept of a one-eyed giant after discovering an elephant skull. The large central nasal cavity in the skull looks like an enormous eye socket.

Mind Over Matter

> Sing to me of the man, Muse, the man of twists and turns
> driven time and again off course, once he had plundered
> the hallowed heights of Troy.
> Many cities of me he saw and learned their minds,
> many pains he suffered, heartsick on the open sea,
> fighting to save his life and bring his comrades home.
> But he could not save them from disaster, hard as he strove . . .
> Launch out on his story, Muse, daughter of Zeus,
> start from where you will—sing for our time too.
> (Homer, 800 B.C./1996, p. 77)

These lines begin the *Odyssey*—a 12,110-line-long epic poem, a pillar of Western literature, and a nearly 3,000-year-old adventure story. Almost everyone has heard of the *Odyssey*, a work referenced everywhere from the Odyssey minivan, to James Joyce's novel *Ulysses* (Ulysses is Latin for Odysseus), to the common term *odyssey*, meaning a long journey. Although there are film adaptations, novelizations, and books like the one you are reading now that retell the *Odyssey*, the best way to experience the epic poem has been and always will be actually *reading* it. Unlike the *Iliad* (Homer's other epic poem about the Trojan War), which can drag in places, the *Odyssey* clips along at a brisk pace and reads more like a modern novel—never failing to entertain. The poet Homer, just as he captured the nature of war in the *Iliad*, perfectly captures the excitement of a magical sea voyage:

> Suddenly wind hit full and the canvas bellied out
> and a dark blue wave, foaming up at the bow,
> sang out loud and strong as the ship made way,
> skimming the whitecaps, cutting toward her goal. (Homer, 800
>   BC/1996, p. 106)

Like the other veterans of the Trojan War, Odysseus sets out homeward for Greece from Troy, yet unlike the others, he spends 10 long years lost on the seas, tossed this way and that by Poseidon, held captive by supernatural females, and constantly hampered by the foolishness of his men.

The Greeks who lived after Homer analyzed his two great poems in and out. Even though they highly prized the human intellect, wily Odysseus was not necessarily their favorite character. Achilles and the other heroes of the Trojan War received top billing, and although Odysseus was noted for his wisdom, some criticized him for being cowardly. After all, even the Greeks had to admit that sneaking out of a wooden horse and slaughtering sleeping Trojans was not a noble way to win a war. And whose idea was that? Odysseus'. In fact, it was the *Iliad*, not the *Odyssey*, that earned a central place in Greek society as *the* text that defined what it meant to be Greek. Great men quoted its lines, treated its characters as real historical figures, and lived their lives according to its values. Young men were expected to learn whole passages by heart and recite them on command. Alexander the Great even slept with a copy of the poem under his pillow. In contrast, the Greeks viewed the *Odyssey* as an entertaining fantasy, the lesser work of a great author, but not the same instructional manual for being a man that the *Iliad* was.

Over the centuries, both poems have remained popular, but in the modern world the *Odyssey* has nudged its way ahead of the *Iliad*. It may be that people's tastes have changed over time. The *Iliad* is all about war and death and glory; the *Odyssey* is about journeys, home, friendships, and family. Another possible reason for this preference change is the charm of Odysseus. Most people cannot easily identify with the *Iliad*'s protagonist Achilles, the world's greatest warrior whose nymph-mother dipped him in the River Styx to make him invincible. After all, we are normal, *vincible* people. We may *want* to be Achilles, but we are more like Odysseus. Odysseus is an *everyman*, an ordinary character, and we can also identify with his mission. He is not on a quest to slay a monster, conquer a kingdom, or find a treasure; he is a tired, middle-aged man who just wants to return home to his family.

Modern audiences enjoy an underdog story. Odysseus is somewhat short, not the strongest, not the fastest, and definitely not the richest (his home in Ithaca is a simple place), yet his mind proves to be his greatest asset. Homer describes Odysseus as the "man of twists and turns." There is no mythological character who puts his mind to better use than Odysseus. As you know, Odysseus' mind power triumphed over the Cyclops, a creature with more brute strength than you could shake a stick at (but maybe not "jam a stick into"). In a David-and-Goliath moment, Odysseus proves that the bigger they are, the harder they fall.

The War at Troy

It is important to know at least something about the *Iliad* and the Trojan War before reading the *Odyssey*. Because the war spanned 10 years, the abbreviated play-by-play below is a bare-bones outline of the conflict:

- While visiting Sparta in Greece, Prince Paris of Troy elopes back to his homeland with Helen (the most beautiful woman in the world).
- King Menelaus, Helen's husband, rallies all of the kings of Greece to cross the sea to Troy and get her back.
- During the war, Achilles is the greatest warrior for the Greeks, and Prince Hector (Paris' older brother) is the greatest warrior for the Trojans.
- The war rages for 9 years, and neither side gains a victory.
- Finally, Achilles challenges Hector to a duel and kills him.
- Shortly after, Prince Paris kills Achilles by shooting him in his only vulnerable spot, the heel. Paris is killed soon after.
- Odysseus and Ajax, Achilles' cousin, argue over who should get Achilles' amazing Hephaestus-made armor. Agamemnon, the commander of the united Greek army, decides that Odysseus should get it. Ajax is insulted and kills himself, but not before going insane and murdering a few cows.

- To end a war that still will not quit, Odysseus engineers the idea of the Trojan Horse.
- The Greeks pretend to sail away while Odysseus and a detachment of men hide inside the giant wooden horse that appears to be a tribute to the sea-god Poseidon.
- The Trojans discover the horse, take it for a god tribute, and wheel it inside the city so that it will bless them instead of the Greeks.
- The Greeks sneak out of the horse at night and completely annihilate the Trojans. Most of the royal family of Troy is murdered or taken into slavery. Helen is taken back to Greece by Menelaus.

Previously on the *Odyssey*: The Lotus Eaters

By the time Odysseus encounters Polyphemus the Cyclops, he and his men have already made it through several obstacles on their ill-fated journey home. (It will eventually take Odysseus 10 years to get home. That makes 20 total years he's been away: 10 at the Trojan War, 10 getting home.) One of these obstacles is the land of the Lotus Eaters, where all of the inhabitants eat of the intoxicating lotus plant and forget everything else.

Nine whole days
I was borne along by rough, deadly winds
on the fish-infested sea. Then on the tenth
our squadron reached the land of the Lotus-eaters,
people who eat the lotus, mellow fruit and flower.
We disembarked on the coast, drew water there
and crewmen snatched a meal by the swift ships.
Once we'd had our fill of food and drink I sent
a detail ahead, two picked men and a third, a runner,
to scout out who might live there—men like us perhaps,
who live on bread? So off they went and soon enough
they mingled among the natives, Lotus-eaters, Lotus-eaters
who had no notion of killing my companions, not at all,

they simply gave them the lotus to taste instead . . .
Any crewman who ate the lotus, the honey-sweet fruit,
lost all desire to send a message back, much less return,
their only wish to linger there with the Lotus-eaters,
grazing on lotus, all memory of the journey home
dissolved forever. (Homer, 800 BC/1996, p. 214)

The effect of the lotus flower is so addicting that Odyssey has to literally drag the men back to the ship and tie them to their rowing benches.

DISCUSS
• What could be a modern parallel for the Lotus flower? Explain.

Witchy Woman

There are only two witches in all of Greek mythology. You have already met one, Medea; the second was her aunt, Circe, the daughter of the sun. When a party of Odysseus' men go ashore on the island of Aeaea to scout for supplies, they discover Circe's house, a villa circled by tame wolves and lions. The beautiful witch greets them kindly and invites them in. Her nymph attendants offer the men food and drink, and while they drink their drugged drinks, Circe touches them each with her wand—transforming them into pigs. One suspicious man who did not enter Circe's house runs back to the boat to tell Odysseus what has happened.

Even though Odysseus has no idea how to save his men or keep himself from the same fate, he strikes out for the witch's house. On his way, the god Hermes appears to Odysseus and gives him a magical herb called moly that will protect him from Circe's transformative magic. When Odysseus arrives at the house of Circe, the witch greets him as she had previously greeted his men. A herd of swine has joined the tamed animals of the household. Circe offers him drink, which he takes, but before he drinks, he sprinkles the moly herb over it. The witch is amazed when Odysseus does not transform as she had expected. She is even more shocked when Odysseus draws his sword and threatens her with it. Realizing that the man before her must be beloved by the gods, the witch begs for mercy, promising to restore Odysseus' men to their rightful forms. Instead of leaving the island, Odysseus and his men decide to stay with Circe and her nymphs for a time. Odysseus chooses to become Circe's lover and remains on her island for almost a year.

DISCUSS
• If Odysseus truly desires to reach his home (and his wife), why does he choose to stay on Circe's island much longer than necessary?

MYTH-WORD
The word *circle* is closely related (according to some, derived from) Circe's name.

Dead Men *Do* Tell Tales

At last Odysseus and his men tire of the continuous feasting at Circe's house. Circe advises Odysseus that before continuing his journey, he must first sail to the border of the Underworld and consult the soul of Tiresias, a famed blind prophet. Following the witch's suggestion, Odysseus sails to the very edge of the world, and going ashore on the unearthly ground he finds there, he digs a trench and sacrifices a ram and a black ewe so that their blood fills it to the brim. Sensing the fresh blood of the animals, ghoulish figures appear on the horizon—souls from Hades—and crowd in close around Odysseus' offering. The silent spirits frighten the adventurer by pressing in so closely, and he swings his sword, warding them off from the blood until the soul of Tiresias arrives.

The blind prophet finally appears and comes forward to drink of the animal blood. Once he has done so, the soul of the prophet regains the power of speech. Tiresias tells Odysseus that he still has many more dangers ahead and will only reach his home when he regains Poseidon's favor. He also comforts Odysseus by telling him that he will not die upon the sea.

After his prophecy has been delivered, Tiresias fades away and many more familiar faces from Odysseus' past press forward and drink of the blood in order to tell their tales. The ghost of Agamemnon appears and tells his old friend how he died: The king had arrived home in Greece, only to be murdered by his wife and her lover. He tells Odysseus: "The time for trusting women's gone forever" (Homer, 800 BC/1996, p. 265).

Achilles is there, too, among the dead, and Odysseus hails his mournful spirit by praising the honor the warrior won in life.

> But you, Achilles,
> there's not a man in the world more blest than you—
> there never has been, never will be one.
> Time was, when you were alive, we [Greeks]
> honored you as a god, and now down here, I see,
> you lord it over the dead in all your power.
> So grieve no more at dying, great Achilles. (Homer, 800 BC/1996, p. 265)

Achilles does not agree with Odysseus' evaluation of his glorious life. It is better to be a slave and see the sun, the hero laments, than to be the greatest king in Hades. Achilles asks Odysseus pressing questions about his elderly father, Peleus, and his son, whom he never had a chance to see grow up. "Oh to arrive at father's house—the man I was," the spirit of Achilles mourns, "for one brief day" (Homer, 800 BC/1996, p. 265). The warrior Ajax is there, too, behind his cousin Achilles. Odysseus tries to hail him, but Ajax refuses to speak. He still holds a grudge against Odysseus over Achilles' armor.

The most shocking ghost Odysseus encounters is that of his mother, Anticlea, who has recently died of grief over her son's absence. She tells Odysseus that his wife Penelope still waits for him and has not taken another husband. Three times Odysseus desperately tries to embrace his mother.

> Three times I rushed toward her, desperate to hold her,
> three times she fluttered through my fingers, sifting away
> like a shadow, dissolving like a dream . . . (Homer, 800 BC/1996, p. 256)

Heartbroken and disturbed after conversing with many famous souls, Odysseus returns to his ship and sails back to Circe. The witch sets a course for him: He must first make it past the dreaded sirens, creatures whose song is irresistible. These creatures—whom no man has seen and lived to tell about—lure sailors to their island, never to return. To save Odysseus and his crew from this fate, Circe instructs Odysseus to plug the men's ears with beeswax. The witch gives Odysseus further instructions about the obstacles he will face after the Sirens and sends him and his men on their way.

DISCUSS
- What does Odysseus' adventure in the land of the dead have to say about the Greek afterlife? Explain.
- Why does Achilles regret his short but glorious life? What lesson is Homer trying to teach by this? Explain.

The Sirens

> Now with a sharp sword I sliced an ample wheel of beeswax
> down into pieces, kneaded them in my two strong hands
> and the wax soon grew soft, worked by my strength
> and Helios' burning rays, the sun at high noon,
> and I stopped the ears of my comrades one by one.
> They bound me hand and foot in the tight ship—
> erect at the mast-block, lashed by ropes to the mast—
> and rowed and churned the whitecaps stroke on stroke.
> We were just offshore as far as a man's shout can carry,
> scudding close, when the Sirens sensed at once a ship
> was racing past and burst into their high, thrilling song:
> "Come closer, famous Odysseus—[Greece]'s pride and glory—

moor your ship on our coast so you can hear our song!
Never has any sailor passed our shores in his black craft
until he has heard our honeyed voices pouring from our lips,
and once he hears to his heart's content sails on, a wiser man.
We know all the pains that the Greeks and Trojans once endured
on the spreading plain of Troy when the gods willed it so—
all that comes to pass on the fertile earth, we know it all!"
So they sent their ravishing voices out across the air
and the heart inside me throbbed to listen longer.
I signaled the crew with frowns to set me free—
they flung themselves at the oars and rowed on harder.
Perimedes and Eurylochus springing up at once
to bind me faster with rope on chafing rope.
But once we'd left the Sirens fading in our wake,
once we could hear their song no more, their urgent call—
my steadfast crew was quick to remove the wax I'd used
to seal their ears and loosed the bonds that lashed me. (Homer, 800
  BC/1996, p. 276-277)

DISCUSS
- Why does Odysseus leave his own ears unplugged?
- How is the test of the Sirens similar to the test of the Lotus Eaters?

ANALYZE

Homer does not describe the Sirens' appearance, but later myth-makers described them as half-woman, half-bird creatures similar to the Harpies. Others said they were mermaid-like creatures. (In every case they were described as female.) How do you picture the Sirens? Is it more or less effective to leave their appearance ambiguous? Explain.

MYTH-WORD

Our word *siren* is derived from these mythological creature. In contrast to the mythic sirens, most modern sirens serve as a warning instead of bait for a trap and use a "song" that is shrill and loud instead of melodic.

Between a Rock and a Hard Place

Before the traveler leaves the witch's isle, Circe warns Odysseus of a treacherous strait he must navigate. Two monsters live in this narrow seaway. Three times a day, a gigantic underwater monster, Charybdis, opens its gullet, sucking the surrounding waters into the vortex of its mouth. When the terrifying whirlpool subsides, Charybdis then sprays the consumed water high into the heavens, destroying whatever has fallen into its clutches. If a ship keeps close to the rocky edge of the strait in order to avoid Charybdis, it faces another monster named Scylla, a creature with six dog-faced, snake-necked heads, who picks sailors off the passing ships as an easy snack. Those who pass through the

DISCUSS

- Is it fair that Odysseus did not warn his men about the danger of Scylla?

FUN FACT

According to another myth, it was actually the sorceress Circe who was responsible for creating a monster out of Scylla, who had once been a beautiful maiden. Circe grew jealous of Scylla's beauty and transformed the girl into a hideous beast.

MYTH-WORD

"Between Scylla and Charybdis" is a saying that refers to a challenging situation where there are two possible solutions and neither one is pleasant. This saying is similar to "between a rock and a hard place."

strait must choose between the twin terrors—between Scylla and Charybdis.

Odysseus sets sail. He and his men soon approach the strait that houses Scylla and Charybdis. They hear the roar of the whirlpool far away. Odysseus warns his men to row close to the shore. Although he plans to tell them of the threat of Scylla, he realizes that this would only terrify them further, so he keeps this knowledge to himself. The whirlpool monster appears ahead, sucking the sea down into its belly. The crew rows hard to shore, keeping the craft as close to the rocks as possible, avoiding the swirl of the current. As they do, Odysseus keeps his eyes on the cliffs overhead. He knows Scylla is lurking there. Perhaps they will escape her notice.

At that moment Scylla strikes. Six rowers disappear from their posts in the same instant. The crew, covered with their comrades' blood, stare helplessly as the six terrifying heads of Scylla swallow her captives down raw, barely chewing with her razor sharp teeth. "Row! Row!" Odysseus yells. "Before the monster takes us all!" With one final burst of speed, the ship passes through the strait—beyond the reach of Scylla and Charybdis—and out of danger.

Where's the Beef?

Circe had warned Odysseus that if he did in fact make it past the strait of Scylla and Charybdis, he would come to the isle of Helios, her father. Odysseus and his men should not harm the cattle they find there, for these were Helios' cattle. If Odysseus and his men harmed them in any way, the gods would take revenge.

Once Odysseus and his men are through the perilous strait, the island of Helios comes into view. Odysseus knows they should simply sail on by, but his men beg him to stop. They are hungry and exhausted from the day's work. He reluctantly agrees with a warning: "Do not touch the golden cattle of this land."

His men obey, and they camp on the island for the night. In the morning they find the winds blowing against them. Many days pass in this way; the wind continues to blow against their port, and they cannot sail. Supplies grow short, and Odysseus' men begin to hungrily eye the shining cattle that graze on the nearby hillside. When Odysseus goes into the hills one day to call out to the gods, the men snap: They slaughter the cattle of Helios and cook their golden meat. Even on the spit, the cattle continue to moo, and the cuts shine as the men gulp them down. When

Odysseus returns and sees what has been done, he knows they are all doomed.

Soon enough the winds stop, and the ship takes to sea, yet they do not sail far before a raging storm overtakes them. Helios has informed Zeus about the death of his cattle. As the black clouds boil overhead, the Lord of the Gods himself aims a thunderbolt at Odysseus' tiny craft. In a spray of planks and salt water, the ship is destroyed. Men fly into the brine. Only Odysseus survives—clinging to the single surviving piece of his vessel.

Pleasure Island

Shipwrecked and wave-tossed, Odysseus washes up on the beaches of Ogygia, the island of a "lovely-braided" sea nymph named Calypso. Enamored by the handsome mortal, Calypso takes Odysseus prisoner and keeps him as her lover for 7 years.

> In the nights, true,
> he'd sleep with [Calypso] in the arching cave—he had no choice—
> unwilling lover alongside lover all too willing . . .
> But all his days he'd sit on the rocks and beaches,
> wrenching his heart with sobs and groans and anguish (Homer, 800
>   BC/1996, p. 157)

Even though Odysseus is living out a deserted-island fantasy with a beautiful female, he misses his wife, son, and home. At last the goddess Athena, Odysseus' Olympian ally, appeals to her father Zeus for Odysseus to be freed from the nymph's island and allowed to at last return home. Zeus agrees and sends Hermes to deliver the unpleasant news to Calypso: "Release him at once . . . steer clear of the rage of Zeus! Or down the years he'll fume and make your life a hell." (Homer, 800 BC/1996, p. 156). The nymph responds indignantly, stressing the irony of the situation:

> Hard-hearted
> you are, you gods! You unrivaled lords of jealousy—
> scandalized when goddesses sleep with mortals,
> openly, even when one has made the man her husband . . .
> You gods, you train your spite on *me*
> for keeping a mortal man beside me. The man I saved,

DISCUSS
- Do Odysseus' men deserve to die?

ANALYZE

In a previous episode of the *Odyssey*, Odysseus and his men visit King Aeolus, an earthly king to whom Zeus has given the power of controlling the winds. As a present, King Aeolus traps into a bag all of the winds of the world—except one, the wind that will blow Odysseus and his men directly back to Ithaca. Odysseus keeps the bag of wind a secret from his men. They are almost back to Ithaca when Odysseus' men steal the bag while he sleeps and, thinking that it must be filled with treasure, open it. All of the violent winds of the world are released in a fit of tornadic fury, and the ship is blown far off course. How is this episode similar to that with the cattle of Helios?

riding astride his keel-board, all alone . . .
And I welcomed him warmly, cherished him, even vowed
to make the man immortal, ageless, all his days . . .
But since there is no way for another god to thwart
the will of storming Zeus and make it come to nothing,
let the man go—if the Almighty insists, commands—
and destroy himself in the barren salt sea! (Homer, 800 BC/1996, p.
156)

DISCUSS
- Calypso offers Odysseus everything some men would ever want. The fact that Odysseus leaves her behind tells us what about him?
- Why does Odysseus choose *not* to be immortal?

Calypso recognizes the double standard at work here; the male gods of Olympus can take lovers, even ruin their lives, but when the female deities do so, they are rebuked and their love destroyed. In spite of her indignation, she honors the will of Zeus. Odysseus at once begins work on a new ship, and when it is completed, leaves his immortal lover (and his own chance of immortality) behind.

Polyphemus: The Horrible Host

To the Greeks, one of the most shocking things about the Cyclops Polyphemus is the fact that he was such a horrible host! It seems strange, but the Greeks held the obligations of a host to be most sacred. In the Greek religious system where there *weren't* many laws to live by, "Thou Shalt Be a Good Host and Guest" was one of the few commandments. Zeus himself commanded it, and plenty of Greek myths tell about the horrors that befall those who murder or dishonor their guests. It was the duty of every host to give anyone, even complete strangers, a good meal, a warm bed, and in some cases, a guest-gift. In a time when there were no inns and many people traveled the roads on foot, this type of law ensured the safety of the traveler. If hosts violated their duties or guests dishonored their hosts, then they risked the wrath of Olympus. (So you can imagine how much wrath *eating* your guests would stir up!)

Part of Odysseus' cleverness is that he defeats the Cyclops by performing his half of the guest-host relationship. Odysseus offers Polyphemus the strong wine as a return gift, a thanks-for-the-hospitality gift that guests often gave their hosts (even though the monster has given them nothing but cruelty). Polyphemus doesn't catch on, and the Greeks—like us—feel no pity for him when he gets a red-hot stick jammed in his eye. He got what was coming to him for being such a horrible host.

In the next chapter, you will read about another violation of the sacred Greek host-guest relationship. The *Odyssey* shifts from Odysseus and his men to show what is happening to Penelope and Telemachus, his wife and son, in his absence. A group of suitors have shown up to Ithaca, Odysseus' island kingdom. All of them want the hand of Queen Penelope—or more accurately, they want control of Ithaca. Everyone believes that Odysseus is dead, but Penelope holds onto the hope that he lives. To ward off the suitors, Penelope makes excuse after excuse. In the meantime, she must honor the host-guest tradition and provide them with lodging and food. The suitors, a bunch of impolite thugs, take advantage of her hospitality and basically hold the Ithacan household hostage. In contrast to Polyphemus, who was a horrible host, these suitors are violating the guest end of the bargain by their actions. Like the Cyclops, they *may* get what is coming to them, but you will just have to wait and see . . .

CHAPTER 9

Fathers and Sons

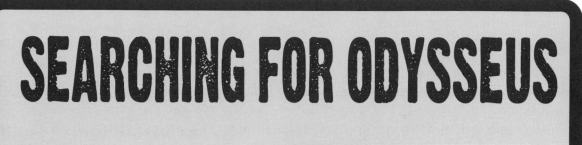

SEARCHING FOR ODYSSEUS

Cast

Telemachus *Son of Odysseus, prince of Ithaca*

Penelope *Wife of Odysseus*

Antinous *Suitor to Penelope*

Eurymachus *Suitor to Penelope*

Menelaus *King of Sparta*

Odysseus *Famous adventurer*

Helen *Queen of Sparta*

Athena *Goddess of wisdom*

Nestor *Wise old king of Pylos*

Pisistratus *Son of Nestor*

NARRATOR: I am Telemachus. These days all of the bards have their favorite song—a song about a man who spent 10 years at sea, trying to get home. I'm mentioned in the song. I have quite a big part in it actually. But the true star is Odysseus, as always.

People have always said to me, *It must be amazing to have a father like Odysseus!* They, of course, are talking about his amazing adventures. They know nothing of the man himself. And for much of my life, the man was even a mystery to me.

Odysseus left for the Great War at Troy long before I was old enough to remember him. My mother said he wasn't a tall man. She said that he wasn't the strongest or the fastest, but he *was* clever. I remember she used to say:

PENELOPE: Telemachus, my son, if there is a man who could find his way home from Troy, it is your father. Athena has always loved his crafty mind. She will guide him home safely.

NARRATOR: Growing up, this gave me hope, and when I was 10 years old, the first news of Greek victory reached us. Troy had fallen. The united kings of Greece had won

the war. Odysseus would soon return, or so we thought. But as the tides brought many ships home filled with fathers—none came for me.

PENELOPE: Continue to watch the seas, Telemachus. Above all things, your father is faithful.

NARRATOR: As weeks turned into months and yawned into years, I guess my innocence melted away. I had to face facts. Despite what mother said, Odysseus *wasn't* coming home, and it would be me—only me—in charge of our island kingdom, Ithaca. Mother never showed despair in front of me, though I could see it there in the rims of her eyes.

PENELOPE: Telemachus, I worry about you, my son. Why do you not make friends? Why do you not chase the girls as other boys do? Drink deep. These are your carefree days.

TELEMACHUS: We must face realities, Mother. Odysseus is not coming home.

PENELOPE: Telemachus! He is *father* to you.

TELEMACHUS: Father? I never even knew the man. He is a stranger to me.

PENELOPE: He knows *you*, Telemachus. He will return to us—no matter what. He is faithful. He is faithful.

TELEMACHUS: Are you telling me that? Or yourself?

NARRATOR: A distraction from our long wait of grief came soon enough. Vultures descended. A herd of young nobles from the surrounding islands—108 to be exact—came knocking on our door. They were suitors for my mother's hand, but only in name. They only lusted for the crown she represented.

ANTINOUS: Odysseus is dead, my lady! It is time you marry again.

PENELOPE: Not dead, good sir. Only delayed. Because my husband is still living, I cannot remarry. But I welcome you to await his return here at Ithaca in our humble halls.

NARRATOR: The suitors smiled at my mother's polite offer. So they moved into our halls, eating our food, killing our livestock, guzzling our wine, and romancing our serving wenches. It wouldn't take long for delicate Queen Penelope to break, snap under the pressure of rudeness. They were rough men. They were cruel men. They were pigs. Mother was a woman. I was just a boy. We were at their mercy. Years came and went. I was 17 . . . then 18 . . . then 19. Even though the suitors made a game of depleting our resources, they tired of mother's tricks and refusals. But even though she managed to evade their advances, each day without Odysseus eroded away a bit of her resolve, like a wave impacting upon the beach.

ANTINOUS: The King of Ithaca is dead! Choose a new king from among us!

NARRATOR: I was nearing manhood. The suitors knew, as the rightful heir, I was growing dangerous. This was their last offer of "peace" before they risked open war. Mother saw this as well.

PENELOPE: I will choose . . .

EURYMACHUS: Yes! Finally!

PENELOPE: *(continuing)* As soon as I have woven a shroud for my father-in-law, Laertes.

EURYMACHUS: What?

PENELOPE: The years lie heavily upon him. I must finish his shroud before death reaches him. Surely you understand.

NARRATOR: How could they understand? They were practically barbarians.

ANTINOUS: *(shrewdly)* Fine! Let her weave for the old coot. How long could it take?

EURYMACHUS: Hopefully not longer than the wine holds out! *(laugh)*

NARRATOR: This would be her final diversion. Her last-ditch evasion. Mother took to her loom. In her weaving, she put the image of the sea, and Odysseus' ship tossed upon it. Even in all her despair, a thread of hope still survived.

I could not explain it, and I know it must have been some trick, but though she sewed for the span of each day, her tapestry was never completed. Each morning there was more work to be done, and the suitors' ambitions were thwarted for yet another day.

TELEMACHUS: Mother! What will happen when your weaving is completed? Will you really marry one of those . . . those . . . pigs?

PENELOPE: To keep you safe, my son, I would do anything. But your father will return first though. I feel it.

TELEMACHUS: I cannot stand it. These men eat up our food, drink up our wine, and lie with our women. They have turned our noble home into a brothel. We still have friends in our own household, don't we? Let me drive these suitors from our home!

PENELOPE: Friends? Telemachus, we have no friends. Only a few here at Ithaca remain loyal to us. All of the others have been bribed or frightened into corruption.

TELEMACHUS: Then I will go to get help elsewhere!

PENELOPE: Yes, go! But if you go, do not return. Do not return until your father has come home and made Ithaca safe again.

NARRATOR: I intended to leave and return with an army. Odysseus had many friends among the other kings of

Greece. Surely there would be one who would help me. But a goddess found me first.

An old sailor came to our hall, his head bare and his beard a grizzled mess. His skin was burnt and swollen by endless hours beneath the sun. That was his outward appearance at least. His eyes were gray. How many sailors have you seen with gray eyes? I knew it was Athena at once.

Those who later told the story said that Telemachus had no idea he was in the presence of a goddess. Odysseus could always see through her disguises, but Telemachus—dumb Telemachus—never the match of Odysseus—was completely fooled. I *allowed* Athena to play her little trick.

ATHENA: *(old man voice)* Young man. I am an old sailor, Mentes, a friend of Lord Odysseus for many years. I seek the hospitality of your hall.

NARRATOR: The gods always think they're so clever—poking their noses into everyone's business.

TELEMACHUS: You come at the wrong time, old man. This hall has given all the hospitality it can. My mother, the queen Penelope, has been made a prisoner in her own home.

NARRATOR: I filled "Mentes the sailor" in on the entire situation—how the suitors had crawled out of every surrounding hole-in-the-wall island and converged on Ithaca. It was all a farce, really. Here was a teenage boy telling information that his listener already knew to a goddess acting out a disguise that the boy had immediately seen through. We were both playing our respective parts.

ATHENA: *(angrily)* I've known Odysseus forever! He wouldn't dare stand for this!

TELEMACHUS: Odysseus is not here, old man. His bones lie out in the waves somewhere, I imagine.

ATHENA: *(strangely)* No! No! I know that he is alive. It must be some prophecy that the gods have placed in my brain, but I know that he is alive. Someone—or something—holds him captive across the wine-dark sea. But he will return.

NARRATOR: I stared into her gray goddess eyes.

TELEMACHUS: If *you* say so, my friend, then I will believe it.

ATHENA: *(happily)* So you are Telemachus! My, how you have grown! I see much of your father in you.

TELEMACHUS: *(bitter laugh)* Mother has always told me that Odysseus was my father. But who in this world ever truly knows who gives him life? My friends call me lucky—to be the son of such a famous father. I say the lucky ones are those who see their fathers grow old in the midst of their possessions. I must be the most unlucky son who ever lived.

NARRATOR: It was then that something in her voice changed. Even a fool could have heard the difference.

ATHENA: *(angrily)* Unlucky? Whose blood flows through your veins? Your father would not give up so easily, Telemachus! You are no longer a whining boy! You're a man! Send these suitors packing! Gather them together and *command* them to leave!

TELEMACHUS: They will only refuse. I know it.

ATHENA: Of course they will, but they will also see how close you are to becoming a man—a dangerous man. Then, after you have delivered your message, take a crew of trusted sailors and seek elsewhere for news of your father.

TELEMACHUS: Just leave my mother behind?

ATHENA: Yes, Telemachus.

TELEMACHUS: Where should I go?

ATHENA: At Pylos seek out King Nestor. He was one of your father's greatest friends. Then travel to Sparta and speak with King Menelaus. Between the two of them, you just might hear word of your storm-tossed father.

TELEMACHUS: *(shrewdly)* Tell me, sailor, what gives you such clairvoyance?

NARRATOR: The gray eyes flashed, and the shape of the sailor melted away. The goddess winged herself away, transformed into a high-flying owl.

TELEMACHUS: *(laughs)* The gods are definitely a dramatic lot.

NARRATOR: The bards always say that at this point, I was beside myself with wonder. I had been in the presence of a goddess all along! Stupid Telemachus.

I returned to the common hall, where the suitors had set up their never-ending feast. It stunk like overspiced food, unmixed wine, and sex—the three vices of men.

TELEMACHUS: (angrily) Suitors! Neighbors! Men of the surrounding isles! I am Telemachus, the son of Odysseus, ruler of Ithaca.

NARRATOR: The drunken slobs turned. Some hung limply in the arms of the serving wenches. Some disrespectfully continued their feasting.

TELEMACHUS: Too long have you haunted my mother's hall. I command that you leave this palace. Surely Odysseus is dead, but *I* am his heir, and Ithaca is mine.

NARRATOR: The two ringleaders, a couple of boars called Antinous and Eurymachus, began to howl with laughter.

EURYMACHUS: (drunkenly) And if we don't, what's a limp-wristed creampuff like you going to do about it?

ANTINOUS: (fake respect) We follow the will of the *gods*, boy! You have no authority here!

EURYMACHUS: Yeah! (hiccup)

TELEMACHUS: (violently) The gods? For your rudeness here, I pray that the gods strike you down!

NARRATOR: This sobered them a bit. They had never seen such strong words from me.

TELEMACHUS: My mother is an honorable woman, and you—

ANTINOUS: (growling) Your *mother* is a *harlot*, boy! A deceiver! Don't you know what's she's been up to?

EURYMACHUS: (yelling) Tricked us! Tricked us all!

(shouts of approval from the suitors)

ANTINOUS: Silence! She's had no intention of completing that shroud she's been weaving. Every night she's been pulling loose her day's work.

EURYMACHUS: The lying wench!

ANTINOUS: Learn to hold your wine! (to Telemachus) Her very own maids ratted her out. Even *they* were appalled by her deceit.

NARRATOR: That was a laugh. The maids of Ithaca had become more like prostitutes.

ANTINOUS: Now she's caught! And she *will* marry one of us. Her excuses are done.

NARRATOR: I could only sneer as they returned to their revelry.

My part had been played. I had taken my stand and proved powerless. It was time to begin my journey.

Old Eurycleia, my nurse and Odysseus' nurse before me, was the only one I told of my plan. She poured unmixed wine into jars and sewed up bags of barley for my voyage and kissed me upon the forehead before I left.

By the sea, a ship and crew was already waiting (Athena's doing, I later discovered) and standing nobly beside the beached vessel was Mentor, Odysseus' right-hand man. When Odysseus had left for Troy, he placed Mentor in charge of Ithaca and, consequently, in charge of me. There stood Mentor now to be my guide.

Or so it seemed. Once again, it was *not quite* Mentor. His sea-gray eyes gave him away.

ATHENA: (man voice) Few sons are the equals of their fathers. Many fall short. Too few surpass them. But in you, Telemachus, I see Odysseus' cunning.

NARRATOR: And so we took to sea, Athena-Mentor at my side. We steered a course toward Pylos, home of Nestor, oldest and wisest king of Greece.

I thought of Odysseus. If what Athena had said was true, what force could be powerful enough to keep him away from his family and his home? Or perhaps we only *thought* that he wanted to be home. Perhaps he preferred the adventure of the open sea to home and hearth.

We found Nestor in his palace, and I thought he must be one of the deathless gods. The man had reigned over his people for three generations of men and still his eyes blazed with youthful glory. A banquet was in progress, and he welcomed us to it, even without formal introductions.

ATHENA: *(whispering)* When the time is right, Telemachus, ask of Nestor your question. Remember: He is far too wise to lie.

TELEMACHUS: *(whispering)* What should I say? I've never spoken in front of a king!

ATHENA: Your father would find the words. *You* must do the same.

TELEMACHUS: But I'm *not* Odysseus. Why does everyone keep assuming . . . ?

NESTOR: *(addressing Telemachus)* Tell me, young traveler, what brings you to sandy Pylos?

NARRATOR: I rose, practically shaking with terror.

TELEMACHUS: *(grandly)* Noble Nestor, I have heard many tales of your wisdom—a man who has lorded over many men. I see in this hall many of your noble sons. I'm sure your heart swells with pride when you behold them. I have come to your hall seeking not a son, but a father, Odysseus—I believe you know him well.

NARRATOR: The old king stared at me, impressed.

NESTOR: Never before have I heard a young man speak in such a way! So much grace! I believe I see your father in you, my boy. I see his majesty—his majestic demeanor. Are you not the son of Odysseus?

TELEMACHUS: You have guessed it, my lord.

NARRATOR: I told Nestor of the suitors and the plight of my mother. He fumed with indignation, yet when the conversation turned to Odysseus, he could offer me little news.

NESTOR: Odysseus was one of my dearest friends. After the fall of Troy, the Greek kings departed those shores in separate groups. One left swiftly behind the flagship of Menelaus, while the other tarried behind with Agamemnon. I was in the first group, and the last I saw of your father was on the beaches of Troy.

TELEMACHUS: Can you tell me no more?

NESTOR: King Menelaus is whom you should seek. Perhaps he has heard more news than I.

TELEMACHUS: But you said he left the same time as you.

NESTOR: He did, but we were foolish to depart without the blessing of the gods! So hasty were we to return home with the spoils of Troy! In anger, the gods cursed Menelaus. He wandered a full 7 years upon the sea with his golden bride. Agamemnon, who stayed behind to make all of the proper sacrifices, received a swift trip home to Mycenae. Unfortunately, only death waited for him there.

TELEMACHUS: Agamemnon is dead?

NESTOR: Struck down by his wife's lover. I thought all of Greece had heard of the murder of its greatest king. Queen Clytemnestra took Agamemnon's cousin Aegisthus into her bed shortly after her husband's departure, and together they hatched a plan to seize his throne.

TELEMACHUS: What would drive a wife to do such a thing?

ATHENA: The murder of a loving daughter.

NESTOR: Your friend speaks truth. With Menelaus lost at sea, it fell to Orestes, son of Agamemnon, to avenge his father's murder. He did so. He put the lover and his very own mother to the sword. It took determination! You, my boy, should strive to be such a son!

NARRATOR: The old man's eyes became soft.

NESTOR: I remember your father before the Great War. I've never seen a man more content. He loved his Ithaca and his Penelope. I remember him holding you lovingly in his arms before he left—vowing to return. If any man would wish to return home, it would be he. I hope he still lives.

NARRATOR: Though I did not will them, tears beaded in the corners of my eyes. I wiped them angrily away.

ATHENA: *(grandly)* Then the course is clear: Go to Menelaus, Telemachus. He will give you the information you seek. Farewell!

NARRATOR: The gray-eyed Mentor rose, and his robe melted into a covering of feathers. Athena once again winged herself away—to the shock of all present.

NESTOR: *(in shock)* By the gods! My boy! You are truly favored to have a goddess as your companion!

NARRATOR: Nestor and his sons stared at one another in shock over Athena's circus trick. The bards say that even the second time, I fell for Athena's disguise. Stupid, gullible Telemachus.

NESTOR: *(laughing)* Even with my long years, I have never seen such a sight! Telemachus, tonight you will sleep here at the palace. Tomorrow I will have my son Pisistratus take you by chariot to Sparta. *(laughing to himself)* By the gods! What a night!

NARRATOR: Pisistratus was a nice enough fellow—the kind of young man who gains his identity from his heritage. He wanted to know everything about Odysseus. What first gave him the idea for the Trojan Horse? How did he cultivate such an enormous intellect? What would it be like to have the bards sing of you in your own lifetime?

I spent most of our chariot ride from Pylos to Sparta silent. How did I know? I honestly had no answers for him. He was asking the wrong person.

As Nestor's palace at Pylos had dwarfed the hall of Ithaca, Lacedaemon, the fortress of Menelaus, dwarfed the latter. Crowds of people thronged through the streets. *(cheering of a crowd)* Pisistratus stated the obvious:

PISISTRATUS: Must be some kind of celebration.

NARRATOR: We were admitted to the palace, where an enormous feast was being held. Because of our noble bearing and some haughty words from Pisistratus, we were admitted into the royal banquet hall without question. There I beheld the red-haired king himself, Menelaus.

MENELAUS: *(happily)* What splendid young men! The guards told me two boys had arrived who looked like the gods themselves! I must say they weren't exaggerating!

PISISTRATUS: What is this happy occasion?

MENELAUS: *(laughing)* Today, my daughter has been wed! Have a seat! Feast with us!

NARRATOR: He whisked us to a seat among the revelers, promising to soon return. He was beside himself with duties on such a special day.

PISISTRATUS: Father told me of this marriage. Hermione, the daughter of Menelaus and Helen, was given to Pyrrhus, the son of Achilles. A good match, I say.

TELEMACHUS: Any daughter of Helen must be a jewel among women.

PISISTRATUS: I saw her once. She's fair enough, I guess. Father will make a better match for me—I'm sure of it.

NARRATOR: The noon feast began to give way to the evening feast, and at last Menelaus appeared at their side, winded and somewhat drunk.

MENELAUS: A wedding! There's nothing like it! Now tell me, lads, where do you hail from?

PISISTRATUS: I am Pisistratus, the son of Nestor, and this is Telemachus, son of . . .

MENELAUS: *(in shock)* Odysseus! Of course! How did I not see it before?

NARRATOR: Pisistratus looked away in annoyance. Odysseus' name always seemed to get a bigger reaction.

MENELAUS: Slave, fetch Queen Helen! Clear away these guests. We wish to speak privately with our special guests.

NARRATOR: Menelaus eyed me like a beggar who had found a pearl.

MENELAUS: My boy, what a pleasure! To meet the son of Odysseus! I have never met a finer man!

TELEMACHUS: That is why I have come to you. I hope one day to meet him myself.

MENELAUS: Oh yes. *I* had my own troubles reaching home, which I shall tell you shortly, but first allow me to introduce my wife. Perhaps you have heard of her? Helen of Sparta.

NARRATOR: As many men claim, after setting eyes on Helen of Troy, or Sparta, or wherever, it is impossible to describe exactly how she looked. Long after our encounter with her, I had to hear Pisistratus stammer over himself trying to describe her features, contradicting himself until he finally resorted to one word: *beautiful*.

HELEN: Yes, my dear. Helen of *Sparta*. How nice it sounds! Who are our young guests?

MENELAUS: These are mighty princes, my dear. The son of Nestor and the son of Odysseus.

NARRATOR: Her eyes locked onto mine. There's a certain feeling you get when you lock eyes with Helen: a kind of worthlessness. You realize how unworthy you are of such a woman. Of course, that just makes you want her all the more.

HELEN: I see that. I remember your father well, my boy. Before the fall of the Troy, he snuck into the city disguised as an old beggar man, scouting out the best way to lay the Greeks' trap. As the daughter of a god, I could see through his disguise, of course, but I raised no alarm. No, when I saw him and how sharp his mind was—that great Greek mind—I grew homesick. I know what you are thinking: Yes, I, Helen the one who started a war for her own shameless lust. Whore that I am, I missed Greece. Aphrodite's spell had held me for 10 long years, and its magic at last grew thin. I yearned to sail back home—be reunited with the husband and the daughter I had left behind.

NARRATOR: She took her husband's hand.

HELEN: Thanks to Odysseus, I saw reason.

MENELAUS: But Odysseus has still not returned to Ithaca, my dear.

HELEN: No? How unfortunate. Did we not hear news of him?

MENELAUS: We did. After we left Troy, Telemachus, the winds of the gods blew us far off course, all the way to the shores of Egypt. There we languished in exile. We knew that some god was holding us there until we repented . . .

HELEN: Tell him of Proteus, dear.

MENELAUS: I was just coming to that, my sweet. Proteus, the Old Man of the Sea, a creature who has the ability to assume the shape of any creature, was rumored to

appear on those shores. He—a god himself—would be able to tell us how to return to Sparta.

Not far from where we were moored, Proteus came up out of the belly of the ocean each morning to sun himself upon a rock. I knew in order to get Proteus to tell me what I wished, I must wrestle him. He would change from form to form, trying to loosen my grip. If I held on until the bitter end, I could ask him any question, and he would be forced to answer.

NARRATOR: Menelaus and Helen continued to tell their story like a couple of newlyweds, interrupting and laughing. Who would have thought this was a man and his adulterous wife?

HELEN: *(proudly)* And so my noble husband hid himself upon the rock, and when the Old Man of the Sea came out of the depths, Menelaus jumped upon him, and the two wrestled fiercely.

MENELAUS: It was no easy contest! He transformed himself into a lion, a serpent, a leopard, and a pig!

PISISTRATUS: *(excited)* Fantastic!

HELEN: He even assumed the shape of a swift-flowing stream!

MENELAUS: It almost drowned me to hold on!

HELEN: Then Proteus grew into a tall tree! But there was Menelaus clinging fiercely to his highest branches!

MENELAUS: I held on! That was his final form, and his shape-shifting stopped! Then I asked my questions of him. He told me the path to get home, how to make amends with the gods I had offended. I asked after my brother, Agamemnon, and Proteus told me of his death. He also mentioned a Greek king who was lost at sea: your father.

NARRATOR: Finally, the news I had been waiting for.

TELEMACHUS: What did he tell you?

MENELAUS: Proteus said that your father had been a prisoner for many years on the island of Calypso, the sea nymph.

NARRATOR: That night in Menelaus' palace I fought sleep. All these years, all these waiting years, we had thought

Odysseus was dead. But in reality he was the prisoner of a nymph? It seemed too far-fetched to believe. For all his cunning, Odysseus could not escape that? Or maybe he didn't want to escape. Perhaps he had found a mate he loved more than his Penelope—or even me.

We stayed in Sparta for weeks. Pisistratus loved rubbing elbows with the likes of Menelaus and Helen, but I was restless. Menelaus' news held little hope for me or my mother.

One morning, I woke, and a gray-eyed woman was standing over me. She wore glistening armor, and an owl perched on her shoulder. Finally, the goddess and I were past disguises.

ATHENA: *(booming)* Telemachus, return to Ithaca at once. I have beseeched Zeus to free your father. Hermes has gone to the isle of the sea nymph Calypso and commanded her to release him. Your father is on his way home even as we speak.

NARRATOR: Very well, I told myself. I guess I will finally meet this man. This Odysseus. But first some questions for him and his divine helper.

TELEMACHUS: Lady Athena. I openly admit that you are wiser than I, but I must ask why? What was the point of this? This wild-goose chase across the sea? Why didn't you just tell me what I need to know?

NARRATOR: The goddess smiled sweetly.

ATHENA: Oh, Telemachus. Nothing in this life is ever simple. Your whole life you've lived with a space where a father once fit. You've tried to fill that space with many things: despair, anger, even hatred. Now your father is coming home. *Odysseus* is coming home. Don't you wish to know this noble man whom the mightiest kings of Earth praise? Don't you wish to know the man who brought Troy to its knees? The man who could make fickle Helen dream of home? Don't you wish to see the man that other men see in you?

TELEMACHUS: *(surprised)* I do.

ATHENA: Then your quest is complete. Hurry home. A father is waiting.

NARRATOR: Menelaus offered me passage home, and Athena instructed me not to return to the palace at Ithaca, but to seek out the hut of the swineherd Eumaeus. Eumaeus was always a loyal servant. He smelled a bit, of course, but he was always loyal.

When I found Eumaeus' dwelling, he had company. Some dirty old man sat in the corner of his hut, running his hands through the pig droppings. Eumaeus was eager to help me, so I sent him on to the palace to tell my mother that I had returned safely.

After he had gone, I experienced yet another miraculous transformation. The old man in the corner seemed to shift, his wrinkles dissipating, his spine straightening, his eyes growing brighter—eyes that some said could resemble mine.

ODYSSEUS: *(emotionally)* My son!

NARRATOR: I had always wondered what would happen when we finally met. Would we clasp hands? Embrace? Would it be the awkward meeting of two strangers? But it was just the opposite. He held me in his arms—as he had 20 years before—and cried tears of happiness upon my head.

Odysseus and I spent hours talking. He told me of his whole journey: the Cyclops, Scylla, Charybdis, the mystical song of the Sirens that only he had heard. I could only sit there like an enchanted 5-year-old and listen to the amazing story of his voyage.

As he spoke, I was there with him—in Troy, on Circe's isle, on Calypso's island, on the very edge of the Underworld.

ODYSSEUS: But tell me of how it goes here, my son. *(laughing)* My son! How great it is to speak those words!

NARRATOR: I told him of the suitors, of mother's tricks. When I spoke of her tapestry, his proud smile told me everything. His affairs with Circe and Calypso may have satisfied his body, but never his heart.

ODYSSEUS: There is not a finer woman under the sun than Penelope! Now listen, my son, we must form a plan!

NARRATOR: It was amazing to watch the man's mind in action. Ten years of wandering had only strengthened his wits. Odysseus would disguise himself as a beggar and make his appearance at the court of Ithaca. I would go to mother, tell her of my quest, but offer her no hope of Odysseus' return.

ODYSSEUS: Penelope must not know that I live! The shock would be too great for her to conceal!

NARRATOR: With Odysseus hidden within the court, I would remove the weapons from the palace storeroom. Then, when the time was right, we would strike and end the suitors' lives.

The plan worked perfectly. My return caused quite a stir among the suitors. They were more determined than ever to destroy me. Mother nearly melted when I told her that neither Menelaus nor Nestor offered any hope of Odysseus' return.

PENELOPE: *(weakly)* He *is* faithful.

NARRATOR: Not too long afterward, Odysseus made his entrance. A shaggy shock of hair and a tangled beard covered his face. He'd smeared himself in the dung of swine and hobbled like a hunchback. The suitors instantly made him the butt of their jokes—kicking and jibing at him, forcing him to dance for their merriment. Mother took pity on him, of course.

How strange to see their first glimpse of each other after 20 years! Odysseus didn't miss a beat and acted his part. Mother never had a clue. A weaker man would have never had such patience, but Odysseus did. The only unexpected twist in our plan came from mother.

PENELOPE: Men of the surrounding isles! Lords who desire my hand! I have reached a decision. Before he left, Odysseus commanded me—In his absence—to select a mate when Telemachus had reached manhood. Because it seems that my husband will never return, I have decided to chose from among you.

NARRATOR: At first I thought she would ruin everything.

PENELOPE: Because I refuse to wed a man who is not the measure of my husband, I will only marry one who can string the bow of Odysseus and shoot an arrow through 12 axe rings.

NARRATOR: Clever mother.

The bow was brought forth—a rough and hardened weapon, nearly inflexible. In all of my days I had never seen it strung. Of course, as with everything to do with Odysseus, there was a trick to it. The 12 axes were driven into the floor, their rings lined up perfectly. The contest was ready.

EURYMACHUS: Back, you dogs! I'll try it first!

ANTINOUS: I'm next.

NARRATOR: The 108 suitors fell over one another to have their chance. They grunted and tugged until the veins bulged out in their foreheads. Try as they might, none of them could pull the string tight enough to secure it. Even I had my turn. If I proved myself here, there might be an end to the contest. I struggled against the hardened weapon, but it was no use. I was not Odysseus. After all had tried and tired, the cracked voice of the beggar was heard.

ODYSSEUS: *(old man voice)* I'll have a try.

(loud jeers and laughing)

NARRATOR: How they howled at him! And I had to chuckle as well. Here was Odysseus' final trick. As the beggar stepped forward to try the bow, I moved silently and bolted the door to the hall.

EURYMACHUS: *(howling with laughter)* Look at this fool!

(laughter from the suitors)

NARRATOR: The beggar took the bow into his gnarled hands. He placed one end beneath his foot and began to slowly bend the bow as he pulled the string-loop upward. The suitors stopped laughing.

ODYSSEUS: *(regular voice)* You see, gentlemen. Things are not always as they appear. You thought that *I* was an old beggar, but nothing could be further from the truth.

NARRATOR: The beggar—who now looked nothing like a beggar—turned, bow and arrow and man. He took the axe rings into his sights and let the shaft fly. It clipped neatly through all 12 rings.

(gasping from everyone)

NARRATOR: My mother covered her shaking mouth.

ODYSSEUS: Hmmm. Appearances can be deceitful. A fine lesson for any man to learn.

EURYMACHUS: *(screaming)* It's Odysseus! Zeus preserve us!

NARRATOR: The next arrow of Odysseus found its mark in Antinous' throat.

ANTINOUS: *(hacking and gurgling)*

ODYSSEUS: A lesson, gentlemen—that you will not live long enough to use. *(cries of panic)*

NARRATOR: I unsheathed my own sword and stepped between the fleeing suitors and the bolted door. And then Odysseus and I slaughtered them—*just like pigs*.

After the carnage was done, we cleansed the household. Those who had remained faithful to Odysseus were spared. The others found their necks noosed and stretched. The 10 treacherous maids of the household met their fate this way, as well as many devious servants.

When the episode had ended, and Odysseus and mother had wept in each other's arms, and Eurycleia, the old nurse, had wept over Odysseus and then wept over me, Odysseus turned, placed his firm hand upon my shoulder, and said these words like he'd journeyed 10 years just to say them:

ODYSSEUS: I'm proud of you, my boy.

NARRATOR: I grinned, ear to ear.

TELEMACHUS: Thank you, Father.

DISCUSS

- With Telemachus acting as the narrator, what can you tell about his character? What kind of tone does he use when he narrates?
- What was the purpose of Telemachus' voyage? What did it add to the *Odyssey*?
- Telemachus' portion of the *Odyssey* can be viewed as a coming-of-age story where a young character matures during the course of events. Can you think of any other coming-of-age stories in literature or film?

MYTH-WORD

Mentor, the man whose identity Athena takes as she leads Telemachus on his voyage, gives us the term *mentor*, which we use to mean "a counselor or guide." The term *monitor*, which means one who watches, is closely related to *mentor* as well.

VIEW

- View *The Odyssey* (1997), directed by Andrei Konchalovsky, a television miniseries adaptation of Homer's poem. What changes have been made to the original story? Do these changes help or hurt the story? Explain.
- View the film *O, Brother, Where Art Thou?* (2000), directed by the Coen brothers. Which episodes from the *Odyssey* can you pick out in this film?

RESEARCH

- Interview a friend of one of your parents. What does this person have to say about your parent? Did this help you see a different side of your parent?
- Research an earlier part of your parent or guardian's life. Does this help you understand him or her better?

ANALYZE

The meaning of Odysseus' name is connected to a Greek verb that means "to cause suffering." Some have said Odysseus means "much suffering" or even trouble. How does Odysseus cause suffering or trouble to those he encounters on his journey? How does Odysseus himself suffer on his journey?

Identity

Identity is a theme that runs throughout the *Odyssey*. Many times Odysseus changes his identity to play a trick. The goddess Athena changes her identity several times to instruct the characters. Telemachus is a young man trying to establish his identity through his father. Odysseus uses a fake identity or name to fool the Cyclops, then foolishly reveals his true identity. Penelope asks Odysseus to prove his identity twice: first by shooting an arrow through 12 axe rings, and then by knowing the secret of the bed they shared 20 years before.

DISCUSS
- What are some other instances of identity being important to the story?
- What does Odysseus discover about his identity on his journey home?
- What does Telemachus discover about his identity through his own adventure?

Fathers and Sons

The Greeks myth-makers understood that the relationship between a father and son is an important one, and the lack of a father figure can affect a person's destiny. So many sons in Greek mythology are the sons of famous (yet absent) fathers. (More often than not these missing fathers are the gods themselves.) Most of these young men try to fill the void left by their fathers—some seek a reunion with the father, while others journey on a quest to prove (either to their father or themselves) that they truly are their fathers' sons.

In one myth, a young man named Phaethon has lived his whole life as the son of a single mother. Finally, nearing the brink of manhood, he discovers the true identity of his father: Helios, the god of the sun. Phaethon sets out at once. His destination—the radiant palace at the far end of the world, where Helios, the chariot driver of the sun, comes to rest his fiery horses every night. Phaethon's quest is to prove once and for all that Helios is truly his father.

Once Phaethon reaches his father's palace, their reunion starts off well; the god is both proud and overjoyed that his son has sought him out. Even though Helios verifies that Phaethon is indeed his son, the boy is not satisfied. His whole life he has been teased and picked on because of his lack of a father. Now he is desperate to prove that he has one—and an immortal one at that. He asks Helios to grant him any wish. After all, it is the least the god could do after being a deadbeat dad for 18 years. Helios swears by the Styx to honor any request, but is soon horror-stricken at his son's request. Phaethon asks to drive the chariot of the sun. In spite of his father's extremely convincing warnings, Phaethon stubbornly refuses to back down, and Helios can do nothing but stand by and let his son destroy himself.

Needless to say, Phaethon's chariot ride does not go well. The boy is ill-equipped to handle the fiery horses—he is no god—and the team runs amok. First the chariot lunges too high, bumping the stars, and then plummets too low, causing the sea to boil. It swings low over the region of Sahara and reduces its lush vegetation to scorched earth—as it is still. At last Zeus sees that the world will be destroyed if this reckless chariot driver is not stopped. He aims a thunderbolt at Phaethon and lets it fly. We can only wonder what goes through Phaethon's mind as he plummets down to Earth—blazing like a falling star. Maybe he thinks of his friends, who would definitely believe that he is the son of the sun now. Maybe he is thinking of the shame he brought to his newfound father or the mother he would never see again. Maybe he is only wishing he would have never known his father at all.

Phaethon illustrates a maxim that is spoken by the goddess Athena in the *Odyssey*. "Few sons are the equals of their fathers," she says. "Most fall short, all too few surpass them" (Homer, 800 BC/1996, p. 102). She is speaking to Telemachus, the teenage son of Odysseus, who has vowed to go on a search for his father. The young man barely knows who he is looking for. After all, his father left Ithaca for the Trojan War when he was only an infant. What he does know is that he has lived in the man's shadow his whole life. Like some sons would, he resents being compared to someone he has never met. From an early age, Telemachus has taken on the job of man of the house. His father is missing and presumed dead, his grandfather is nearly mad with grief, and a band of bullying lords have moved into his household and taken over.

All of the other fathers have long ago returned from Troy. It has been years without word from Odysseus. Telemachus' mother, Penelope, hangs onto the hope that Odysseus has been delayed. But Telemachus is starting to doubt. How can you trust someone you have never met? Telemachus sets out on his own journey—partially to find out news of his father and partially to discover exactly who the man is.

The *Telemachiad*, the portion of the *Odyssey* that deals with Telemachus' journey, is often glossed over. Granted, it is not nearly as exciting as the episodes with Odysseus—what could compete with the blinding of the Cyclops?—but Homer thought it important enough to include it in his poem, so it must serve a purpose. Some experts have suggested that the *Telemachiad* is one of Homer's great displays of genius: When we begin the *Odyssey*, we have the same questions as Telemachus: Exactly who is this Odysseus? Why is he so important? And where the heck is he? These are the questions that Telemachus' journey answers, and as we ride alongside him, we learn alongside him as well. By the time that Telemachus returns to Ithaca after visiting Nestor and Agamemnon, we have learned what we need to know and our appetites are whetted—we want to begin Odysseus' part of the story, and that is what we get. The scene shifts to Odysseus and gives him a chance to tell *his* story thus far.

During his journey, Telemachus matures as he discovers what his father means to other people and realizes the hardships that he must have suffered. Before Telemachus sets out, he even questions whether or not Odysseus is really his father. By the time Telemachus returns, he is willing and ready to accept his father and also to forgive him for his 20 years of absence. It is not until the end of the poem that Telemachus and Odysseus are reunited, and it is a moment worth waiting for. In the squalid hut of Eumaeus the swine-herder, father finds son and son finds father. And it is exactly what both have been searching for.

Homer Is a *Her*?

There is a great deal of mystery surrounding Homer, the poet who probably lived around 800 B.C. and has his name attached to two epics, the *Iliad* and the *Odyssey*. So much, in fact, that the mystery even has its own name: the Homeric Question. The question turns out to be many questions rolled into one. Here are just a few: Was Homer a real person? Was Homer just one person? Was Homer male or female? Did Homer write both the *Iliad* and the *Odyssey*? When were the poems written and for what purpose?

These epics originated from an oral tradition where poets chanted thousands of lines of poetry from memory before a live audience. (Whether Homer was actually literate and able to write the *Iliad* and the *Odyssey* down, or if he dictated it to someone else is another debate.) These bards, who must have had enormous memories, and an uncanny knack for ad-libbing when the need arose, traveled from one royal court to another performing their songs. In Book 8 of the *Odyssey*, Odysseus listens as one of these bards, a blind poet named Demodocus, sings about the destruction of Troy. The poet's talent is so great that it moves Odysseus to tears. For centuries, readers assumed that this episode was Homer inserting *himself* into his story, and this assumption led to the tradition that Homer was a blind poet.

Another debate concerning the two poems is whether or not they are composed by the same author. The name *Homer* is connected with both, but in ancient times authorship was sketchy at best, with artists

DISCUSS
- Is the bond between father and son important? Explain.
- How is Phaethon's quest for his father similar to Telemachus'? How is it different?
- Analyze another father-son relationship from Greek mythology. How is it similar to or different from that of Odysseus and Telemachus?

WRITE
Write a short piece about your father or a father figure in your life. How important is this person to you?

ANALYZE
Athena's quote, "Few sons are the equals of their fathers," shows a society where the older generation is superior to the younger. For example, Telemachus does not have the power to rid Ithaca of the suitors, but his father does. In Greek mythology, each generation of gods and men is less powerful than the one that came before. The heroes who lived before the Trojan War were mightier than the warriors who fought at Troy. Likewise, the gods were born less powerful than the Titans. Has this philosophy flip-flopped today? Does society believe that younger generations will always surpass the older? Explain. Why has this changed?

frequently attaching a more famous artist's name to their work to boost its popularity. It has even been suggested that Homer was another way of saying John Doe.

If the two poems are written by the same author, it would make the *Odyssey* one of the most successful sequels of all time. But many have their doubts. In terms of tone, the *Iliad* is much different than the *Odyssey*. The *Iliad* is a war poem full of warriors, grit, glory, and death. Men and gods furiously duke it out against one another as they bring the 10-year-long Trojan War to a close. Contrast this with the *Odyssey*, where home and family—not glory and victory—are the ultimate goals. Some explain this discrepancy between the two poems' themes with the theory that Homer wrote the *Iliad* as a young man and the *Odyssey* in his later years. After all, Achilles, the hero of the *Iliad*, is a young man, while Odysseus is middle-aged.

The Victorian author Samuel Butler wrote *The Authoress of the Odyssey* (1897) to make the argument that Homer was a young woman living on the island of Sicily. To back up this very specific theory, he argued that the author of the poem showed very little knowledge of sailing, knew more about domestic life (e.g., weaving, household chores) than a Greek man would have, and filled the poem with an overabundance of "female interest." It is true that the *Odyssey* has much more "female interest" than the *Iliad* does. The war poem has only a handful of female characters, and for the most part, they stay on the sidelines. Contrast this with the *Odyssey*, which is filled with strong, crafty female characters—Penelope, Circe, Calypso, Athena—and has themes of faithfulness, love, and perseverance. Butler argued that another female character, the young princess Nausicaa, who discovers Odysseus when he washes up on the beaches of her kingdom, is actually the true author of the *Odyssey*, inserting *herself* into the poem.

These theories make for lively discussion, but there will never be any way to definitively prove that Homer was literate or illiterate, male or female, one author or two authors, blind or sighted. All credible details of his life are lost in antiquity. What we can hear is his voice—the way he masterfully tells a story—and while we may not know much about the man (or woman) behind these great works, the art will remain.

DISCUSS
- What do you think about Butler's theory that Homer was actually a woman?
- Do details about authors' lives or backgrounds help readers better understand their work? Explain.

Penelope, the Virtuous Wife

For centuries Penelope has been praised as the ultimate example of a virtuous wife. In the *Odyssey* she remains faithful to a husband, whom most consider dead, for 20 long years. A woman under extreme pressure—from a father who begs her to be remarried and a group of strong-armed suitors—Penelope rises to the challenge of faithfulness and keeps her cool. She also shows herself to be her husband's match in intelligence and cunning. A trick nearly as famous as Odysseus' Trojan horse is Penelope's tapestry, which she weaves during the day and unravels at night.

Could a woman this crafty really be fooled by Odysseus' disguises? Some believe that Penelope actually sees through Odysseus' disguise when he appears in court dressed as a beggar. Why else would she immediately propose an archery contest that she knows only her husband can win? Maybe she is playing along with her wily husband. Even after Odysseus has revealed his identity, Penelope refuses to believe him until she puts him to another test. The marriage bed that Odysseus crafted 20 years before used a live tree—still rooted to the ground—as one of its legs. Penelope casually mentions that the bed has been moved to another room, and Odysseus cries out in shock: Did she saw the bed loose from the tree? His shock at her statement proves that he is really Odysseus, and she welcomes him home.

Penelope is not given a voice in Homer's poem, and we are left to imagine her inner thoughts for ourselves. Modern writers have often tried to reinterpret the story from Penelope's point of view. What was going through her mind during these many years of separation? Did she ever doubt Odysseus' loyalty to her? If not, should she have?

Journey's End

The return is an important part of every hero's journey. As heroes reach their destinations, they think back on the journey, the many perils escaped, the many wonders seen, and the lesson learned along the way. In this light, "getting there is half the fun" takes on a whole new meaning. These heroes realize that it is not the destination that makes a journey, but the stops along the way.

For Odysseus, the return is the ultimate goal of his journey. With wife and son back in his arms, his kingdom safe and secure after many years of insecurity, Odysseus reaches his journey's end.

Many people compare life to a journey—an odyssey—and like Odysseus' journey, life is filled with many twists and turns and changes of fortune. When we reach the end of our life, we want to look back and appreciate the trip. We will remember the stops we made along the way, the occasions that we took time to have fun amid a hectic schedule. We will

FUN FACT
- In other versions of the same story, Penelope was not such a virtuous wife. They say that instead of remaining faithful to Odysseus, Penelope actually gave into the crude advances of the suitors. Because of this she gave birth to a deformed son—the half-man, half-goat creature Pan.

DISCUSS
- Read the poem "Penelope" by Dorothy Parker and answer the following questions.
  ◊ Do you sense any irony in the last line of the poem? Why is Penelope just as brave as Odysseus?
  ◊ Is there more than one type of bravery?

- Some view Penelope as a male-created stereotype because she stays faithful even while her husband is having wild affairs. What do you think of this assessment?

WRITE
Write a letter from Penelope to Odysseus.

remember past friends and loved ones whose voyages diverged from our own. We will remember the many obstacles that we overcame along the way—that, in the end, made us a better person. If we can look back on our journey fondly, then the next journey will not be so frightening, the one that leads into uncharted waters.

Excerpt From "Ithaka" by Constantine Cavafy

As you set out for Ithaka
hope the voyage is a long one,
full of adventure, full of discovery . . .

Keep Ithaka always in your mind.
Arriving there is what you are destined for.
But do not hurry the journey at all.
Better if it lasts for years,
so you are old by the time you reach the island,
wealthy with all you have gained on the way,
not expecting Ithaka to make you rich.

Ithaka gave you the marvelous journey.
Without her you would not have set out.
She has nothing left to give you now.

And if you find her poor, Ithaka won't have fooled you.
Wise as you will have become, so full of experience,
you will have understood by then what these Ithakas mean. (Savidis, 1992, p. 36)

DISCUSS
- What is the message of this poem?
- Is life a journey? Explain.

Odyssey II: The Sequel

It is not only Hollywood that is sequel-crazy. The ancient Greeks were not satisfied with Odysseus simply reaching his home and settling down for old age. They thought there should be more to the story. After all, Odysseus has an adventurous heart, so ordinary life would not be for him. The *Telegony*, a lost poem that exists only through summary, tells the events that occur after the *Odyssey*. Rather than settling down like everyone expects him to, Odysseus goes back to sea, leaving Telemachus in charge of Ithaca, and sails around on another series of adventures. Meanwhile, Odysseus' long-lost son, Telegonus, whose mother is Circe the witch, arrives in Ithaca searching for his father. Odysseus returns to Ithaca but, through a misunderstanding, is killed by Telegonus. Once true identities are revealed, Telegonus laments the fact that he has killed his own father. He takes Telemachus and Penelope back to Circe's island, where Telemachus is married to Circe and Telegonus himself marries Penelope. Circe makes all four of them immortal, and they live happily ever after. This goofy story should be enough to show you that sequels are rarely a good idea. Homer never mentions (nor apparently has any knowledge of) these events, and they only complicate the perfectly fine ending of the *Odyssey*.

One Journey's End Is Another Journey's Beginning

Many authors, and not just ancient ones, have wondered what exactly happened after the *Odyssey* comes to a close. Like the author of the *Telegony*, they find it hard to believe that Odysseus would settle down to live an ordinary life once he had a taste of high adventure. They picture him to be like J.R.R. Tolkien's Bilbo Baggins from *The Hobbit* and *The Lord of the Rings*, who refused to go back to a humdrum life after so many adventures. The Victorian poet Alfred, Lord Tennyson, made Odysseus (Ulysses) the subject of one of his most famous poems, "Ulysses." Odysseus has grown older and itches to return to the open sea. He compares himself to metal that is rusting over; he declares that he will drink "life to the lees" (the last drop); he will knock the rust off his body and shine again; he will follow "knowledge like a sinking star, beyond the utmost bound of human thought."

> It little profits that an idle king,
> By this still hearth, among these barren crags,
> Match'd with an aged wife, I mete and dole
> Unequal laws unto a savage race,
> That hoard, and sleep, and feed, and know not me . . .
> I cannot rest from travel: I will drink
> Life to the lees . . .
> How dull it is to pause, to make an end,
> To rust unburnished, not to shine in use!
> As though to breathe were life . . .
> Come, my friends,

DISCUSS

- Do you perceive Odysseus to be a restless wanderer? Explain.
- Do the events of the *Telegony* seem like they fit with the events of the *Odyssey*? Explain.
- The last four lines of Tennyson's poem are often used as a motto. What is inspiring about them? What other lines are worthy of note?

'Tis not too late to seek a newer world.
Push off, and sitting well in order smite
The sounding furrows; for my purpose holds
To sail beyond the sunset, and the baths
Of all the western stars, until I die.
It may be that the gulfs will wash us down:
It may be we shall touch the Happy Isles,
And see the great Achilles, whom we knew
Tho' much is taken, much abides; and though
We are not now that strength which in old days
Moved earth and heaven; that which we are, we are;
One equal temper of heroic hearts,
Made weak by time and fate, but strong in will
To strive, to seek, to find, and not to yield. (Tennyson, 1842/1961,
        p. 284–286)

CONCLUSION

As the journey of Odysseus reaches its close, so does the journey of this book. I hope that you have learned something along the way. The Greeks were a complicated, yet fascinating, people whose myths have laid the foundation for Western literature, language, music, and art. At the very least, maybe you have gained an appreciation for these stories and their impact on modern times. My true hope is that you have learned to love the classical myths by experiencing them in a new way—and that you have seen the truth in myth.

Underworld Find-It

Items to Find:

1. Argo
2. Bats
3. Heracles' bow
4. Calydonian Boar
5. Cattle
6. Chained Titans
7. Charon
8. Chimaera
9. Crows
10. Flying ram
11. Flying sandals
12. Ghosts
13. Giant snake
14. Girdle of Aphrodite
15. Golden Fleece
16. Gopher
17. Gray Sisters
18. Hades
19. Harpy
20. Heads of Cerberus
21. Helmet of invisibility
22. Heracles
23. Hermes
24. Homer
25. Icarus
26. King Midas
27. Medusa
28. Mini Trojan horse
29. Minos
30. Minotaur
31. Missing eyeball
32. Narcissus
33. Orpheus
34. Pegasus symbol
35. Persephone
36. Pie
37. Pig
38. Rat
39. Severed heads
40. Skulls
41. Sphinx
42. Spider
43. Thunderbolt of Zeus
44. Tiny snake
45. Tiresias
46. Toad
47. Tree of dreams
48. Trident
49. Waldo
50. Worm

Answers on p. 191.

Underworld Find-It Answer Key

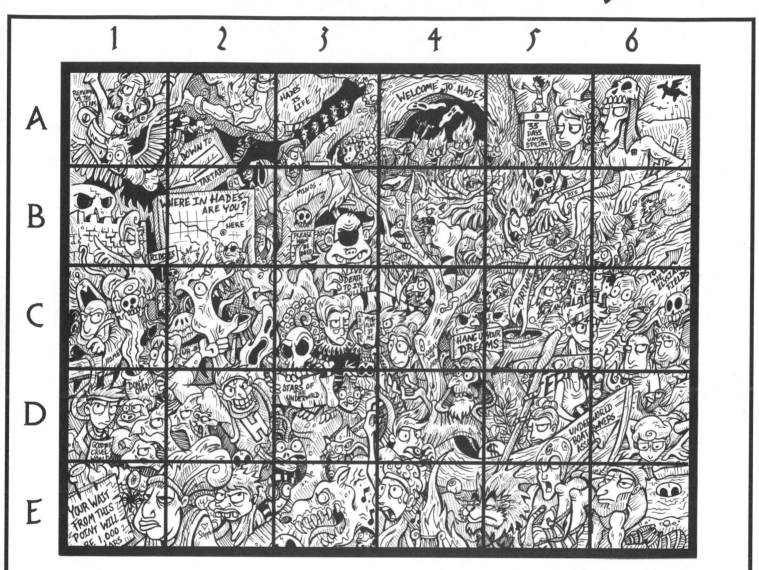

Where to Find Items:

1. Argo B3
2. Bats A2, D3
3. Heracles' bow D3-4
4. Calydonian boar C4
5. Cattle C5-6
6. Chained Titans A1-2
7. Charon D4-5
8. Chimaera E4-5
9. Crows B4, D6
10. Flying ram A3
11. Flying sandals A2, C6
12. Ghosts A4, A-B5, C2
13. Giant snake B4
14. Girdle of Aphrodite B2
15. Golden Fleece C3
16. Gopher A3
17. Gray Sisters C4-5

18. Hades A6
19. Harpy B5
20. Heads of Cer. B4, C2, E3
21. Helmet of invisibility C1
22. Heracles D2
23. Hermes A4
24. Homer C1
25. Icarus A1
26. King Midas C6
27. Medusa D3
28. Mini Trojan horse E6
29. Minos A-B3
30. Minotaur C2-3
31. Missing eyeball E4
32. Narcissus D6
33. Orpheus E4
34. Pegasus symbol A6

35. Persephone A5
36. Pie C2
37. Pig D1
38. Rat D2
39. Severed heads D3, D5
40. Skulls A6, B1, B3, B5, C1, C3, C3, C6, D2, E3, E6
41. Sphinx B1
42. Spider E1
43. Thunderbolt of Zeus A6
44. Tiny snake D5
45. Tiresias B2
46. Toad E3
47. Tree of dreams B-C-D4
48. Trident C-D6
49. Waldo E2-3
50. Worm C4

PRONUNCIATION GUIDE

Achates	(UH-KAY-TEEZ)	**Argos**	(AR-GOS)
Acheron	(ACK-UH-RUN)	**Argus**	(AR-GUS)
Achilles	(UH-KILL-EEZ)	**Ariadne**	(AIR-EE-AHD-NEE)
Acrisius	(UH-KRIH-SEE-US)	**Artemis**	(AR-TUH-MIS)
Actaeon	(ACT-EE-ON)	**Astyanax**	(UH-STY-UH-NAX)
Æetes	(EE-UH-TEEZ)	**Atalanta**	(AT-UH-LAN-TUH)
Aegeus	(EE-GEE-US)	**Athena**	(UH-THEE-NUH)
Aegina	(EE-JY-NUH)	**Atreus**	(UH-TRAY-OOS)
Aeneas	(EE-NEE-US)	**Avernus**	(UH-VERN-US)
Aeneid	(EE-NEE-ID)	**Bacchus**	(BAHK-US)
Aeolus	(EE-OH-LUSS)	**Bellerophon**	(BEH-LEHR-UH-FUN)
Agamemnon	(AG-UH-MEM-NON)	**Briseis**	(BRIH-SEE-US)
Alcema	(AL-SEE-MUH)	**Cadmus**	(KAHD-MUS)
Alecto	(UH-LEHK-TOE)	**Calchas**	(KAL-KUS)
Amata	(UH-MAY-TUH)	**Calliope**	(KUH-LY-O-PEE)
Anchises	(AN-KY-ZEEZ)	**Calydon**	(KAL-IH-DUN)
Andromache	(AN-DRAH-MUH-KEE)	**Carthage**	(KAR-THIJ)
Andromeda	(AN-DRAH-MEE-DUH)	**Cassandra**	(KUH-SAN-DRUH)
Antigone	(AN-TIG-UH-NEE)	**Castor**	(KAS-TER)
Antinous	(AN-TIN-YOO-US)	**Centaur**	(SEN-TAUR)
Aphrodite	(AF-RO-DY-TEE)	**Cerberus**	(SER-BUH-RUS)
Apollo	(UH-PAW-LO)	**Charon**	(KAH-RUN)
Arachne	(UH-RAK-NEE)	**Charybdis**	(KUH-RIB-DIS)
Ares	(AIR-EEZ)	**Chimaera**	(KY-MEE-RUH)

Chiron	(KY-RUN)	**Helle**	(HEH-LEE)
Chryseis	(KRY-SEE-ISS)	**Hephaestus**	(HEH-FESS-TUS)
Clio	(KLEE-OH)	**Hera**	(HAIR-UH)
Clytemnestra	(KLY-TIM-NESS-TRUH)	**Heracles**	(HEHR-UH-KLEEZ)
Colchis	(KOL-KISS)	**Hercules**	(HER-KOO-LEEZ)
Creon	(KREE-ON)	**Hermes**	(HER-MEEZ)
Cumae	(KOO-MEE)	**Hylas**	(HY-LUS)
Cupid	(KEW-PID)	**Hypaepa**	(HY-PEE-PUH)
Cyclopes	(SY-KLOPE-EEZ)	**Hyperborean**	(HY-PER-BOR-EE-UN)
Daedalus	(DAY-DUH-LUS)	**Icarus**	(IH-KAR-US)
Danaë	(DUH-NAY-EE)	**Iliad**	(IH-LEE-AD)
Delphi	(DEL-FY)	**Ilium**	(IH-LEE-UM)
Dictys	(DIK-TUS)	**Ino**	(EYE-NO)
Dido	(DY-DO)	**Iphigenia**	(IF-UH-JUH-NY-UH)
Diomedes	(DY-O-ME-DEEZ)	**Iris**	(EYE-RIS)
Dryad	(DRY-AD)	**Ithaca**	(ITH-UH-KUH)
Electra	(EE-LEK-TRUH)	**Iulus**	(YOO-LUSS)
Eris	(EE-RUS)	**Janus**	(JAY-NUS)
Eros	(EE-ROS)	**Jocasta**	(YO-KAS-TUH)
Eumaeus	(YOO-MAY-US)	**Juno**	(JOO-NO)
Eumenides	(YOO-MEN-IH-DEEZ)	**Jupiter**	(JOO-PIH-TUR)
Eurycleia	(YOOR-IH-KLEE-UH)	**Kithairon**	(KIH-THY-RUN)
Eurydice	(YOO-RIH-DIH-SEE)	**Laertes**	(LAY-AIR-TEEZ)
Eurymachus	(YOO-RIM-UH-KUS)	**Laius**	(LAY-US)
Evander	(EE-VAN-DER)	**Latinus**	(LUH-TY-NUS)
Gorgon	(GOR-GUN)	**Latium**	(LAY-SHEE-UM)
Hades	(HAY-DEEZ)	**Leda**	(LEE-DUH)
Harpies	(HAR-PEEZ)	**Lemnos**	(LEM-NUS)
Hecate	(HEK-UH-TEE)	**Lethe**	(LEE-THEE)
Hector	(HEK-TER)	**Leto**	(LEE-TOE)
Hecuba	(HEK-YOO-BUH)	**Lyre**	(LY-ER)
Helenus	(HEL-UH-NUS)	**Maenad**	(MAY-NAD)
Helios	(HEE-LEE-OS)	**Maron**	(MAH-RUN)

Marsyas	(MAR-SAY-UHS)	**Perdix**	(PER-DIX)
Medea	(MEE-DEE-UH)	**Perseus**	(PER-SEE-US)
Medusa	(MEH-DOO-SUH)	**Philoctetes**	(FILL-OK-TEE-TEEZ)
Melanion	(MUH-LAY-NEE-UN)	**Phineus**	(FIN-EE-US)
Meleager	(MUH-LEE-UH-JER)	**Phoebus**	(FEE-BUS)
Melpomene	(MEL-PAH-MUH-NEE)	**Phrixus**	(FRICK-SUS)
Menelaus	(MEN-UH-LAY-US)	**Phrygia**	(FRIH-GEE-UH)
Mercury	(MER-KOO-REE)	**Pisistratus**	(PIH-SIH-STRAH-TUS)
Mestra	(MEH-STRUH)	**Plautus**	(PLAW-TUS)
Minerva	(MIH-NER-VUH)	**Pluto**	(PLEW-TOE)
Minos	(MY-NUS)	**Polybus**	(PO-LEE-BUS)
Minotaur	(MY-NO-TAR)	**Polydectes**	(POLLY-DEK-TEEZ)
Mycenae	(MY-SEE-NEE)	**Polydeuces**	(POLLY-DEW-SEEZ)
Myrmidon	(MER-MIH-DON)	**Polyphemus**	(PO-LEE-FEE-MUS)
Naiad	(NY-AD)	**Poseidon**	(PO-SY-DUN)
Narcissus	(NAR-SIS-US)	**Priam**	(PRY-UM)
Neptune	(NEP-TOON)	**Proserpine**	(PRO-SER-PEEN-UH)
Niobe	(NY-O-BEE)	**Proteus**	(PRO-TEE-US)
Odysseus	(O-DIS-EE-US)	**Pylos**	(PY-LOS)
Oedipus	(ED-IH-PUS)	**Pyrrhus**	(PEER-US)
Oeneus	(EE-NEE-US)	**Remus**	(REE-MUS)
Orestes	(O-RES-TEEZ)	**Rhea**	(REE-UH)
Orpheus	(OR-FEE-US)	**Romulus**	(ROM-YOO-LUS)
Ovid	(OH-VID)	**Rutulia**	(ROO-TOO-LEE-UH)
Pactolus	(PAK-TOE-LUS)	**Satyr**	(SAY-TER)
Pallas	(PAL-US)	**Scylla**	(SIHL-UH)
Pandarus	(PAN-DARE-US)	**Scyros**	(SKY-RUS)
Parnassus	(PAR-NAH-SUS)	**Seriphos**	(SEHR-UH-FUS)
Pasiphaë	(PASS-IH-FAY-EE)	**Silenus**	(SUH-LY-NUS)
Patroclus	(PAH-TRO-KLUS)	**Styx**	(STIKS)
Peleus	(PEE-LEE-US)	**Tantalus**	(TAN-TUH-LUS)
Pelias	(PEL-EE-US)	**Telemachus**	(TUH-LEM-UH-KUS)
Penelope	(PEH-NEL-O-PEE)	**Thalia**	(THUH-LY-UH)

Thebes	(THEEBZ)	**Tiresias**	(TY-REE-SEE-US)
Theseus	(THEE-SEE-US)	**Tyndareus**	(TIN-DARE-EE-US)
Thessaly	(THEHS-UH-LEE)	**Urania**	(YOO-RAY-NEE-UH)
Thetis	(THEE-TIS)	**Zephyr**	(ZEH-FER)
Tiber	(TY-BUR)	**Zeus**	(ZOOCE)

REFERENCES

Auden, W. H. (1979). *Selected poems* (E. Mendelson, Ed.). New York, NY: Vintage.

Anderson, M. J., & Stephenson, K. F. (1999). *Collective biographies: Scientists of the ancient world.* Springfield, NJ: Enslow.

Brunet, S., Smith, R. S., & Trzaskoma, S. M. (Eds.). (2004). *Anthology of classical myth: Primary sources in translation.* Indianapolis, IN: Hackett.

Bulfinch, T. (1967). *Bulfinch's mythology.* New York, NY: Dell. (Original work written 1855)

Burns, Ken. *Mark Twain.* Florentine Films, 2002.

Butler, S. (1922). *The authoress of the Odyssey.* London, England: Jonathan Cape.

Homer. (1996). *The odyssey* (R. Fagles, Trans.). New York, NY: Penguin. (Original work written circa 800 BC)

Ovid. (1958). *The metamorphoses* (H. Gregory, Trans.). New York, NY: Signet. (Original work written 8)

Savidis, G. (Ed.). (1992). *C. P. Cavafy: Collected poems* (E. Keeley & P. Sherrard, Trans.; Rev. ed.). Princeton, NJ: Princeton University Press.

Sophocles. (1977). *Antigone* (D. Fitts & R. Fitzgerald, Trans.). Orlando, FL: Harcourt. (Original work written 442 BC)

Tennyson, A. L. (1961). *The idylls of the king and a selection of poems.* New York, NY: Signet. (Original work published 1842)

The George Lloyd Society. (n.d.). *Repertoire guide.* Retrieved from http://www.georgelloyd.com/georgelloydsociety/index_biography_repertoireguide.htm

ABOUT THE AUTHOR

For the past several years, Zachary Hamby has been teaching mythology to high school students through the use of reader's theater plays. When he first began teaching his mythology course, he was discouraged by student reaction. Zachary felt the subject matter could be made much more interesting. After developing a series of plays covering the same material, Zachary has found that even secondary students enjoy reading aloud, role-playing, and learning together. He is also a consultant for the National Writing Project and has presented his reader's theater approach at multiple academic conferences. He lives with his wife and two children in the Ozarks.